Dynamics in Chinese Digital Commons

The book provides an up-to-date, comprehensive, and critical explanation of digital commons in China.

It aims to reshape the theoretical discussion of digital commons, stressing the significance of digital mode of production and power division structure between government and digital platforms—both characters shed light on how China has developed its digital economy and maintained a relatively innovative cyberspace during the past 20 years. This book could serve as a foundational analysis for future studies on China's Internet.

The book will appeal to scholars, entrepreneurs, and policymakers interested in digital commons, governance of cyberspace, and China's political economy.

Hu Ling is Associate Professor of Law in Peking University, and holds a Ph.D. from Hong Kong University. His major research area is cyberlaw and legal theory. He has published numerous books, articles, and review essays on issues related to Internet governance.

Dynamics in Chinese Digital Commons

Law, Technology, and Governance

Hu Ling

Routledge
Taylor & Francis Group
LONDON AND NEW YORK

First published 2025
by Routledge
4 Park Square, Milton Park, Abingdon, Oxon OX14 4RN

and by Routledge
605 Third Avenue, New York, NY 10158

Routledge is an imprint of the Taylor & Francis Group, an informa business

British Library Cataloguing in Publication Data
A catalogue record for this book is available from the British Library

Library of Congress Cataloging in Publication Data
Names: Hu, Ling, (Law teacher), author.
Title: Dynamics in Chinese digital commons: law, technology, and governance / Hu Ling.
Description: Abingdon, Oxon [UK]; New York, NY: Routledge, 2024. |
Includes bibliographical references and index. |
Identifiers: LCCN 2024037933 (print) | LCCN 2024037934 (ebook) |
ISBN 9781032935119 (hardback) | ISBN 9781032935263 (paperback) |
ISBN 9781003566243 (ebook)
Subjects: LCSH: Open source software–Law and legislation–China. |
Free computer software–Law and legislation–China. |
Computer networks–Law and legislation–China. |
Open source software–Economic aspects–China. |
Open source software–Government policy–China. |
Technology and law–China. | Subcontracting–China.
Classification: LCC KNQ1183 .H85 2024 (print) | LCC KNQ1183 (ebook) |
DDC 343.5109/99–dc23/eng/20240815
LC record available at https://lccn.loc.gov/2024037933
LC ebook record available at https://lccn.loc.gov/2024037934

ISBN: 978-1-032-93511-9 (hbk)
ISBN: 978-1-032-93526-3 (pbk)
ISBN: 978-1-003-56624-3 (ebk)

DOI: 10.4324/ 9781003566243

Typeset in Times New Roman
by Deanta Global Publishing Services, Chennai, India

Contents

Introduction

Research background

Digital technology has brought a flourishing commons in cyberspace. As the technology disseminates across the globe, we see different forms of digital commons generated by various participants and mechanisms. In China, as the Internet was introduced domestically and spread through layers of infrastructure, it seems a digital commons could bring a universal benefit to all people, but how such commons came into being and developed at both macro- and microlevels still needs to be explored and answered. At the macro-level, the book wishes to highlight the importance of power division between the government and platform companies; at the microlevel, the book wishes to further explore the mechanism of digital production and labor process. Based on Chinese experience, this book tries to provide a detailed explanation in this regard, particularly from a legal and political–economic perspective, concerning the following main research questions: (1) How such a digital commons is created in terms of digital mode of production, promoting the liquidity and movement of digital resources? (2) How such a digital commons is sustained by organizational, institutional, and legal means in China? (3) How law and policy help to solve disputes and conflicts concerning ownership, collaborative opportunity, and benefit distribution, during which process the relevant rules also changed gradually.

Information technology, represented by the Internet, is rapidly spreading throughout society, expanding space and time, and absorbing more factors of production and resources into the production and circulation process regulated by digital platforms. This process is widely recognized as a new type of production that is different from the traditional industrial mode of production, encompassing production, distribution of goods/services, and consumption, which are traditionally separated in space. And this process has formed into a new type of public space, mixed with public and private interests, namely, digital commons. It started with information content services and was later extended to more physical factors to facilitate mobility. How such new mode of production was generated is an important topic in political economy. Based on previous study, this book tends to regard the digital commons as (1) a process of resource productive mechanisms and mobility, emphasizing that the modular combination of different resources based on low-cost information technology is embedded into the networked productive

DOI: 10.4324/9781003566243-1

process of matching, its rapid flow and circulation process is very critical to the generation of value, and the acceleration of technology brings about a huge scale effect; (2) a platform for the organization of productive enterprises, emphasizing that the transformation of mode of production is a process of organizational adjustment, and that the platform company itself plays an important role in resource matching and control as an organizational force; (3) an infrastructure for digital market, emphasizing that in order to realize the orderly movement of resources, the commons need a strong market infrastructure (such as payment, logistics, and credit) to provide effective support; (4) a legal and public policy process, recognizing that the survival and growth of the new mode of production is not as natural and smooth as it seems, and emphasizing the need for the legal rules to protect the interests of unique economic processes, confirm their legitimacy, and appropriately resolve conflicts between old and new interests. Of course, since these perspectives cover quite a range of aspects on modes of production and digital commons, we need to put these explanations together and allow one to visualize the dynamics of paradigm shift as a whole. Therefore, this chapter will try to propose a systematic framework to understand the digital commons in China, including dimensions of production, control, ownership, division of power, infrastructure, and distribution of interests. Some dimensions are similar to traditional commons, while others are quite new and unique.

This book will start from least three correlated trends of existing works, corresponding to the three main themes of this book: architecture, commons and culture production. The first trend is the theories of Internet architecture and its effects upon endpoint innovation and cultural production.[1] Cyberlaw scholars have long found the "code" or information architecture has great influence on the end devices and their generativity since the advent of the Internet. The retrieval of doctrines such as "end-to-end" argument even ignites the far-from-ending debates on net neutrality in the United States. This stream of works provides insights in exploring the Internet architecture in China and how it affects mass cultural production.

The second trend of works is about knowledge as a kind of digital commons and key element for a robust public domain.[2] The distributed architecture of the Internet facilitates the peer-based production of knowledge and culture. Such mass production has grown out of ethic practices such as trust and cooperation rather than economic calculation, in other words, it is based on gift economy rather than

1 For example, Lawrence Lessig, *Code: Version 2.0*, Basic Books, 2006; Jonathan Zittrain, *The Future of the Internet—And How to Stop It*, Yale University Press, 2008; Schewick, Barbara van, *Internet Architecture and Innovation*, MIT Press, 2012.

2 For example, James Boyle, *The Public Domain: Enclosing the Commons of the Mind*, Yale University Press, 2008; A. Broumas, *Intellectual Commons and the Law: A Normative Theory for Commons-Based Peer Production*, University of Westminster Press, 2020; C. Fuchs, "The Digital Commons and the Digital Public Sphere: How to Advance Digital Democracy Today", *Westminster Papers in Communication and Culture* 16, no. 1 (2021), 9–26; Jeremy Rifkin, *The Zero Marginal Cost Society: The Internet of Things, the Collaborative Commons, and the Eclipse of Capitalism*, St. Martin's Press, 2014.

commercial economy. However, as with media companies, modern copyright law renders our culture a danger that private culture enterprises could possess knowledge production exclusively and claim for culture ownership, which is a threat for both democracy and cultural innovation. How copyright law is impeding the mass creativity and innovation and how people could get access to knowledge is also being heatedly discussed in Western countries. By analyzing the digital cultures in China, this book will further discuss whether such a cultural commons has flourished in confrontation of modern copyright law and what kind of commons it turns out to be.

The third trend of literature is the critical theory of communication and culture.[3] It has been studied intensively that how culture production has become a capitalist industry through modern technology and propaganda before the invention of the Internet. Many people cheered when the Internet brought them more freedom and a seeming public sphere. However, this might prove to be a myth. It is true that ordinary people are greatly empowered to complete imaginable tasks. But the traditional giants and information empires are fighting back and trying to grasp more influence in cyberspace. The Internet has been commercialized since the mid-1990s and the business model of various services has shaped the way how it works, how we receive information, and how we interact with the world. The new "cognitive capitalism" is making profit out of mass' free labor and leisure time. Old and new media corporations are under close cooperation to tame the cyberspace with even powerful tools and ambitious goals. Although it is difficult to evaluate exactly whether the Internet amateur culture is good or bad, we are able to identify the process and private basis of cultural production on the Internet. Such inquiry helps to clarify the nature of digital commons and public domain in contemporary China.

Theoretical framework

This book tries to develop a rough theoretical framework aiming to provide a detailed explanation of the formation and development of digital commons in China. It includes double-layer analysis: on the one hand, the digital mode of production is crucial for the formation of digital commons, including (1) market infrastructure, (2) data and other productive resources, and (3) platform as organization and market system; on the other hand, the stable relationship between the government and platforms, including (1) institutional mechanism for mode of production transformation, (2) institutional mechanism keeping the platform open and close, and (3) distribution among digital labors. The framework will combine these factors together to contribute to current studies. The above six dimensions could fully

3 For example, S. Zuboff, *The Age of Surveillance Capitalism: The Fight for a Human Future at the New Frontier of Power*, PublicAffairs, 2019; Dan Schiller, *Digital Capitalism: Networking the Global Market System*, MIT Press, 1999; N. Srnicek, *Platform Capitalism*, Polity Press, 2017; T. Scholz, *Platform Cooperativism: Challenging the Corporate Sharing Economy*, Rosa Luxemburg Stiftung, 2016.

cover all the important issues for the digital commons growth and give sufficient explanations to China's Internet development and governance.

The main theme of this book is to deal with the relationship between technological system as a new mode of production and its governance system, including law and public policy. It starts from conflicts between old and new interests due to the "illegal rise" of the Internet and reflect on this short but significant process through the practices and controversies surrounding digital property rights as an example. The common features of digital property/assets are as follows: (1) *Limited mobility*: Social and economic value is generated in constant mobility and reuse process, the core of which lies in the platform's algorithm-driven precise matching, but the flow of these resources within the platform architecture is prioritized over the cross-platform flow, which has formed a certain kind of commons contributed by the masses; (2) *Exclusive use*: The platform reduces mobilization costs as much as possible but profits exclusively from it, thus implying that the value of the labor devoted by platforms in their technical design and arrangement activities takes precedence over the value of the labor used to produce those goods/services by users; (3) *Aggregated entitlements*: Only data analysis over a large amount of goods/services can produce the required aggregate values that take precedence over individual values and are effectively implemented by privately built infrastructures. These three features actually find their ideological and institutional roots in traditional legal and economic theories and rules. However, in the era of platform economy, the new mode of production has led to a very flexible and dynamic, but not uncontrolled, form and mechanism for this new type of commons, which is perfectly demonstrated by data. "Illegal rise" focuses on the conflict between two paths and mechanisms for viewing this new type of property/asset, which is reflected in the alternation and choice between property rule and liability rule in law.

Technological system forms an open platform oriented toward market mechanisms, but this market is gradually moving toward closedness by the platforms through various ways of strengthening their management and control. Initially, this market took the form of some kind of single-service market, but with the discovery of two-sided markets and networked patterns of cross-externality, Internet portals have all gradually shifted to platforms. Platform-based markets first face the problem of attracting user traffic with sufficient high-quality productive resources, which is achieved through the "illegal rise" of low-cost access to unauthorized or infringing works. Once a large number of users are attracted by the free content or services, they can slowly become content producers or service providers, forming a network of trading and cooperation, thus realizing a rapid economic cycle from production to consumption. At this stage, the Internet began to profit from the so-called mobility, which has double meaning. Firstly, mobility means digitizing non-digital content (for instance, converting traditional records, books, and broadcasts into standardized bytes of 0 and 1). Second, it also means fragmenting the time and space of the mass people, who devote different amounts of time and energy to different service processes, which are integrated and matched by algorithms without the need to participate in the whole process. Along with the rise of sharing economy, the flow of information content resources in the virtual space also extends to the fragmentation and flow of human and physical resources. The acts of digital riders and gig workers providing labor services endure mobility both in physical space and in the sense of decentralized fragmentation of labor.

Low-cost mobility undoubtedly brings value to the digital economy, not only from the sum of surplus value resulting from the scale and fragmentation of labor at the disposal of the platforms, but also from the efficiencies of precise matching and targeted ads pushing, which contribute to an accelerated cycle of the economy and legitimize the claims of the new mode of production to be capable of increasing productivity. With increasing scale, large digital platforms in particular gradually have an incentive to reduce mobility. The underlying rationale is that, first, mobility allows productive resources to profit from different platforms, but large platforms want to keep producers and consumers on the same platform for all of their time, covering all the main services constantly tracked and exclusively produced for the platform, namely, monopolized in the usual sense of the word. This has led to the emergence of widespread "choosing one from two" tactic (e-commerce platforms) and non-job-hopping clauses (live-streaming platforms) in the digital economy, in the hope of reducing resource mobility. Second, from the perspective of normal market operation, in order to enable resources to flow in a more secure and orderly manner, and to reduce potential fraud, counterfeiting, brushing, black market, and other disruptions to the market order, it is necessary to monitor and manage the trustworthiness of the market participants, and the security of the transaction process. Such demands have given rise to a number of digital infrastructures oriented toward information functions, such as identity authentication, matching and connection, reputation scoring, third-party payments, logistics, behavioral regulation, dispute resolution, and so on. These mechanisms aim to provide stable expectations for resource transactions and labor, increase the time spent within the platform, and actually form a whole new set of labor infrastructures.

In traditional offline markets, we need laws to regulate property and contracts in general, and provide registration and management of market players. We need courts to settle disputes, exchanges to provide specialized trading services, financial institutions to provide funding. We also need postal and logistical transportation to deliver goods, regulatory agencies to enforce the law, and other necessary infrastructure that helps reduce transaction costs while ensuring transaction security, market order, and willingness to trade in the future. On digital platforms, these infrastructural services are beginning to be provided by private platforms, enhancing the scale and efficiency of transactions and increasingly favoring automation. As large amounts of data are generated by human producers and consumers, AI can improve these infrastructures more rapidly through data analytics and pattern learning, such as face swipe authentication, automated matching and scoring, automated payments and shipping via unmanned logistics, and so on. In this sense, the new employment form of labor is constantly providing intelligent machines with metadata as raw productive materials.

The digital market in this sense has two dimensions. On the one hand, the continuous digitization of productive resources through private platforms promotes the process of digitizing the economy and society, and establishes a standardized digital infrastructure that contributes to the orderly mobility and connectivity of resources within a given industry and jurisdiction, and creates a semi-closed order of production by organizing production in such a way as to make the pie bigger. On the other hand, as the competition of the platforms intensifies, infrastructure can help create some sort of anti-mobility mechanism, while mobility oriented solely on efficiency creates larger negative externalities for the market, society, and workers. For instance, while infrastructure stabilizes production, it raises the cost of start-up compliance, causing data traffic from small- and medium-sized platforms (which are unable to build infrastructure) to gradually converge on larger platforms, contributing to market concentration. Efficiency-oriented algorithms inevitably tend to assign orders to laborers who spend more time on work, thus turning more and more people into full-time workers. Laborers are required to bear their own share of risks encountered in the course of a service or transaction. The gig platforms are less likely to bear the costs of the tools of production for them. The "architecture" tends to be closed and maintains the legal boundaries of the system through numerous disputes over unfair competition, gradually turning the market and its productive resources into private property at the disposal of the platforms, even though it still formally emphasizes the autonomy of the workers and the informed consent of the users of the form contracts.

As a result, digital infrastructure and resource mobility are in fact two sides of the same coin: The digital economy requires the continuous digitization of unorganized resources that have not yet been digitized into the productive mechanisms of the platforms. As the productive resources increase, the platforms need to intervene as market managers to develop the infrastructure to regulate and control it. The ideology of the digital marketplace has continued to package the digital economy as an acculturated innovation enterprise that can exist in a vacuum, as if innovation will continue to be incubated if enough capital is invested. This ideology generates two fallacies. First, innovation in the form of technological systems cannot survive on its own, and needs to rely on effective market operation and order. No market can form order spontaneously, but requires external intervention to build public infrastructure services and institutional construction. In traditional markets, numerous market resources have been regulated by the state (such as labor, prices, financial system, intellectual property, competitive order and monopoly, social credit) to enable the market to operate and expand effectively.[4] In the digital marketplace, platforms play the role of public institutions to a certain extent, not only as "private power" in the legal sense, but also as a comprehensive force that influences the activities of large-scale market resources and demands that national laws serve its interests. Second, ideology attributes digital innovation and monopoly to the hard work and fierce competition of digital platforms; however, it is the state that actually provides the upgraded infrastructure and operational support for the digital economy. For instance, Taobao Village relies on ubiquitous telecom base stations,

4 See Steven K. Vogel, *Marketcraft: How Governments Make Markets Work*, Oxford University Press, 2018, pp. 15–19.

third-party payment relies on the state's financial licenses; authentication relies on the state's provision of a unified and trustworthy identity. Even the flexible labor model itself relies on existing social security mechanisms and the urban–rural dichotomy to survive.

Given digital markets operate in such a logical manner, many of the legal issues we see involving technological systems essentially occur within the framework of this orderly flow of resources. Law and public policy actually intervene at different levels. This is how the law intervenes into the digital commons governance.

Outlines

Chapter 1 focuses on the digital mode of production and "illegal rise" of the Internet in China. The 30-year history of the Internet in China is a history of illegal rise and constant lawbreaking, which does not refer to the simple violation of existing legal rules, but is more reflected in the fact that the Internet, as a new mode of production, constantly connects all kinds of productive resources, both online and offline. In this process, the rules reflecting traditional productive relations and interests are challenged by illegal actions, and the law as superstructure thus gradually changes to help establish the legitimacy of new types of economic interests representing advanced productive forces, and to harmonize the conflicts between old and new interests. From the perspective of the external relations of the new economy, new entrepreneurial entities not only need to continue to creatively and illegally obtain resources that have not yet been digitized from the physical world and traditional industries, but also need to obtain resources that have already been digitized from other competitors, so as to reduce their own costs and enhance their competitive advantages. The law's choice between innovation and order thus has become a key issue, which is centered in a series of judicial cases of unfair competition around content, data traffic, social capital, and so on. These phenomena definitely require a legal response to the legal status, usage arrangements, and status of the property/assets that can be mobilized by platform companies. Therefore, this chapter focuses on the initial internal incentive for the digital commons in China. It adopts a political–economic analysis and case study method to illustrate how illegal rise of the Internet occurred during the past decade. It will introduce the beginning of the digital commons in China and set the first part of the framework.

Chapter 2 focuses on the architecture of digital commons in China. Architecture, as a metaphor, can be viewed from multiple perspectives, each of which can help to reconceptualize the qualities of cyberspace and how it impacts law and governance. There is a need to look beyond the electronic screen and explore the specific implications of architecture in a larger context and break it down into meaningful legal issues. This chapter tries to show, both horizontally and vertically, what is digital architecture that is compatible with the control/production process in cyberspace around the "account-data-rating" mechanism as the core, in order to form a complete theory of architecture. The shortcoming of early Code Theory is that, while it recognizes the "regulability" of architecture, it fails to more accurately abstract from what architecture means in general. The boundaries of technical architectures seem to be clear from everyday Internet experience, but in reality are controversial. Therefore, this chapter aims to provide a more systematic and comprehensive categorization of architectures in which the boundaries of each category are discussed.

Chapter 3 focuses on the collaborative networks in digital commons. "Network" has a long history in human life, especially in the form of social relationships among people, which subtly influence our daily behavior. The network is not only a spontaneous social relationship between social subjects, but also a productive relationship consciously shaped and facilitated by the platform company, and the social capital thus formed and accumulated has become an important medium and asset for the platform to exert control and matching power over the actors in the network, and can even be described as a kind of "infrastructure". The creation, protection, and distribution of this intangible asset has become an important issue in the law and economics of digital commons. The current digital network can be designed and shaped by platform companies, and embodies the typical features of "commercialization" and "platformization", thus changing the productive process of the digital economy. This changes the relations in the productive process of the digital economy, which itself becomes part of the mode of production, and "control" is an important factor behind this process. This chapter will reflect on the productive orientation of law and how traditional sociality is being reshaped and mutated through its role as a network of mode of production/relationships.

Chapter 4 talks about how to build efficient and robust digital infrastructures for flourishing commons. Infrastructural development is critical in the maintenance of any commons. The particularity of digital commons lies in the fact that, on the one hand, platform companies, as private entities, have the ability to design and manage their operations; on the other hand, in cyberspace shaped by the platforms, a large number of resources are being matched and traded in a market-based manner. The infrastructure of a digital commons thus extends beyond the traditional physical or technical infrastructure to the market system that sustains the effective operation of the system. Digital markets do not form naturally in the vacuum, but rather rely on established production networks and infrastructures to collaboratively advance and evolve, and require a variety of supporting mechanisms like trusted identity, logistics, financial support, market credit, convenient payment, and so on. The functions of infrastructure in the usual sense are to confirm the true and unique identity of market participants, to realize the effective matching of resources, and to ensure the orderly and safe movement of resources. In order to achieve these functions, it is necessary to integrate and utilize the information of the players entering the market networks. For example, if the real identity of market participants cannot be confirmed officially, then fraud, counterfeiting, copyright infringement and other misbehaviors may occur, providing actors with unstable expectations. For another instance, if there is a lack of evaluation of the historical behavior of market participants, opportunists in one-off transactions may appear very soon, thus not helping to improve the behavioral standards of players on the whole. From a historical perspective, new digital infrastructures have risen from technical solutions to institutional norms. This chapter finds that new digital infrastructures of the commons are more often developed by private digital platforms and help to create scale and network effects; but after reaching a certain market size, platforms may also develop anti-liquidity mechanisms that restrict resource movement across platforms, thus requiring state intervention and regulation. Adopting a political–economic analysis and case study method, this chapter tries to illustrate the critical role of infrastructure in the shaping of digital commons, how it is able to help manage the mobility and order of digital resources. This chapter will focus on two cases—third-party payment tool and consumer financial credit system—-to illustrate how market infrastructures have been established by platforms and finally backed up by the government.

Chapter 5 discussed further about ownership issues of resources like data in digital commons. The digital commons is not a static but dynamic market system that is constantly undergoing fluid changes. The way in which effective resource movement is promoted and incentivized in this system becomes so critical. Traditional economic and legal theory believes property with full ownership protection is the foundation for a healthy market economy. This chapter argues that there is not necessarily a strong correlation between the realization of digital resource market and ownership per se, that is, effective market operation does not necessarily require information/data rights in the strict sense, as long as the market function is well-satisfied by digital infrastructures. In this way, this chapter tries to jump out from the legal issue of resource ownership, which is of particular interest to lawyers, and focuses on the theoretical issue of its antecedent, that is, how to form a mature market that permits the free flow of all kinds of productive resources, data included. According to the traditional thoughts in law and economics, only by clarifying property rights through the law and making them understandable and acceptable to all market players can stable universal transaction expectations. However, this chapter will argue, at least on the basis of the platform's practice in China, that the formation of digital market order and resource movement do not depend on the clear identification of property rights, and that more sustainable resource trading or exchange can only be realized through effective infrastructure design that ensures the security and order of digital commons. On the contrary, ownership for digital assets could cause tragedy of anti-commons that is popular in traditional economies. The establishment of digital market and data ownership are separate issues. The former is more critical than the latter. Since data cannot generate value separately without other productive resources, this chapter tries to focus on market process and order that facilitate resource liquidity. It is the mature infrastructure in the market that facilitates production, circulation, and consumption, against which background various measures of making good use of data could gradually come into being. This chapter will pick legal cases to discuss to what extent the platform needs certain kind of data ownership as well.

Chapter 6 moves from virtual properties to more tangible labor issues. Along with the continuous proliferation of information technology represented by the Internet, more and more new industries have emerged on the basis of new media, generating a lot of incremental value. The current labor law system has been responding to the changes brought by the digital commons at the margin, but the characteristics and consensus of the digital labor process need to be further refined, since mode of production on which the new business labor relies has not yet been fully fixed and understood. This chapter discusses how the relevant legal mechanisms adapt to the changes in mode of production, explains how the "productivity" nature of labor law is reflected in the two core elements of "mobility" and "integration", and at what institutional level it needs to be addressed. It argues that while market logics around publicity and commons (for instance, market infrastructure and public resource sharing) can help to increase the incomes of workers in new forms of employment to a certain extent, they also need aid from secondary distribution. Market issues cannot be solved purely in a market-oriented manner, as they are also social issues that need to be considered in the larger context of the relationship between the market and society. Therefore, the digital commons require us to adopt the following measures, including to further implement a fair employment system and eliminate employment discrimination; to improve the minimum wage and payment guarantee system, and to promote the inclusion of workers in new forms of employment that do not fully meet the requirements for establishing a labor relationship, and so on. This chapter will also discuss how to establish a set of social security and distribution rules for the gig workers, which is an intrinsic need and guarantee for effective digital commons.

Chapter 7 turns to the external governing structure of digital commons with Chinese style called "subcontracting". From China's experience in the development of the platform economy, the rapid and effective formation of digital mode of production cannot be achieved without a fully developed production organization and a coordinated external environment, a process that is in fact made possible through some kind of "subcontracting" or "outsourcing" governance mechanism, whereby the state consciously adopts a strategy of inclusiveness and prudence in the course of the rise of the Internet, by permitting platform companies to explore the development of their own mode of production without restricting market entrance and investment access. At the same time, the state allows platform companies adopt a variety of means of self-regulation to take on the responsibility for online activities and risk management. The platform subcontracting regime is the inevitable result of the maturity of digital commons, and it also confirms and protects the new type or mode of production and organization, which gradually dissolves the existing problem of illegitimate emergence, and retains the state of illegitimate emergence within the platform economic system through the contracting authorization, thus shifting the problem of legitimacy to the question of how to promote the effective flow and utilization of factors, which turns into a problem of innovation within the system. Therefore, this chapter illustrates how the platform subcontracting system and the administrative contracting system could become two grips for the central government to regulate socioeconomic complexity and a nationally harmonized market. The two systems represent two types of existing modes of production, and could then compete, constrain, and cooperate in different policy areas. Platform companies are already carrying out autonomous governance activities in response to resource mobility and infrastructure development, and have proposed new governance proposals in data ownership, credit management, and infrastructure-building.

Chapter 8 goes back to the original architecture of the Internet and discusses the dynamics of openness and closeness of digital commons in China. Ever since the birth of the Internet, "openness" has become an enduring ideology across the globe, claiming it helps with the formation of digital commons. But should the Internet be always kept open? To what extent? When digital technology has gradually become embedded in all aspects of sociopolitical and economic life, continuously facilitating the connection of all kinds of social resources and things, and forming an increasingly complex network, it is difficult to give a simple, one-size-fits-all answer to this question. People also often ignore some given basic assumptions, thus ignoring the interests behind the open-closed discourse, intentionally or unintentionally. The open-closed discourse is constantly evolving around some kind of abstract architectural interests, and there is a need to go beyond the purely platform-centered open-closed discourse, and return to the essence of the issue, namely, how the Internet facilitates the liquidity of productive resources and builds a robust infrastructure for the digital commons, and how to further explore to institutionalize the system to ensure a greater range of digital markets and societies for the safe and orderly flow of resources. Therefore, this chapter reshapes the open-closed discourse from existing literature, arguing that such discourse actually directs to the original architecture of the Internet, and that it is necessary to see how the architecture has been transformed from a simple technology of connectivity to a complex political economy of interest. This chapter continues to adopt a political–economic approach and briefly review the ideas, ideologies, and problems of the original open architecture of the Internet, leading to a number of societal factors and risks that have caused closeness of the commons. Changes in modes of production have played a key role during the process. Finally, it will go further to see what the China state could do to prevent further fragmentation of digital commons.

The final chapter and conclusion part extend the framework developed in this book to other jurisdictions such as the European Union and the United States. Given the diverse economic, social, and cultural contexts that influence the development of digital commons, comprehensive multidimensional comparisons are essential to enhance our understanding of this dynamic field. This book seeks to transcend the conventional comparative approach and reframe the experiences and lessons learned from the EU and US Internet governance through the lens of digital commons. While the United States and China exhibit similar regulatory approaches, both harnessing the power of large platform companies to promote and build the digital space, the EU's heavy reliance on US platforms prevents it from fostering its own. First, at the data level, the EU's GDPR and other data flow restriction policies have impeded the growth of the digital economy. In contrast, the United States has taken a more pragmatic stance in promoting data element flows. Second, at the infrastructure level, the EU's efforts to establish a unified digital market through the *Digital Market Act* have been hampered by cultural, linguistic, and other factors. This has hindered the emergence of global Internet companies, leading to a less-effective market infrastructure. Third, both the European Union and the United States have experienced the illegal rise process for the digital mode of production, but the manifestation of legal disputes differs due to varying degrees of rule of law development. Finally, the relationship between the central government and large Internet companies, as well as their political processes, helps explain the contrasting digital economy governance models adopted by the European Union and the United States. Despite the ideologies in regulatory approaches between China, European Union, and the United States, the theoretical framework presented in this book can help revisit the convergences and differences in the development of the three leading digital empires.

1 Digital commons and "illegal rise" of the Internet

1.1 Introduction

The 30-year history of the Internet in China, from its introduction to development, is a history of "illegal rise". This does not mean simply violating the existing legal rules, but mainly reflects the fact that the Internet, as a new type of mode of production, constantly connects online and offline productive resources of all kinds and mobilizes them within the scope of the society to be matched, thus generating new ways of utilizing resources creatively and efficiently, as well as disrupting the pattern and order of the forming or established industrial interests.[1] In this process, rules reflecting traditional productive relations and interests are no doubt challenged. The law as a superstructure is thus required to establish the legitimacy of new economic interests representing advanced productive forces. The law is also asked to harmonize conflicts between old and new interests thereafter.[2] Both legislative, judicial, and regulatory actions serve more or less similar functions in China all these years.

If looking closely, we will find that the "illegal rise" has manifested itself very differently at different stages of development of the Internet. In the early age, new economic infringement started from the cultural industry and gradually spread to other offline industries, a process of gradually "digitizing" all kinds of resources, and a process that is still unfolding through various sharing economies.[3] "Digitization" does not only mean that enterprises simply use information technology to organize and manage production, but also implies a change in the mode of production: Various resources are extracted from traditional industries and attracted

1 Hu Ling, "Public sphere or private asset? The nature of digital commons in China", *Peking University Law Journal* 11, no. 2 (2024), 185–198.

2 For similar studies on Western countries, see Anupam Chander, "How Law Made Silicon Valley", *Emory Law Journal* 63 (2014), 677; Julie E. Cohen, *Between Truth and Power: The Legal Constructions of Informational Capitalism*, Yale University Press, 2019. Specifically, the extent of legal change depends on the relative dominance and voice of particular traditional industries compared with the new economy.

3 A typical example is Google's digital library initiative, see Nanna Bonde Thylstrup, *The Politics of Mass Digitization*, The MIT Press, 2019. For a similar study of online literature in China, see Huijuan Chu, *Storytellers and Dream Factories: Technology, Law, and Online Literary Production*, Social Science Literature Press, 2019.

DOI: 10.4324/9781003566243-2

to open digital platforms, which process reduces the competitiveness of traditional industries and forces them to undergo a more thorough digital transformation, and finally manifests itself in the form of Internet platforms. With numerous unauthorized use of intellectual property or unfair competition against traditional industries, this stage could be regarded as version 1.0 of "illegal rise". As the Internet enters the mobile stage, the new economy further explores and establishes mode of production, dynamically tracking users and resources, and strengthening data analysis through expanding the platform architecture. By "disruptive innovation" (a popular notion since Joseph Schumpeter), the sharing economy continue to promote infringement and unfair competition around data resources and user's attention. This could be regarded as version 2.0 of "illegal rise". In contrast to the first stage, the second stage is occurring more often between competitors who both are Internet companies while the law is not clearly biased in favor of innovative infringing companies, but rather tends to recognize and promote the legitimacy survival and development of new mode of production as a whole.

From the perspective of external relations of new economy, digital enterprises not only need to continue to creatively and "illegally" obtain resources that have not yet been digitized from the physical world and traditional industries, but also need to obtain resources that have already been digitized from other competitors, so as to reduce the cost of entrepreneurship and enhance their competitive advantages. The choice of law between innovation and order becomes a key issue, which is centered in a series of unfair competition cases around data, traffic, social capital, and so on. In terms of internal relations, platform companies constantly need users as free laborers and consumers to provide behavioral data to be tracked and monitored. Meanwhile, the platforms do not want them to obtain the status of equal subjects, but rather the recipients of service agreements, and to carry out production and consumption activities under the platform's permission, which is centrally embodied in the discussion of data ownership and confirmation of labor relations cases. It is in such dual relations between the internal and external forces that a new type of productive relation is expanding, capable of satisfying the interests of the new economy as a whole while avoiding disruption of the competitive order within it. "Illegal rise" 2.0 objectively ensures that the process of digitization of society as a whole continues as ever, while protecting the existing platforms internally from the same logic, which in turn provides a key safeguard for the self-adaptation of underlying infrastructures and mode of production. These require a legal response to the legal status of property/assets that can be mobilized by platform companies.

A number of studies have emerged on data property rights,[4] particularly on the debates over whether intellectual property mechanisms can be applied to big data,[5] with a normative analysis mainly on the rights construction rather than value

4 A. Perzanowski and J. Schultz, *The End of Ownership: Personal Property in the Digital Economy*, MIT Press, 2014.

5 See Cui Guobin, "The Underlying Theory of Limited Exclusion Rights in Big Data", *Legal Studies* 5, no. 5 (2019), 3–24.

production. Chapters 5 and 6 of this book will focus on details of data property issue. This chapter briefly reinforces the view that legislative entrenchment of data property/assets (and other types of digital property) may misunderstand the essence of digital economy and increase the cost of production and mobility. It is not so much the existence of ownership that matters, but rather the orderly process of productive resources mobility and aggregation. The law should try to minimize such costs during productive process, while at the same time curbing the ever-reinforcing moat of the platforms.

Sections II and III briefly describe and compare the two stages of "illegal rise", arguing that the evolution from 1.0 to 2.0 reflects not only the unchanging nature of digital economy, but also how the law actually chooses to maintain a balance between order and innovation. The new economy has always been characterized by the paradoxical dichotomy between the need to expand and absorb new resources to create new markets and the need to build a gated garden to prevent other competitors from trespassing and invasion into its borders. If low-cost expansion stagnates, innovation across the Internet could be undermined and development will come to a halt; but if unfair competition is allowed to go unchecked, the market and the productive process will become disorganized as well, giving rise to adverse selection. The issue of data property highlighted in "illegal rise" 2.0 reflects such a two-way movement and different demands. Section IV concludes with a vision for the future of production in the digital economy, reflecting on how the law can provide incentives to further mobilize idle productive resources.

1.2 Illegal rise 1.0 in early age of the Internet

1.2.1 Stages of illegal rise

The theoretical significance of this political–economic concept of "illegal rise" lies in understanding, from the perspective of production, how law is called upon to adapt to the prevailing mode of production representing advanced productive forces and to protect the interests behind them. At a time when the industrial economy's mode of production was unable to meet the needs of the information economy, by relying on its own low-cost organization to deploy productive resources, and thus changing the relationship between workers and productive organizers, the Internet consequently transformed the attributes of the legal relations that reflect productive relations as well as of the various types of rights that arise from the process of production. Thus, what appeared at the time to be an "unlawful" infringement was actually a manifestation of the advanced productive forces, which required the law to recognize and protect this unlawful model.

In the two decades since the introduction of Internet to China, tremendous changes have taken place, and some of the basic elements of the new economy have been widely practiced and accepted. For instance, the model of "free + advertisement + value-added service + subscription" has been firmly established. The status of data as a basic productive resource and enterprise's asset has been discovered and explored. Along with the rise of platform-based enterprises, "connecting everything together" has become the main goal of Internet development.

The "cloud-network-end device" framework has been promoted as a new type of information infrastructure. The "sharing economy" has become mainstream ideology that everyone is talking about. In any case, it is difficult to hide behind the complexity of innovations an obvious logic on which Internet businesses are based: The acquisition of free content or labor at low costs.

In its early stages, the Internet developed out of a so-called cyberspace, which, because of its focus on the dissemination of information and its detachment from physical world, led to debates about whether governments should regulate this space.[6] However, similar theoretical reflections did not occur at the beginning of the introduction of Internet in China. Rather, the rise of the Internet was driven more by national effort to pursue technology modernization and commercial forces, which clashed with traditional industries from the outset. During the process, Internet companies not only violate domestic laws, but instead also wanted the law to recognize and protect their arising business model.

This conflict is not difficult to understand: In order to attract users in the early days, it was necessary to gather a large amount of free content in a short period of time, which was not only the need for capital expansion, but also a consensus gradually reached by the state and entrepreneurs. From the beginning, the Internet looked similar to traditional media model, which adopted the profit model of free content and advertising. Most of the free content comes from unauthorized use of books, music, and movies published and distributed through traditional channels, which are digitized for free use. This conspicuous infringement along with venture capital helped to realize the original accumulation of the new economy and attract a large amount of loyal users since then. It serves at least two functions: First, it invests a large amount of cost to digitize human works, laying the foundation and standard for subsequent users to directly produce digitized works accordingly. Second, it creates the impression in the minds of users once and for all that basic Internet services are free, setting the tone for the entire Chinese Internet development model.[7]

As China strengthens its protection of intellectual property rights after Beijing Olympic Games in 2008, access to free content requires more licensed inputs. In order to save costs, Internet companies have turned to a large number of users and encouraged them to produce for the Internet, entering a stage called "web 2.0" featuring in online interaction among users. Turning users into free labor is a major innovation in the new industry. It has far-reaching significance: First, users are tightly bound to information technology devices, with their identity transformed into "prosumers" who can either produce original works, or be encouraged to provide pirated works. Second, a new mode of production different from traditional publishing channels is gradually being explored. Online contents broke physical

6 John P. Barlow, "A Declaration of Independence of Cyberspace", available at https://www.eff.org/cyberspace-independence.

7 This model extends to the offline world. The consequences are even more far-reaching: under capital collusion, two or three oligopolies have been formed in many market areas, or have been invested or acquired by giant platforms. At the same time, free of charge has become a sharp weapon to defeat the traditional competitors.

limitations of traditional books and music as a whole piece of product, becoming more fragmented and facilitating mass production. Third, the boundaries of the traditional productive organization—the enterprise—that traditional economic theories focus on are dissolving. Its productive activities are becoming increasingly decentralized and outsourced to the public in large quantities, forming a long-tailed chain in terms of value, which has brought about innovative ideas in economic theories.[8] Lastly, individualized production (or "peer-production" has become the predecessor of the "sharing economy", which has provided a reference model for the rapid expansion of the Internet into offline service industry.

In the second following stage, with the rapid replacement of desktop-era Internet by mobile Internet, digital economy is firmly established and is beginning to shift from an information-sharing platform to the connection and sharing of financial, human labor, and physical resources. The control of traditional money, labor, and physical resources was in the hands of established economic organizations and not fully utilized and matched with consumers, thus it could not be used effectively due to the high cost of information. Through digital platforms, these productive resources are extracted and utilized in a wider context beyond traditional organizations, enhancing the efficiency of their use. At the same time, platforms are gradually becoming new channels and organizations for algorithm-driven resource mobility, or integrating old organizations into the platform chain as a whole. Similar to the first stage, in the process of productive resources flowing from established organizations to new platforms, they are inevitably constrained by established legal rules, which in turn trigger conflicts between old and new productive organizations, requiring the law to reconfirm the boundaries of interests.

As can be seen from the above description of the stages of development in new economy, the Internet is essentially a way of exploiting the productive resource and labor in society at low cost and accumulating data on their use and matching (through unauthorized use, value-added services, mobilization through information platforms, piracy, and unfair competition). Since platforms do not exercise tight ownership over these productive resource and labor, they prefer to claim that they do not assume any responsibilities of traditional organizations (such as employer liability), but rather are a kind of "connector" of the resources and allows them to flow as freely as possible. In this sense, the logic of the Internet, which opposes all laws and institutions (including national borders) that impede the free flow from bits to atoms, has always been commercial rather than political. The more recent sharing economy is but a by-product of the Internet's evolution to a more massively collaborative stage, where cloud storage capacity, precise algorithmic capabilities, and control over decentralized resources have been greatly enhanced.[9] The digital commons has thus emerged with such model.

8 Yochai Benkler, *The Wealth of Networks*, Yale University Press, 2006.

9 For instance, through credit evaluation and certification mechanisms, platform companies can manage the resources moving through them in a more dynamic manner, complemented and protected by mechanisms such as insurance.

The need for the Internet to attract users with high-quality content is the main reason why the revolution in the information economy first took place in mass media. The Internet has gradually explored unique business models, from self-provision of content to mobilization of user-generated contents to agorithmic production in the future, with illegal behaviors such as piracy and copyright infringement as a constant core issue. It is necessary to distinguish between the early sporadic individual acts of piracy and the mass domination of invocation as a new mode of production, even though the latter is regarded as more serious by traditional right holders. From the perspective of new economy, the mobilization of assets through accurate matching of information is a more creative way of generating value, offering a wide range of opportunities for cooperation and increasing overall economic efficiency.[10] The "illegal rise" of the Internet is more of a transformation in the mode of production, raising specific questions for legislators and regulators about how to recognize the legitimacy of such mode of production and distribution of benefits, as well as highlighting key issues of self-regulation within the new economy.

Illegal rise 1.0 took place in the first decade or so of the proliferation of the commercial Internet in China, which saw the emergence of a large amount of copyright infringements and piracy against the cultural industry. First, both domestic policies and laws at the time tacitly endorsed digitization, with the implicit premise that "free + advertisement" approach and on-demand customization could attract users and create a wider network effect. Second, although the disputed sources of free content need to be carefully identified, many infringing websites often evade liability from vague rules, taking advantage of safe harbor rule in favor of new model and the cost of litigation for the parties involved.[11] Third, the creation of a new type of copyright, "right of communication through information network", has brought crucial support to digital production, providing legal protection for Internet companies to collect, produce, and disseminate online works. As long as large amounts of information can be accessed at low cost, and the channels and licenses for dissemination and access are restricted, non-scarce resources can be made artificially scarce, bringing the economics of the physical world back into play. The main result of illegal rise 1.0 is that the new economy is largely recognized for its legitimacy at a time when the law and related supporting institutions are not yet complete.

Moreover, whether illegal rise 1.0 implies that the new economy is unfair competition against traditional industries is no longer a controversial theoretical issue. A growing number of researchers have recognized that increasing production and distribution efficiency through improved technology is consistent with competition principles and objectives, and could contribute to the overall welfare of society in

10 The term "sharing economy" has been overly abused to the extent that more attention has been paid to the allocation of existing productive resources (mobilizing idle resources) than to the distribution of benefits (the division of benefits from the use of information platforms by producers).

11 More controversial is the issue of the form and effectiveness of the notification.

the long run, even though it may result in "creative destruction" or degradation of traditional industries. Nonetheless, traditional industries (and the people who work with them) can still create thorny social problems in the short term by reducing competitiveness and compromising profitability, which is why the law has to balance the interests of the old and the new economy by pushing the new economy to accelerate the absorption of resources from the former, while requiring a reduction in the speed and scale of the digitization of physical resources in areas of public interest, so as to avoid over-aggressiveness and the creation of more interlocking social problems.

1.2.2 Organizational phase change

As a physical phenomenon, "phase change" means that due to changes in the external environment, the substance itself will undergo a change in state (for instance from solid to liquid), but the basic elements that constitute the substance remain unchanged. It is only the internal structure of the substance and the state of motion that could endure a transformative process. With the help of such perspective, this chapter argues that the change in mode of production brought about by technology is more similar to the process of phase change. Namely, the productive resources occurring in the traditional mode of production, along with the reduction of the cost of internal cooperation and matching, will be attracted out of the organization to recombine for new value, thus gradually forming another seemingly different productive organization. In the process of such mode shift, our understanding of the legal attributes of the resources and the legal relationship between the subjects will change (for instance, from employment relations to cooperation relations). The current digital economy model has changed from a centralized productive organization to a loose but controllable one, where the relationship between resources and productive organizations and the connection between resources have become more flexible. However, they are able to cooperate with each other to generate value on a large scale, which improves the efficiency in the economic cycle. In this model, the phenomenon of what the economists call "infinite supply" has emerged, a metaphor for the continuous availability of resources, which is closer to streaming services than to the mere transfer of possession of fragmented goods. Of course, software and operating systems can be made more powerful with a given amount of computing power, but the labor and resources behind are still finite, and marginal returns can be incremental in the digital economy because platforms need to incorporate both producers and consumers who can bring value at scale.[12]

Under the traditional industrial organization-dominated mode of production, property can be understood in terms of both means of production and consumption. As far as the means of production are concerned, the enterprise relies on the basic productive tools such as machinery, plant, land, intellectual property, and so on, and a large number of resources are incorporated into the enterprise organization to

12 W. Brian Arthur, *Complexity and the Economy*, Oxford University Press, 2014.

be processed and formed into new commodities for sale to the outside world. The production–distribution–consumption nexus are separated. In the case of means of consumption, the transfer of ownership occurs when the consumer buys goods in the market. The consumer can possess and dispose of his private property and even sell it in second-hand market. Property in the sense of consumer goods is irrelevant to the producer as soon as it is produced, and its physical characteristics determine the period of use and specific warranty requirements. In the context of industrial-era productive processes, the social functions of property also include providing a stable order and expectation of production, ensuring the security of transactions, protecting privacy and autonomy, reducing transaction costs, and stabilizing the social order. Thus, property rights have shaped an imaginary of production and consumption order.

In this sense, property, as we usually understand it, always revolves around physical objects with boundaries that can be quantified and transferred, and often tends to view particular objects in isolation. Digital mode of production, however, are more inclined to demonstrate a networked way of imagining property. Namely, the value of a single resource is much lower than the value that shapes the entire network of transactions and collaborations. Realization of a particular piece of resource value is not that important, but enhancement of the entire network value through the continual promotion matters a lot. This is difficult to grasp in economic processes in the physical world, where consumer data is primarily obtained through market survey conducted through traditional business channels, but becomes relatively easy in the digital world. Both virtual and physical goods can be viewed as product of a circular flow along a particular network (or architecture) of platform company, which can be used to satisfy a wider range of needs at the same time or over a period of time.

The process of transformation of traditional industrial organizations into platform organizations is briefly described below. First, platform organizations use mass peer production to capture value, and producers increase in scale; second, platform companies effectively connect production, distribution, and consumption segments, so that the information economy cycle is greatly accelerated around stable transaction and distribution networks; third, the platform infrastructure has been gradually consolidated, not only as a market mechanism for the orderly flow of various resources, but also as a technological basis for the effective use of resources themselves, thus exerting more control over the use of resources; finally, the boundary between the means of production and consumption has become blurred, and producers are also consumers in the process of the digital economy, so that people can instantly consume the information content produced by others and create more new contents. Similarly, the sharing economy encourages people to share specific physical goods (information goods are not required to be shared), namely, retaining ownership of the original idle resources and making full social and circular use of them in a solid way. Under sharing economy, the boundaries between purchasing for consumption and subletting for profit become further blurred. For instance, online car renting platforms has gradually moved from the early sharing to a model of directly providing car rental services, or even providing loans for external drivers to purchase cars.

1.3 Transformation to illegal rise 2.0

Illegal rise 2.0 embodies a logically peculiar two-way movement. Externally, it continues to follow the logic of 1.0 to further expand the scope of new economy as a whole, so that the cyberspace gradually covers the physical world and continues to absorb and compete for resources to develop new services, which reflects the relationship between new economy and traditional industrial economy. Internally, it starts to recognize the right of a more solid "architecture" to stabilize the order of production, thus ultimately establishing the basis for the existence of new productive relations, which reflects the relationship between platforms and users within the new economy. In illegal rise 1.0, the main conflict surrounding the Internet was the question of legitimacy, namely, in which areas the Internet was allowed to exist and expand as a business model; while in illegal rise 2.0, legitimacy as a political issue was no longer critical, and the main conflicts became legal issues of delimiting the boundaries of property rights within the new economy, such as unfair competition, labor relations, and information/data ownership. Production issues gradually shift to reproduction and distribution.

Interestingly, it is precisely the logic of external expansion that leads directly to the claim of intrinsic rights, because the logic of "illegal rise" of external expansion applies perfectly well within the new economy later on. For platform companies that survive through stage 1.0, there is a need both to fend off unfair competition from new entrepreneurs and to build new types of infrastructure to ensure that legitimate production can be sustained, with sufficient legal protection. The abstraction on which this dual objective is based is called "architecture", which goes beyond the narrow notion of a computer system to refer to the controllable boundaries within which platform companies are able to track their users by means of "account-data-algorithm-rating" mechanism, both as a spatial implication and as a logical notion of extension of production/control power.

Compared with stage 1.0, although stage 2.0 involves a different legal environment,[13] the fundamental theoretical issue remains unchanged, namely, how the law needs to reflect advanced productive forces and protect productive relations accordingly. When productive relations representing advanced productive forces expand steadily, in line with slow change of law in physical world, then it will not cause too many problems in a relatively stable period of time. However, if the productive order is constantly challenged by the disruptive nature of emerging tech-

13 Stage 2.0 places greater emphases on the formal rationality of user' agreements (although courts are still lax in conducting substantive review), with growing judicial and law enforcement capacity, a better external rule of law environment, and more importantly, a degree of self-help capability within the digital architecture itself, especially if the law fails to provide effective protection. Civil remedies often fail to provide effective protection, relying more on the protection provided by criminal law.

nologies or business models, the intrinsic security and stability values of law will be impacted, thus requiring consideration of whether to support innovative practices representing advanced productive forces or to protect competition order.[14] The answer to this question in the stage 2.0 is to maintain the new economic mode of production as a whole, allowing the logic to expand further, while not permitting the common ground to be weakened by law.[15] The alternative solution is to recognize the vested interests of large platform companies, to ensure the orderly flow of productive resources, to ensure the orderly expansion of the architecture, and to promote the creation of infrastructural services. If the history of stage 1.0 was simply too rapid and chaotic to be summarized in terms of legal rules, stage 2.0 demonstrates more sharply how the law protects platform architectures, implying that the illegal rise is no longer a question of legitimacy in normative sense, but a question of redefining the boundaries of rights in details.[16]

Illegal rise 2.0 undoubtedly responds to the core needs of the new economy. According to classical law and economic principles, the effective functioning of the market requires clearly defined private property rights, a system of property transfer and exchange based on contracts with consideration, a productive process that can continuously provide productive value, with effective judicial protection. In digital economic environment, after stage 1.0, the legitimacy of the productive process has been initially established, but the productive mechanism has not been fully finalized. The ownership of productive resource is still unclear, and the courts lack strong incentives to protect for legitimate use of productive resources. These problems have been answered to a certain extent in stage 2.0, but they reflect characteristics that are quite contrary to traditional principles.

First, productive resources like data no longer require clear property rights and can still flow efficiently and generate significant value. Second, labor value does not require explicit informed consent or an employment relationship, and there is a large common pool of "free" and flexible laborers. Third, the norms for data possession and use (access) are merged, protecting the right of platform to control its aggregated data. However, for users, they can only share with platforms in the

14 A recent example of this is the short video and long-form video debate, where video platforms that used piracy to attract data traffic in the early days have now become movie and TV series copyright holder, with incentives to discourage the secondary creative practices of compressing long-form content and their associated short-form video platforms, even though the latter are more popular with the younger generation.

15 This is why this chapter argues that the beginning of the 2.0 phase was the Tencent and Qihoo's war in 2011, in which the Supreme Court blocked for the first time Qihoo's attempts to tear apart the legitimacy of the Internet (namely, its natural monopoly) from an internal position, laying the groundwork for the expansion of the platform in the mobile Internet era. A handful of antitrust cases have followed challenging WeChat's market position, while all unsuccessful under the influence of such precedent.

16 In China's statutory law tradition, this tendency translates into relying heavily on abstract principle-based provisions, most notably the first two paragraphs of Article 2 of the *Anti-Unfair Competition Law*, which has 105 words that bear as much impact on China's Internet as Section 230 of the *Communication Decency Act* has had on the US Internet.

fruits of their labor. Lastly, it is the judiciary rather than the legislature that is progressively pushing for the protection of property rights in data, responding to the needs of platform companies, and thus being progressive and efficient in solving new problems posed by technology.[17] In this sense, cyberlaw as a whole is beginning to be constructive rather than destructive, thus transforming the concept of "illegal rise" from a critical political–economic concept into an operational law and economics one.

This constructiveness can be partly explained by the distinction between property rule and liability rule in law and economics, which explains how the early new economy was able to transform productive resources in the physical world from atoms to bits at low cost, and to utilize them efficiently.[18] A large amount of intellectual property infringements helped to facilitate the digital transformation of resources and the exploration of viable business models. Objectively, the use of such resources was closer to a liability rule than a property rule, whereby the law dealt with possible infringements *ex post*, depending on the circumstances of the case, but did not effectively prevent the (creative, but unlawful) use of resources *ex ante*. This provided institutional incentives and sufficient space for cooperation with mass innovation and drove the Internet industry to prosper. But after that, the demand for licensing and aggregated property rights by dominant platform companies contributed to return from liability rule to property rule, with courts increasingly less inclined to support the former, generally increasing the level of protection of data resources and raising the costs of data use by public.

Overall, the law relating to illegal rise 2.0 is characterized by (1) a tendency for property rules to take precedence over liability rules for particular platform companies, requiring property rules to protect their vested interests, but remaining a liability rule (namely, opting out) for free data and labor from users; (2) an emphasis on protection of abstract "architecture" and its aggregated values, recognized through default user agreements; (3) a series of measures around competition law (extensive use of principle-based provisions of *Anti-Unfair Competition Law*) that have been continuously improved, sufficient to ensure that platforms' aggregated property interests are protected; (4) less dependence on antitrust laws that have not been applied as frequently as in Western countries to avoid fluctuating impacts on the continuity of the Internet model and digital infrastructure; and (5) a process in which giant platforms continue to transfer responsibilities and risks to productive resources and society on the one hand, and emphasize their social responsibilities, on the other hand, creating an unbalanced redistribution and compensation mechanism.

17 Not to mention that the state has specifically established Internet courts to provide specialized trial jurisdiction over Internet-related cases.

18 Guido Calabresi and A. Douglas Melamed, "Property Rules, Liability Rules, and Inalienability: One View of the Cathedral", *Harvard Law Review* 85, no. 6 (1972), 1089–1128; Mark A. Lemley and Philip J. Weiser, "Should Property or Liability Rules Govern Information", *Texas Law Review* 85, no. 4 (2007), 783–842.

1.4 How law responds to the illegal rise

On the surface of it, the Internet is an incremental change, combining and utilizing resources (both inside and outside the system) that were previously beyond the reach of governments and traditional economic organizations. Since the shift is happening so quickly, not only is traditional industrial economic thinking failing to keep up, but so is the managerial thinking of regulators.[19] While the new legal issues superficially impact on the existing social order and management styles, the deeper factors are the ways of economic development in the industrial era reflected behind the existing rules. Namely, traditional enterprises are standard productive organizations occupying large quantities of productive resources. The use of certain resources requires prior consent of the right holders in the form of agreement. Such use also requires regulatory measures from agencies, such as licensing, annual inspections, and so on. Conversely, platform companies demand rapid mobilization of a wider and broader range of productive resources, free from the constraints of established rules, thus indirectly affecting traditional organizations that have not yet adopted information technology for profit, who in turn have an incentive to lobby the government to tighten regulation of the new economy, so as to safeguard vested economic interests and forms of industrial economy. New issues have arisen in many areas of Chinese law, including copyright, data property, privacy, unfair competition, antitrust, labor law, and security regulation.

The new economy has no intention to change the nature of traditional rule, but rather wish to become an exception to that rule, mitigating tort and security liabilities and thus ensuring the new business model survives. Its core proposition is that Internet platforms do not have to own any assets, but are merely information intermediaries for mobilization and matching of the resources, in the hope of forming an ecosystem in which productive resources on the platforms are autonomous, with as little traditional owner or employer liability as possible. The logic of such "separation of ownership and access" has been consistently reflected in all phases of the Internet history. In the early days, the copying of information content from other websites could be considered a type of use (which led to piracy and unfair competition); while more recently, the mobilization of privately owned vehicles and houses through access could still be considered a type of use (which led to violations of existing regulatory rules). The following examples of how the law has responded to the conflicts of interest brought about by the Internet, using two of the most common types of unlawful behavior—copyright infringement and unfair competition, will reveal the complex commercial logic and political economy contexts in which they operate.

In his influential theoretical book *Code and Other Laws in Cyberspace*, Lawrence Lessig argues that the code, as rule in cyberspace, can protect intellectual property rights alongside, or even more effectively than, real-world laws and

19 Angela Huyue Zhang, *High Wire: How China Regulates Big Tech and Governs Its Economy*, Oxford University Press, 2024.

social norms.[20] In particular, under the premise that the law already provides the same protection as in physical space, code can serve a dual protection function, as represented by the then popular Digital Rights Management (DRM) system. Influenced by the US *Digital Millennium Copyright Act* (DMCA), copyright law in China have incorporated anti-circumvention technological protection measures. In the abstract sense, code can be used for copyright protection. But the unspoken question is, whose copyright is being protected? Who is better able to use code for protection? In the early stages of the Internet, digital companies, in an effort to attract users with free content, often pirated works distributed through traditional channels and brought them onto the Internet at low cost. Given the traditional channels' weak ability to integrate resources and collectively defend their rights, they failed to stop the illegal rise of the Internet as a new channel on a national scale. With DMCA, Internet companies have been able to grow under the principle of safe harbor (notice-take down mechanism), and have been given the opportunity to cooperate with traditional cultural industries on the basis of a large number of users, creating a platform that "connects everything together". This history laid the foundations of the Internet industry, where code was used to digitize works distributed in traditional media and exploited through free business models, becoming first and foremost a tool for copyright infringement. The law was called upon to protect the emerging economy against traditional industries, recognizing its overall legitimacy, and this has been successful in the context of the state's desire to develop the information industry. That's not to say that the state hasn't taken steps to strike on online piracy (such as special crackdowns on P2P software), but this has only hit those who share the software for downloading pirated works, but has not shaken more companies like Baidu, which has gone through a number of lawsuits brought by domestic and international recording companies during the years 2004–2008. This echoed the reality that many users at the time were accustomed to downloading digital works to their computers, and online direct browsing had yet to become the dominant mode of production. Neither traditional nor digital publishing was yet mature enough to rely on code to enhance copyright protection.

While infringement of the "right of communication of information network" was a relatively common lawsuit in the early days between the traditional cultural industries and new economy, it is interesting to note that since 2012, more lawsuits for infringement of such rights have been filed on the grounds of unfair competition instead. Such shift is closely related to several important factors. First, these lawsuits are less likely to occur between the old and new economies and more likely within the new economy sphere, say, with video sites that might have been defendants for infringement now becoming plaintiffs. This is mainly due to the fact that the central government is determined to promote the "National Intellectual Property Strategy" to develop cultural and information industries with creative intellectual property rights in the face of both domestic and international pressures. Resource-intensive industries such as online video or literature have seen

20 Lawrence Lessig, *Code and Other Laws in Cyberspace*, Basic Books, 1999.

a trend of large-scale consolidation, and investors have spared no expense in purchasing domestic and foreign licensed works, which has also pushed up the price of copyrights. Giant Internet companies have become the new owners of intellectual property rights, and are more motivated and capable of defending their rights than traditional industries.

However, this does not mean piracy is over, but that the way of infringement has changed considerably. With gradual popularization of 4G networks, Chinese people have become more accustomed to receiving streaming services, with software, games, songs, films, and TV series all appearing in the form of a steady stream of services rather than commodities for sale, which explains the gradual decline in piracy from users over the same period. Traditional online publishing may still rely on digital copies, creating artificial scarcity in an information service with zero marginal cost, which can be protected using DRM. Streaming services, however, have moved away from this mindset altogether. In this new phase, the incentive to pirate through digital tools is rather the start-ups, who lack enough capital to squeeze into a resource-intensive industry, and thus cannot attract users through free content, and have to resort to infringing on other companies' content and exploiting it for free. They will have to grab copyrighted works, user-generative contents, and user data to compete in the same way at the lowest cost. In this sense, the illegal rise is always alive and well. Now it is the turn of the giants with vast resources to be challenged by infringement.

The courts' expansive interpretation of unfair competition on the Internet has also spurred an explosion of such litigation. Infringement of the right of communication of information network is also in a sense an act of unfair competition, even if the infringer and the right holder belong to two different industries (for instance, content service and search engine). Article 2 of the *Anti-Unfair Competition Law* is sufficiently broad to have gained wide support in local courts of major cities with a high concentration of Internet companies. Lawyers representing right holders are also increasingly inclined to bring actions in the name of unfair competition. It is difficult to prove that they have suffered actual damages and their causation, which makes it inconvenient to sue for mere infringement on certain civil rights. In such process, codes are still not widely used for the purpose of protecting one's own resources.

But does the law really provide effective protection? The amount of compensation in most cases is less than a day's worth of advertising revenue for the infringer. Not to mention, it is difficult to prove that the right holder's revenue is necessarily reduced as a result. It could be argued that similar lawsuits are more of a symbol of the right holders' desire for the courts to recognize relevant interests and business models, such as data commons with property rights and the important role of commercial advertising. A recent pattern of unfair competition has been the blocking or removal of advertisements accompanying free video content through browsers or players, disguised as utilizing and intercepting free content to place their own advertisements. Local courts have been inclined to find unfair competition behavior in such activities, which amounts to granting content service platforms the right to review the technical standards of downstream software tools.

This could inevitably lead to further control by those platforms ranging from video players to browsers and even routers to prevent the blocking of advertisements and form "vertical integration".

The social consequences of relying on laws rather than codes for protection can therefore be further summarized.[21] As we have seen, unlike 1.0 stage, the courts in 2.0 stage spared no effort to strengthen protection in online infringement cases, but were ineffective in establishing rules and authority in a rapidly changing market. The court's decision was intended to reduce unfair competition, but relatively weak protection may prompt Internet companies to start investing more in utilizing technological protection measures to prevent their own contents from being captured, as well as creating more vertically closed video players, browsers, and mobile APPs, which will further lead to the fragmentation of Internet content services. However, it should be noted that the first stage of architectural protection appeared in the era when the business model was not yet mature, and the architecture is used to prevent unauthorized use and reduce mobility. Later, the code is built more on the basis of ensuring mobility of the information content from traditional channels so as to maximize the use of these resources within an architecture.

In response, traditional industries have adopted different strategies to deal with such challenges. The most direct option is to negotiate or take a lawsuit for damages. Once they realized that digital economy was unstoppable, they turned to cooperating with Internet companies or entering the Internet industry themselves. In any case, this means that the new mode of production has been widely accepted and has become the social foundation for the government's "Internet Plus" policy. In this process, the Internet business model has been recognized, bleached, and also experienced the refinement and upgrading from rough to fine, further enhancing the competitive ability through algorithms.[22]

1.5 Extended application of the framework

As a theoretical framework, apart from describing and explaining the historical facts, "illegal rise" also needs to have certain applicability, which can be used to predict the possible problems that may arise in the mobile Internet age or even in the future. Historically, the degree of integration and conflict between industries,[23] national policy support,[24] the overall marketization of society and administrative

21 The rise and development of the new economy first requires the protection of laws and external sovereigns, depending on the strategy of the new economy to overcome the old ones. The conflict between modes of production is something that traditional Code Theory does not pay attention to.

22 The Wei Zexi Incident in 2016 led to a vocal denunciation of Baidu's bidding ranking system, essentially a repudiation of such crude business model.

23 The degree of integration and bargaining power of different industries directly affects the degree of Internet penetration into that industry. In addition, the state takes into account the behavioral habits of traditional industry participants when balancing conflicting interests; for instance, to avoid strikes by cab drivers, which would affect social stability, the Ministry of Transportation has adopted a compromise stance in the private car regulatory scheme.

24 National policies such as "Internet Plus", "Open Government Data", and "Sharing Economy".

management, the effect of court judgments, and even the popularity of ICT have all directly or indirectly affected proliferation of the Internet. If the "illegal rise" is primarily a process description of the new economy's continuous erosion of traditional economy, it is easy to see that this process is also playing out within the new economy, which allows this framework to continue to explain the evolution of Chinese Internet.

Competition among Internet enterprises in the platform era mainly focuses on data storage and analysis (cloud), content disseminating channels (network), and terminal hardware (endpoint). In order to attract users, content channels are still the most valuable competitive advantage for start-ups. Given that platform-based enterprises possess a large amount of licensed content resources and user data, small- and medium-sized developers can only obtain productive resource through third-party cooperation or infringement. The mobile Internet maintains the business logic of the Internet in the desktop computer era, and productive resources are still creatively scrambled among platform companies in an aggressive manner.[25] In addition to PC terminals, a large amount of new types of terminals continue to emerge, such as tablets, smartphones, smartwatches, driverless cars, and VR (metaverse). Rapid change has led many Internet giants with substantial resources to focus more on cross-screen competition, utilizing free resources displayed on one screen to another. Transferring content from old terminal channels to new terminals to gain a competitive advantage has also become an unavoidable choice for emerging companies, and its business logic has no difference from the way the Internet encroached on the traditional cultural industry in the early days, or even the logic of sharing economy, which calls for physical resources without permission. As academics have failed to provide a unified theory of unfair competition on the Internet as a guidance, it is impossible to expect the court's decision to provide clear guidelines for future infringements.

The difference may lie in the fact that the early profiting Internet giants have strengthened protection over productive resources from competitors, and have done so through technological measures. It is foreseeable that future legal conflicts will continue to revolve around content resources and data, in addition to conflicts with more traditional industries. From the experience of the past two decades, the impact of the disruptive innovations brought by the Internet to Chinese society has been enormous, and the state has been paving the way for the rise of new economy in terms of both policy and law. However, when platform giants have become vested interests, controlling the entrance to cyberspace and productive resources that serve as the basis for innovation, it is necessary to observe whether lawmakers have really understood the inherent logic of Internet development. The process of innovation is always accompanied by infringement and reshaping of boundaries of productive resources. Balancing the disruption of the market order brought about by unfair competition with the new value brought about by innovation will be core issue in related industrial policy.

25 Deep linking and video aggregation is one of the most typical forms of infringement.

When observing the shift in the process of illegal rise through the lens of digital property, one can conclude that, first, the emergence of the new economy requires that resources remain mobile and low-cost to be illicitly acquired, dynamically accumulating more user behavioral data. Meanwhile, requiring them to stay within its own ever-expanding architecture rather than across platforms, they can be constantly monitored and tracked through the architecture's micromachinery. Externally, it requires that the architecture be free from the law and replace the law by itself. Through all these years of accumulation by judicial cases, the law has made its choice to protect the vested interests, laying down a competitive order outside the architecture.

Second, platform companies are centrally regulated through technology and business models that continuously transform products into services. Labor theory can be regarded as one of the core theories of virtual value generation, and the following question is to recognize and protect whose labor interest: The platform requires a large number of free laborers for low-cost production, while faces users' demand for virtual property and confirmation of labor relationship. However, in terms of confirmation of data ownership, the platforms also similarly demand the right to virtual properties obtained through labor. The law actually makes the choice to protect property rights of platform company and less to recognize the property rights of users as producers, which lays down the production order within the architecture.

Third, data resource not only needs to flow, but also needs to be accumulated in order to form data commons and scale effects. With the rise of rights discourse, both competitors and users have incentives to claim relatively independent virtual property rights, thus increasing the production costs of the entire new economy, and even facing fragmentation of cyberspace. By rejecting the infringer's attempts to bargain in unfair competition cases, as well as the tendency of individuals to take full possession and control of data, the law essentially tends to preserve the integrity of collective rights within the architecture, ultimately stabilizing the order of production through the protection of the architecture and its productive space, which in turn establishes the boundaries of the property rights to data. Such boundaries are continually facilitated through factors such as consumer choice, acquiescence in judicial activity, and ambiguity in legal provisions, and become the result of collective action as a whole.

1.6 Future of digital economy after illegal rise

This chapter explains how a whole new set of property mechanisms have been created in the Internet era, embedded in the new economic productive process, and moving from disorderly use to order. This is the foundation of digital commons in China. The mystery of the new economy lies in how to bring about an orderly mobility of resources and how to prevent disorderly competition after illegal rise 1.0 diverted all kinds of resources from traditional industries or mobilized idle resources. Local courts protect market order not only based on productivity and innovation or consumer welfare criteria, but also incorporate more business ethical criteria. Fragmented data rights or resources are also a form of mobility, but they do not help to generate integrated value. Thus, the new economy takes on two basic dynamics, the constant digitization of offline resources and the embracement of resources to be integrated as much as possible to generate collective value and flow within the same architectural ecosystem. Both the integration of resources and architectures are superior to fragmented property rights. The core issues of new mode of production have thus been legally resolved. The productive relations have not prevented the continued development of productive forces. Future issue could be the design of distributive mechanism, namely, how to evaluate public resources obtained from the public sphere, and how all labors can benefit equally from the digital commons.

If illegal rise 1.0 confirmed the legitimacy of new economy, stage 2.0 goes further and shows how the illicit state can be absorbed into the normal productive order of digital economy and become lawful again. The growth of the Internet required the emergence of illegitimacy as a way of breaking down vested interests and creating new competitors. The next stage of illegal rise may exist in Internet of Things, AI, and more disruptive scenarios. This implies the virtualization of more public space with a certain degree of commoditization, which needs to be taken seriously.

The resulting lesson hereafter is that, in order to promote economic growth, there is a need to reduce the clear delineation and protection of property rights, to continually transform property rules into liability rules, so as to avoid costly authorization and negotiation processes, and finally reduce transaction costs. But the question is whether such processes should be the norm or the exception in the long run. In stage 2.0, local courts have shifted its protections, helping to create a number of increasingly closed and bounded commons of public resources by trying to maintain the legitimacy of resource while preserving new mode of production. As it stands, this process is largely running smoothly, with high-quality resources further concentrated in the giant platforms and the new economy still growing rapidly. The risk is that the concentration of data resources could potentially affect the scale of future innovation, that is, those new business model developments that need to rely on large amounts of low-cost resources. How to maintain the balance and transformation of a small number of giant platforms and a large number of long-tail enterprises is key to ensuring the smooth proceeding of the digital economy in the future.

The contemporary sharing economy mechanism is effective to promote the utilization of resources, aiming to overcome the lemon market by reducing the cost of transaction information.[26] In line with the discussion of data property rights generation in this chapter, a one-size-fits-all complete application of property rules by courts that focus solely on the protection of the economic value of data and market order will not be sufficient to maintain the dynamic balance of this market. It is

26 Adam D. Thierer et al., "How the Internet, the Sharing Economy, and Reputational Feedback Mechanisms Solve the 'Lemons Problem'", *University of Miami Law Review* 70, no. 3 (2016), 1–47.

necessary to see the crucial function of further legitimate mobility of resources between platforms.

This chapter also implicitly concludes that illegal rise will not cease. The reason for this is that the original architecture of the Internet was open, and unless current transmission protocols (such as the World Wide Web protocols) are discontinued, innovators will always have the incentive and the means to engage in illegal rise process, which is not only technologically unstoppable, but is also the logic and driving force behind the Internet's constant competition and growth. When platform companies become vested, they will build moats in the same way, pooling resources on a closed basis so that start-ups have less opportunity to become competitors and challengers. The endogenous disruptive mechanisms of information capitalism in China will occur again and again. It is the task of law to readily adjust to productivity standards in order to discover rules that better accommodate innovation and maintain order. Therefore, it is important for lawyers to reflect on the extent to which the law, as a superstructure, should support the creative destruction of existing markets by innovators, and how its stability should be balanced against innovation. It is unlikely that today's innovators will be allowed to grow wildly through the illegal use of resources, as was the case in the first wave of the Internet, but competition can be fine-tuned in terms of AI and underlying services, as long as regulators ensure that the platform's resources and data remain as mobilized as they should be. This is not only in the interest of the Internet industry as a whole, but also breeds a multitude of possibilities for the commons.

2 Architecture of digital commons

2.1 Introduction

The emergence of cyberspace has gradually brought about changes in the political and economic structure of the whole society, and law as a superstructure is no exception. More and more studies focus on the new problems caused by the Internet, most of which start from various legal rules, but there are relatively few discussions on the overall thinking of governance model of the whole cyberspace.[1] This is not only because changes in technology and business models have created a set of new issues to which the law needs to respond swiftly, but also because the proliferation of new concepts tends to lead to deviation from original issues of cyberspace, and thus to falling into the prevailing ideology.[2] One of the few core concepts that have enhanced our understanding of cyberspace and its governance is "architecture", the design and use of which directly affects the activities of social agents and shapes the new order. This chapter attempts to break the seemingly complex and varied prism of new issues, starting with architecture as the original source of research question, reinterpreting this concept in the light of changing shape of the Internet in China, and systematically linking various legal issues to it.

Architecture, as a metaphor, can be viewed from multiple perspectives, each of which can help to reconceptualize the qualities of cyberspace and how it impacts law and governance.[3] In *Code and Other Laws of Cyberspace*, Lawrence Lessig first incorporated architecture into the sociology of law, elevating it to a level parallel to law, markets, and social norms, systematically describing (and even predicting) how architecture can "regulate" the online behavior of social agents, affecting legal regimes such as copyright, privacy, and speech, thus suggesting that architecture can be used as a metaphor for the law and governance of cyberspace.[4] This

1 For instance, Zhou Hanhua, "On Internet Law", *China Law Journal* 3, no. 3 (2015),1–5.

2 Such as "out of control", "connecting everything together" and "sharing".

3 Regarding the qualities of cyberspace, recent studies have emphasized "data" and "algorithm", see John Cheney-Lippold, *We Are Data: Algorithms and The Making of Our Digital Selves*, New York University Press, 2017. The following will show that these concepts can be integrated within a unified analytical framework.

4 The idea of architecture is nowadays widely used in Internet governance practices, such as automated blocking of illegal online content, technological protection measures in copyright law, privacy by

DOI: 10.4324/9781003566243-3

code/architecture theory in turn raises the fundamental question in cyberspace: Who ultimately controls the production and operation of architectures?[5] Limited by electronic screens and digital terminals, it is easier for users to distinguish between the Internet-mediated cyberspace and the physical world (the online/offline dichotomy), but with the advent of the Internet of Things and the age of AI, the architecture of cyberspace will ultimately cover everything that exists in the physical world. There is thus a need to look beyond the electronic screen and explore the specific implications of architecture in a larger context and break it down into meaningful legal issues. This chapter tries to show, both horizontally and vertically, what is digital architecture that is compatible with the control/production process in cyberspace around the "account-data-rating" mechanism as the core, in order to form a complete theory of architecture. In addition, the architectural design and dynamics of online information dissemination and reception have triggered discussions on democratic communication mechanisms and agenda-setting in the public sphere,[6] the rapid development of artificial intelligence has raised concerns about the "black box" problem,[7] and the cross-border flow of data and jurisdiction issues can also be incorporated into architecture theory to a certain extent.

Architecture theory is not an all-encompassing list of new cyberlaw issues, but centers on the process of architectural construction, composition, and boundaries, and reveals how architectural power emerges from within and spreads like a tentacle. The shortcoming of early Code Theory is that while it recognizes the "regulability" of architecture, it fails to more accurately abstract from what architecture means in general. The boundaries of technical architectures seem to be clear from everyday online experience, but in reality are controversial: Architectures can sometimes extend into unpredictable scenarios, and sometimes they become unfathomable black boxes. In cases where it is not possible to be precise in language, it is important to state clearly the criteria by which the boundaries are recognizable. The meaning of adequate and effective information disclosure becomes crucial, not in terms of how much authority is given to users, but in terms of clearly stating the identifiable criteria of the architectural boundaries and giving users appropriate expectations. We therefore need a more systematic and comprehensive categorization of architectures in which the boundaries of each category are discussed.

---

design (PBD), authentic authentication, and so on. See also Francesca Musiani et al. ed., *The Turn to Infrastructure in Internet Governance*, Palgrave Macmillan, 2016.

5 Lawrence Lessig, *Code and Other Laws of Cyberspace,* Basic Books, 1999. The author's use of the term "code" utilizes a semantic double entendre in contrast to "law", which is made by democratic processes, namely, East Coast Code vs. West Coast Code (in the United States). One of the earliest proposers of such perspective is Joel Reidenberg, "Lex Informatica: The Formulation of Information Policy Rules Through Technology", *Texas Law Review* 76 (1998), 553.

6 For instance, Cass Sunstein, *Republic.com 2.0*, Princeton University Press, 2007; Cass Sunstein, *#Republic: Divided Democracy in the Age of Social Media*, Princeton University Press, 2017.

7 Frank Pasquale, *The Black Box Society: The Secret Algorithms That Control Money and Information*, Harvard University Press, 2015.

This chapter is structured as follows. Section II reflects on how architecture has emerged and grown along with the new economy and architecture enterprises, reflecting the Internet industry's ongoing logic of transcending established rules, a process in which the most central legal safeguards are "opt-out" and "informed consent". Sections III and IV examine the basic horizontal (scenarios) and vertical (layers) dimensions of architecture and three sub-dimensions (network, black box and infrastructure) from which it derives, respectively, with a special focus on the demarcation of the boundaries of architecture.

2.2 Logic of architectural evolution

2.2.1 Rise of the "architecture enterprise"

In the original discourse of Code Theory, architecture is only a metaphor, covering multiple levels from micro-programming to macro-network transmission protocols. Its core lies in the "regulatory power" over the actors within the architecture.[8] In this sense, the expression "code is law" graphically depicts the spatial sense of cyberspace that shapes the behavior of the subject, and even draws an analogy with the structure of physical space. This depiction is more of a static illustration, but as the shape of the Internet itself continues to change. As cyberspace continues to expand intelligently into the physical world, it is necessary to understand architecture in a dynamically generated historical context, and to discover the logic of its formation.

In the abstract sense, architecture is born and relies on scenarios, through which productive resources are aggregated and social relationships of all kinds are formed, leading to more transactions and connections. The continuous formation of architecture relies on the strong competitiveness of the new economy in competing with traditional industries for the means of production, which externally manifests itself in the "illegal rise", the continuous transformation of existing social relations into productive relations (the process of "commoditization"), and the requirement to ultimately rise to the level of enforceable legal relations. This process is a continuation of the traditional capitalist process of production, as well as a continuation of the ongoing fragmentation of all kinds of "solid things" in society by the traditional capitalist mode of production.[9] Platforms use information technology to "digitize" all kinds of means of production, breaking them down into smaller modules and particles, which can be reassembled, reconnected, and creatively used. At the macro-level, the reorganization of particles is reflected in the emergence of the so-called "sharing economy": Platform companies provide opportunities to combine fragmented (or even idle) productive resources in direct transactions, meanwhile improving the understanding of the preferences of the participants, predicting their future behavior, giving them informational guidance, influencing their

8 Lawrence Lessig, *Code version 2.0*, 23–24.

9 "All that is solid melts into air", in Karl Marx and Friedrich Engels, *Manifesto of the Communist Party* (2nd revised ed.), Progress Press, 1977 [1848].

actual choices or facilitating their use by traditional business organizations in a more flexible and low-cost way.[10] At the micro level, it is known as "data mining", which is based on the identification of the behavior of social agents and their re-profiling based on existing behavioral and transactional data, generating future variable social connections and identities, and even new scientific knowledge.[11] Architecture is an important model for the process of particulate reorganization, which is a scenario of activity, a mode of production and a mode of computation.

Micro particle restructuring has given rise to the emergence of platform companies. Such platforms have created a new economic model through the construction of two-sided markets, which have evolved into multilateral markets as platforms have developed more and more service functions.[12] But the structure of transactions and profit patterns is one thing, the production and legal relations between platforms and the resource activities in the architecture is another. In terms of productive relations, the large number of mobile resources undoubtedly contributes tangible and intangible economic value to the platform, and interestingly, civil law relations between resources and platforms are relatively loose, while the platform's administrative obligations are getting closer to those of traditional media gatekeepers. For instance, the works produced by users in public areas of the platforms are obviously not employment works, and do not receive the corresponding advertising share. Accordingly, since the early days of the safe harbor rules, expanding platforms have been striving for fewer administrative obligations and more autonomous rights, because this is how they can fully utilize mobilized resources to gain a competitive advantage, reduce operating costs, and rapidly generate values.[13]

From this perspective, we can see that the economic theory of platforms is unable to depict the operation of real platforms, as it only explains how various types of cross-value chains are generated on the platforms, but it cannot reflect the willingness and constructive efforts of platforms themselves to achieve more transactions, nor can it explain how the disordered social resources released (or "liberated") from traditional organizations become orderly rather than out of control. Besides, it is also unrealistic to blame platforms for trying to mitigate their liability. At least in the case of large, mature platforms, the costs of *ex post* liability have in fact been converted into *ex ante* costs of prevention, which are used to improve the transaction process and reduce the risk of disputes, namely, invested in

10 The background and culture of the development of the sharing economy in China and the United States are slightly different, but in general both are due to the fact that the real economy was affected by the 2008 financial crisis resulting in the unemployment of a considerable portion of society's labor force, which in turn became flexible laborers on the platform of the sharing economy. For a relevant comparative analysis, see Christian Fuchs, *Social Media: a Critical Introduction*, 2nd ed. SAGE Publications Ltd, 2017.

11 David Weinberger, *Too Big to Know*, Basic Books, 2014.

12 David S. Evans and Richard Schmalensee, *Matchmakers: The New Economics of Multisided Platforms*, Harvard Business Review Press, 2016.

13 For a systematic review, see Liu Wenjie, *From Responsibility Haven to Safety and Security Obligation: A Study on the Intermediary Liability of Network Service Providers*, China Social Science Press, 2016.

the construction of the infrastructure as a basic service. In addition, the term "platform" itself may give the audience a certain two-dimensional flatness that does not adequately depict the influence from various dimensions in cyberspace. Therefore, this chapter uses the term "architecture enterprise" as a broader explanatory term that encompasses the economic dimension of platforms, but also places the regulatory capacity of architecture in the context of the shifting relationship between platforms and mobile resources, revealing that such "architecture enterprise" is a kind of "platform" that is not only a platform as intermediary, but also a platform as space shaper and resource organizer. It can also place the regulatory capacity of architecture in the context of the shifting relationship between platforms and mobile resources, revealing how "architecture enterprise" can materially intervene in the process of online transactions and activities, which is a question not further answered by previous Code Theory. This shifting relationship is most notably between the architecture and the users as prosumer. The real boundaries of the architecture are shaped by the interaction between the two.

2.2.2 Shaping the legal relationship with users

Users as consumers can bring about quite different legal imaginations of cyberspace than users as producers/laborers.[14] This chapter mainly focuses on users as consumer and Chapter 6 as laborer. Due to the diversity of architectural powers, we can sense their blurred boundaries. Previous Code Theory tells us that the boundaries of a user's behavior end where the architecture is built, but there is no uniform rule on whether a user can change the architecture based on an agreement or a legal requirement to gain the right to know or even greater autonomy (for instance, property rights). Architectures can be broadly categorized into four types based on the degree of ability users are entitled to.

Type I: Users must accept the basic functions and default settings of the architecture as an infrastructure, which cannot be changed, otherwise the property rights of architecture enterprise will be violated. There is no need to disclose the basic technical information to the users except for the operation information (which belongs to the scope of the regulation). In such a circumstance, users are just simple consumers and users.

Type II: The user accepts the basic functions and default settings of the architecture. The architecture may not be infrastructure, but it cannot be changed as well, otherwise the property rights of the architecture enterprise could be violated. The basic technical information can be disclosed to the user to facilitate the users

14 In other words, whether cyberspace is a playground or a factory, and whether the architecture is a service process or a production line, is another angle for thinking about the qualities of cyberspace. See Trebor Scholz ed., *Digital Labor: The Internet as Playground and Factory*, Routledge, 2012; Trebor Scholz, *Uberworked and Underpaid: How Workers Are Disrupting the Digital Economy*, Polity, 2016.

and their agents to assess the impact of such information to their own rights and interests.

Type III: The user accepts the basic functionality and default settings of the architecture, and can perform selective operations on some of the functionality or change nonbasic settings of the architecture as permitted by the architecture enterprise. The users need to be accountable for their own choices in a given line of circumstances.

Type IV: The user accepts the basic functionality and default settings of the architecture, and can make functional choices or change the basic/nonbasic settings of the architecture without the permission of the architectural organization, or even design their architectures that is different from the original at their will.

The change in the spectrum from Type I to IV is a gradual process in which users gain more autonomy of action and control over certain dimensions of the architecture, and the sharing of responsibilities between the architecture enterprise and the users should change accordingly. First, if the rules of user behavior are written into the architecture and become default settings, it is generally more difficult to alter them, and they can only follow the settings of architecture. The law is more inclined to protect the autonomy of architectural enterprises based on their devotion to business, prior contractual rights, and the legitimacy of business model based on the specific technology. Second, if the behavior of users can break through default settings and have greater behavioral space and control in the architecture, the architecture enterprise needs to assume more obligations to assist and monitor, increasing operational costs thereafter. Sometimes users need the law to intervene in the default power of architecture to match certain social norms. Once the power of architecture absorbs the administrative obligations of public law, it will lead to disputes whether the creation of such obligations will unduly affect the scope of private law obligations.[15]

The above discussions also illustrate that legal safeguards for the emergence of architectures are largely dependent on the process of realizing users' right to information and choice. While the traditional rule in the physical world is a free option on an informed basis (opt-in), the logic of cyberspace is reversed: First, the early Internet industry supported "opting out" by attracting all kinds of offline resources into cyberspace in the name of safe harbor to avoid liability, which facilitated the digitization of a number of traditional industries. In comparison, the "opt-in" approach is very inefficient and may create a tragedy of the anti-commons. The result is that individual user may choose to opt out at some platform that uses human works without authorization, but then ultimately decides to opt in to embrace the Internet. Similarly, the user is merely a link in the chain of production in the new economy, requiring both continuous production of information content as a producer. Opting out provides a formal legal justification for the smooth

15 Zhiwei Yao, "Havens in the Shadow of Public Law-focusing on the Censorship Obligations of Online Service Providers", *Global Law Review* 1, no. 1 (2018), 68–72.

realization of this process.[16] As architectures flip from protecting privacy by default to collecting and making use of privacy by default, traditional spatial/informational privacy gradually ceases to exist.[17] As architectures gain access to more user data, explicit expression of informed consent does little to stop this process.

Second, the right to opt out is often communicated in the form of a user agreement. The vast majority of users do not navigate through the agreement and go to particular service directly, which under the terms of service is tantamount to recognizing the validity of the agreement.[18] In this sense, terms of service is not exactly a contractual agreement, but is more akin to a unilateral notice hung at the entrance to a building. The problem, however, is not so much the authentic legal nature of these texts (whether they are contracts or notices, specific elements can be declared invalid *ex post* for violating consumer rights), but rather the ideological and popular way of thinking that seeks to improve the problem: The assumption that the consumer will rationally weigh the cost and benefit, instead of expanding the ability to make real choices and maneuvering within specific architectures and scenarios, and thus continually demanding greater information disclosure to maximize their formal right to know. The corollary of this path is that user agreements become increasingly lengthy, presented in a way that detracts from the experience, in an all-or-nothing take-it-or-leave-it format, while users are unable to determine what their substance is, preferring to accept whatever the architecture enterprises offer to inform them.[19] Meanwhile, a terms of service written in human language will never be able to cover the full dimensions of the architecture, and will need to be interpreted by local courts in the event of a dispute.

2.3 Horizontal and vertical dimensions of architecture

As exemplified in the previous section, the default architectural boundaries of the current cyberspace are that users have to tolerate tracking and monitoring of targeted advertisements within the architecture, that they cannot completely erase data even if they log out and delete their accounts, and that they have to respect the property rights of the architecture's enterprise, including terminals and servers,

16 Article 43 of *Cybersecurity Law* stipulates: "An individual who finds that a network operator has collected or used his or her personal information in violation of the provisions of laws, administrative regulations or the agreement between the two parties has the right to request the network operator to delete his or her personal information. If he or she finds that his or her personal information has been collected or stored incorrectly by the network operator, he or she has the right to request the network operator to correct it. The network operator shall take measures to delete or correct it."

17 Lawrence Lessig, "The Architecture of Privacy", *Duke Law Journal* 51 (2002), 1783; Ronald Leenes et al. eds., *Data Protection and Privacy: (In)visibilities and Infrastructures*, Springer International Publishing, 2017.

18 The fact that we don't need to view any of the contents of term of service in reality has almost no impact on our smooth use of online service, which just goes to show such agreement has little relevance to user's daily perception and is not primarily used to ask for informed consent.

19 For a broader reflection on mandatory disclosure, see Omri Ben-Shahar and Carl E. Schneider, *More Than You Wanted to Know: The Failure of Mandated Disclosure*, Princeton University Press, 2014.

which are expanding at an imperceptible rate. This section will start with two fundamental dimensions of architecture: Horizontal scenario and vertical layering; the next section builds on them to develop two important derivative dimensions for a nuanced discussion of the realization and boundaries of architectural power.

2.3.1 Horizontal scenarios of architecture

Scenario (or context) is the most basic form of architecture and the basic unit that constitutes the visible part of cyberspace. It is the pattern of architectural enterprises to realize specific service functions, and it creates a "space" for many social subjects' activities online. The evolution of cyberspace is from simple to complex, staying in the one-way communication mode of mass media in the early days, and later trying to restore and shape more and more complex interactive scenes to capture and predict the subject's behavior. The scenario can be either online virtual worlds used through electronic screens or spatial recreations covering physical places with sensors and cameras. It can also be a single application function or a combination of behavioral processes designed by a whole set of codes. We need to use a large variety of APP-based services in our daily working lives, and will continually move from one scenario to another in cyberspace, where architectural design allows us to see what we can and cannot do in a scenario.

The actual activities within the scene produce a large amount of data as by-product, detached from the actual activities of the bubble or false data that cannot bring the effectiveness of the analysis, only the application can be tested. On the contrary, effective data analysis can enhance the number and scale of the actual activities, thus expanding the digital market. Architecture enterprises standardize the data they collect and use themselves as intermediaries to provide third-party developers with the opportunity to data mining and provide a variety of services, which is currently a more efficient approach.[20] Architecture enterprises open portals for certain types of standardized data to third-party developers, who have access to relevant data about users stored in the architecture, but in exchange share with the former the derived data about users' subsequent use of their services.

Unlike a continuous physical space, behaviors in cyberspace scenarios are covered, recorded, and tracked by a number of architectures with horizontal relationships and stored in the corresponding accounts of the scenarios. With the generalization of business logic and the proliferation of business models, a large number of scenarios have the micro-power structure of "account-data-scoring", which implies the constant convergence of cyberspace, where the architectures can be intersected, overlapped, or separated, and the boundaries represent the (exclusive)

20 This is why architecture enterprises are also known as infomediaries, even though they do far more than simply matching information. See Zhang Yicheng, Lv Linyuan, and Zhou Tao, *Reinvention: the Structure of the Information Economy*, Sichuan People's Publishing House, 2018, pp. 43–87.

control power of the architecture enterprises.[21] The need for user convenience (it is difficult to remember dozens of different account passwords) has given rise to the consolidation of tiny scenarios, merging not only virtual scenarios, but also online and offline scenarios, to connect the otherwise fragmented and unconnected contexts. The scenario dimension suggests that cyberspace may not be a natural free world but is composed of countless independent architectures interconnected with each other, realizing only a minimalist uniformity with TCP/IP, WWW protocols, and Windows operating system as the underlying standards. Cyberspace operating under a control/production mechanism is doomed to fragmentation from the start, and the internalization of inter-architectural connectivity through horizontal and vertical architectural consolidation by mega-architecture corporations, or the construction of telecommunication infrastructures by nation-states within a country instead promotes the ease of access and uniformity of user behavior.[22]

It is easy to find that Code Theory is discussing architecture in the sense of scenarios, in terms of its composition, and in addition to (1) transaction process design and auxiliary functions, (2) account-centered behavioral control mechanisms, and more importantly, (3) commercially targeted advertisements that are part of the default settings. All user agreements indicate that users not only need to tolerate the display of advertisements as a business model, but also need to accept that advertisements are constantly identified and targeted for tracking within the architecture. When users have entered the architecture of a certain platform and its advertising alliance, their behaviors are transformed into recognizable and analyzable data, which in turn triggers the targeted advertisements. This does not take place within the private physical space in which the user resides, and thus is not subject to the latter's norms. On the other hand, attempts to disrupt commercial advertising, whether by users or competitors, are prohibited by law, and the relevant architecture enterprises certainly have the right to defend themselves or fight back. Meanwhile, applications that host specific architectural functions are also protected by intellectual property laws, and cracking terminal software or digital works encrypted with DRM could be treated as undermining technical protection measures.[23]

Finally, the scenario perspective can also help to partially understand the evolution of cyberlaw. When regulators or courts try to regulate online behavior, they

21 In the early days of the Internet's development, it was widely believed that different architectural designs would reflect different values and could become very different. It was also emphasized that the mechanism of competition in marketplace would lead to architectures that were free from control, see David G. Post, "What Larry Doesn't Get: Code, Law, and Liberty in Cyberspace", *Stanford Law Review* 52 (2000), 1439.

22 Milton Mueller, *Will the Internet Fragment? Sovereignty, Globalization and Cyberspace*, Polity, 2017.

23 In the early development of the Internet in China, there was a discussion of software users' end-user behavioral privileges, that is, whether users are able to revise the software installed in their personal computer. Although the discussion occurred in the context of targeting foreign companies like Microsoft, its significance has last to today.

either create new rules for what appears to be new activity or simply apply established rules. Given scenarios are just concepts that are closer to physical space, in many cases they will be favored along the usual lines of offline venues, and what triggers this way of thinking is not, in the first place, thinking about how the behavior itself should be scientifically interpreted for characterization, but rather that the similarity of the scenarios in which the behavior occurs triggers legal analogies that can be used to conveniently solve the problem. For instance, the regulation of provocative behavior is extended from offline public places to online space; deep link is considered to have destroyed the scene where the infringed content was originally displayed, and so on. Even in cases that require characterization of illegal behavior, courts are more willing to use architectural boundaries as a criterion for determining whether the behavior is illegal or not, and are less willing to make more distinctions between the nature of particular behaviors.[24]

2.3.2 Vertical layering of digital architecture

Layering theory of the Internet is an important lens for looking at architecture vertically, highlighting the physicality and complexity of cyberspace. The practice of developing the Internet in a layered form and proposing technical standards has a long history.[25] Legal and public policy analyses have also found that this perspective allows for a clear discussion of the different layers of regulation of the Internet and their interactions.[26] They tend to use more general, nontechnical layering, and are mostly based on the PC form of the Internet. Early and influential layering theory categorized the cyberspace into content, logical, and physical layers.[27] The Hourglass Model of the Internet, which builds on this, is used to justify the theory

24 Similar questions have been raised in a series of cases at home and abroad: whether it is trespass or spamming, whether it is invasion of a computer system or theft on virtual property, and whether it is infringement of the architectural property rights of a computer system or infringement of property rights of specific data.

25 For instance, the International Organization for Standardization has proposed a seven-layer standard for the Open Systems Interconnection Communication Reference Model.

26 Methodologically, the different levels of the Internet form different market structures and principles, and even the same legal system concepts involving different levels should be discussed separately and in depth, rather than being generalized and placed under a seemingly uniform cyberspace. For instance, when discussing Internet antitrust case, people tend to put the Microsoft case, the 3Q case, and the Baidu case together, while confusing them at different levels of the cyberspace architecture, and the conclusions reached will be very limited in their scientific nature.

27 Lawrence B. Solum and Minn Chung, "The Layers Principle: Internet Architecture and the Law", *U San Diego Public Law Research Paper* no. 55 (2003); Lawrence Lessig, *The Future of Ideas: The Fate of the Commons in a Connected World*, Vintage, 2002; Andy Yee, "Internet Architecture and the Layers Principle: A Conceptual Framework for Regulating Bitcoin", *Internet Policy Review* 3 (2014), 3.

of "generative Internet"[28] and how the architecture of the Internet facilitates distributed innovation.[29]

In addition to the user, the architecture can be generated and extended through at least seven layers. Unlike horizontal scenarios (content and application layers), vertical layering covers several physical (such as hardware, physical layer, and cloud storage) and logical (such as transport protocols/domain name system) mechanisms that underpin the scenarios, demonstrating how the original Internet's end-to-end distributed architecture shaped the cyberspace[30] and raised a range of new issues, including information security. It also inspires how the current Internet of Things and smart city networks can be expanded through architectural design.[31] On the surface, architectural enterprises develop more types of terminals to adapt to more scenarios and users, making the cyberspace more heterogeneous and diversified. However, by improving computing power and integrating data analysis, the behavior of more subjects can be tracked and analyzed in a wider scope, and each level can be transformed through the "account-data-score" mechanism so that the actual control and service efficiency can be continuously improved meanwhile.[32]

The vertical layering perspective allows us to better understand new issues in digital commons. First, vertical layering itself stretches the dimensions of cyberspace from the everyday accessible endpoints to the invisible cloud, and in doing so creates new types of power relations. For instance, the emergence of cloud computing and streaming service models has permanently altered the legal relationship between consumers and service providers who do not have the ability to technically control the virtual objects (and therefore not property) they pay to use, but can only obtain licenses to use them by agreement. Similarly, a user is unable to arbitrarily manipulate a smartphone that has been "purchased" in a manner that

28 According to such theory, the Internet can continue to create and expand at both the top and the bottom of the hourglass, see Jonathan Zittrain, *The Future of the Internet–And How to Stop It*, Yale University Press, 2008, Chapter 3. Another way to look at the layering theory is that information content and data are transmitted along different endpoints, which has also become an important idea for regulation, see Jonathan Zittrain, "Internet Points of Control", *Boston College Law Review* 44 (2003). Cybercafes in the PC Internet era were important control endpoints that have since declined due to the rise of smartphones, but are likely to be revived in the VR era. New endpoints, such as driverless cars, will also emerge, and the human body also has a tendency to become a "container" of data.

29 Barbara van Schewick, *Internet Architecture and Innovation*, MIT Press, 2012, Chapter 2.

30 J. H. Saltzer, D. P. Reed, and D. D. Clark, "End-to-end Arguments in System Design", *ACM Transactions on Computer Systems* 2 (1984), 277.

31 Jonathan Zittrain, "The Generative Internet", *Harvard Law* Review 119 (2006), 1974.

32 For instance, (1) the Windows operating system was relatively open in the early days and Microsoft had weak control over the software running on it, and now it has become stronger by learning from Apple Store model, trying to exercise control on products like Surface; (2) browsers and any terminal software are converging on business models and becoming capable of influencing the power of the upper content business model; (3) terminals like WeChat are developing mini programs in an attempt to replace the operating system; and (4) telecom companies and terminal companies are also trying to become data vendors, not willing to be overtaken by OTT companies.

allows them to unlock it or crack it.[33] This is a good example of how the boundaries of architecture have intruded into the physical space of traditional life.

Second, layering theory suggests that the architecture does not extend only along horizontal scenarios, but also integrates vertically, which will reshape the legal relationship between data transmission service providers and content service providers, and bring about the net neutrality controversy.[34] By extension, vertical integration highlights the nested nature of architectures, namely, the extent to which underlying architectures have the incentive and ability to influence upstream architectures, redrawing the boundaries of interest between architectures and the extent to which underlying architectures should be legally compelled to be neutral rather than subject to negotiation.[35] A powerful underlying architecture will influence the upstream activists to turn the standards they establish into industry standards, enforceable through technical measures. Conversely, if negotiation fails, boundaries are more likely to be drawn or defaulted through actual infringement. Finally, productive resources within the architecture flow along the vertical architecture just as they would in a horizontal scenario. For instance, data of all kinds may be stored on servers in the cloud, displayed on the screens of smart terminals, or even piped to and from them, creating data commons that architecture enterprises need to be able to readily access, control, and claim legal protection for.[36] Such data is not centralized in a specific location, but is an abstract aggregate property right, the sum of all unspecified data available to the architecture enterprises. This also raises the question of the scope of the state's jurisdiction over cyberspace, namely, the extent to which it can demand access to the physical servers of architectural enterprise.

33 For a detailed description, see Joshua A. T. Fairfield, *Owned: Property, Privacy, and the New Digital Serfdom*, Cambridge University Press, 2017. The 3Q wars have demonstrated that users cannot fully control their endpoints, and can only hand over control to specific software vendors.

34 The United States has gone through the process of net neutrality policy from existence to abolition, but the situation in China is relatively simple.

35 For instance, Apple has made it clear in its latest Security Audit Guide that in-app rewards for original creators are "in-app purchases", and that all payments must be made through the payment method provided by Apple, with a 30/70 split between Apple and the original creators. This not only reduces the income of the original creators of WeChat, but also affects the utilization rate of WeChat Pay. Huawei's Honor Magic cell phone smart service adds hyperlinks to keywords in all kinds of App push information, promotes restaurants based on user tastes, and recommends movies based on user preferences, which triggered friction of interest with Tencent when applied to WeChat's information push service. On the contrary, the mini program platform created by Tencent can also completely challenge the hardware manufacturers. The situation could be even worse when it comes to AI cell phone.

36 Data has two types of meanings, one in the traditional sense, emphasizing numerical values, quantitative values, and related to statistics; the other is a new meaning that has arisen along with digitization, referring to a structured and disposable collection of digital bits, such as databases, data structures, data communications, and so on, which is the concept of a data common pool in the abstract sense.

2.4 Derived dimensions of architecture

This section discusses three derived sub-dimensions that complement the content of the basic architecture, and which represent the specificity of the architecture. The first is a more complex and dynamically networked architecture that cuts across scenarios and layering. The second is a black-box view of the kernel—the algorithms that drive changes throughout the architecture. The last is how to see the architecture as a fundamental service in digital market (not just a utility infrastructure).

2.4.1 Networked architecture

Scenarios are given for static architectures, but most scenarios are created for the purpose of creating connections dynamically, namely, attracting all kinds of productive resources into the architecture to establish links and exchange information, leading to potential cooperation and transactions. As social animals, humans have always been in complex social networks, but the spread of information technology has made such networks (and their power relations and resulting social capital) easier to realize and pursue. Users in cyberspace are in constant connection with others (social networks), service applications (ready to use), and sensors (exchanging data), becoming nodes on an ever-generating network.[37] Behaviors are consequently influenced and constrained, a dynamic lens through which to view the architecture.

Meaningful connections take place in scenarios—the result of constant discovery and creation—which reflect both the social relationships in the architecture and the intent of the architecture enterprises designing for specific scenarios, hoping to transform social relationships into productive relationships that embody economic value. Architectural design can subtly influence information dissemination and connectivity. For instance, the design of microblogs encourages users to produce more and disseminate images and opinions more easily (rather than blog-like long-windedness, limited to 140 characters), which accelerates the emergence of an aristocratic network with network vloggers as the core nodes. Some architecture enterprises go even further to automate sharing service, by pushing (and also delivering) information to users based on their browsing history after they have logged into accounts, predicting preferences and pushing (and also matching) relevant information. These all reflects the huge impact that architecture enterprises are having in shaping network connectivity, integrating B2C and C2C models more and more tightly, and highlighting the fact that networked architecture is not just about the relationship between users, but also between users and architecture.

37 This more or less reflects society's need to accelerate the delivery of services and transactions; as living organisms, human brains and bodies need to rest offline (albeit with less and less sleep), but their accounts (or intelligent agents) need to be always online, recording and reflecting the actual state of the user (including sleep) at all times.

The legal implications of networked architectures are yet to be explored in depth, and can be exemplified for the purposes of this chapter in at least a few ways. First, this perspective highlights the "relational" nature of privacy rather than its purely personal ownership. Both spatial and informational privacy are situated in relationships between individuals and others, and can be shared along specific network flows. The criterion for invasion of privacy lies in the transfer of privacy beyond the expectation/control of the person concerned to flows outside the network.[38] Second, the influence of online speech is closely related to the information channels and architectural design of the dissemination of that speech, which has led to the gradual formation of aristocratic networks, with core nodes becoming important targets of regulation. Meanwhile, social networks can track and quantify specific speech (for instance, rumors) for risk prevention through opinion monitoring techniques.[39] Third, the identities of social subjects are becoming increasingly networked, and new social identities are being formed through interconnections with different kinds of social beings.[40] This leads to the creation of "social credits" in specific scenarios by the government, the essence of which is to predict the future behavior and nature of a certain subject through algorithms based on its historical records in order to reduce risks. The constant flow of data and connections makes the subject's identity more dynamic, giving rise to the current model of public administration based on social credit, which attempts to find constant standards in the ever-changing process of behavior. Finally, the network perspective may also provide new ideas for the identification of relevant markets in competition law. As market behavior becomes increasingly traceable and calculable through networking, the traditional criterion of geographically delineating relevant markets becomes crude, as it is entirely possible for the influence of architecture enterprises to transcend geographic limitations—implicitly exerting a network effect and transmitting value along a particular network.[41]

2.4.2 Architecture as a (algorithmic) black box

The use of the "black box" metaphor is intended to highlight the relationship between architecture and disclosure, rather than focusing solely on algorithmic regulation. For users, the vertical hierarchical structure from cloud computing and algorithms to operating systems and endpoints are all black boxes, which realize certain functions through technology and constitute production processes in cyberspace. Users as layman can only rely on the design of these functions and the limited information disclosed to them to carry out their activities. The example of algorithms is used here to briefly demonstrate how architecture should be viewed

38 Daniel J. Solove, *Understanding Privacy*, Harvard University Press, 2009, Chapter 5.

39 Albert Laszlo Barabasi, *Linked: The New Science of Networks*, Perseus Books, 2002.

40 Oscar H. Gandy Jr. "Exploring Identity and Identification in Cyberspace", *Notre Dame Journal of Law, Ethics & Public Policy* 14 (2014), 1085.

41 See Final Decision of the 3Q War, Civil Judgment of the Supreme People's Court of the People's Republic of China (2013).

through the lens of black boxes, showing that users need to tolerate the reality that black boxes are not completely transparent, nor do they need to be. Algorithms are the decisive force by which architectural power works, determining the matching calls to the means of production, and are also a core trade secret for architecture enterprises. Algorithmic black boxes inherently encompass a technical level of complexity and default usability that is virtually impossible to publicize. However, for the sake of informed consumers and the need for security regulation, it is necessary to disclose the technical composition and functionality to a certain extent, translating it into words understandable to ordinary people, in order to enhance the credibility of the technical product.[42] However, such disclosure needs to be balanced with the property rights of the architecture enterprises.

Similar to the criteria for categorizing architectures in Section II, based on the mandatory information disclosure criteria, architectures that serve as black boxes can be broadly categorized into two types, thus setting up different governance ideas: (1) Users do not have the right to be informed of the technical details of the black box, and they can only use the software program according to the functional settings. If an accident occurs, the responsibility will be judged only on the basis of the behaviors and consequences demonstrated, and they will not be concerned about the design of the black box itself (no matter how intelligent it may be). This is the model that is most consistent with the status quo, relying essentially on market-based operations to drive algorithmic improvements and innovations through competition, and with the general perception of corporate property rights. The arrangement that accompanies this low level of liability regime is prior insurance for users in the case of riskier services.[43] (2) Black boxes are mandated to make a certain level of disclosure. For most users, the technical details of the algorithms are difficult to understand and rely on linguistic explanations, with precise descriptions of the relevant functions and business models mainly through user agreements (or product manuals). Leveraging the expertise of dedicated agents to help with oversight and promoting public–private partnerships, such as disclosing source code or system security vulnerabilities within a specific context, encourages white hat hackers to publicize vulnerabilities within a limited scope so that flaws can be patched in a timely manner. Certain market intermediaries (for instance, software ratings and security software vendors) are also needed to help discover vulnerabilities and enable consumers to make better choices.[44]

42 In particular, it is necessary to "dehumanize" intelligent products, otherwise, once the robots with the same appearance as real people start to communicate and think, it may make users panic and then abandon the use of AI, according to famous "Uncanny Valley" theory.

43 In Beijing's driverless car testing requirements, a human driver is required to assist, and in the event of an accident the driver is legally responsible, but compensated by the insurance purchased by the company. Such two-tiered responsibility could have the consequence of rational idleness on the part of the human driver.

44 These cases may also involve unfair competition by security software vendors, such as "360 Label Insertion Case", see Beijing Higher People's Court Civil Judgment (2013) (Gaozhi Minzheng No. 2352).

2.4.3 Architecture as digital infrastructure

The complexity of the architecture requires a unified and trusted underlying infrastructure to ensure the security and stable continuity of transactions in cyberspace. We have witnessed the process of private digital infrastructures being provided by architecture enterprises in China.[45] These infrastructures are very similar to market infrastructures in the physical world. The way these infrastructures evolve is that they are first developed to solve a specific problem in an architecture enterprise's own business, and then, as the firm grows, there is a need and incentive to scale up the underlying services. The scale effect leads to decreasing marginal costs and increasing benefits.[46] Meanwhile, state licensing of certain basic services has a direct impact on the supply of such services (for instance, third-party payments). The following discussion focuses on four types of basic services, in addition to general technology services, which are more or less geared to the way productive resources flow, as well as more basic trust-enhancing facilities.[47]

Payment and dispute resolution: Payment is the core function to support the digital economy, without fast payment tools, the Internet can only stay in the primary media mode of "free content + advertising", or only allow users to use self-created point cards or virtual coins within a specific service system, and the exchange of value can't be truly integrated into the cyberspace. The history of Chinese Internet development shows that third-party payment services have adapted to the large-scale individual-based remote transactions like Taobao in the early days, which is a powerful supplement to the lack of offline payment means, and has rapidly expanded to all kinds of business scenarios outside of the Taobao system, thus making ubiquitous transactions possible. More importantly, the guarantee function and cumulative scoring mechanism of third-party payment solves the trust problem of stranger transactions, which is especially critical in a social environment with a low level of trust. The subsequent development of nonfinancial institution payment business is more helpful for platforms to reshape payment channels and expand to more new consumer retail scenarios. Some sharing economy businesses also assume the function of unified settlement, implying stronger control over transactions.

Logistics: Logistics has expanded along with the rise of e-commerce, with the core idea that atoms should catch up with the speed of bit transmission, as illustrated by constant innovation from human labor to electric logistics vehicles to

45 The underlying telecommunication and domain name infrastructure is still provided by the Chinese state.

46 Jeremy Rifkin, *The Zero Marginal Cost Society: The Internet of Things, the Collaborative Commons, and the Eclipse of Capitalism*, St. Martin's Press, 2014; Jean-Francois Blanchette, "Introduction: Computing's Infrastructural Moment", in Christopher S. Yoo and Jean-Francois Blanchette, ed. *Regulating the Cloud: Policy for Computing Infrastructure*, MIT Press, 2015.

47 Rachel Botsman, *Who Can You Trust?: How Technology Brought Us Together and Why It Might Drive Us Apart*, PublicAffairs, 2017.

drones.[48] The private courier industry has grown vigorously by taking advantage of low-cost labor, and neither the state-run Postal Express nor the four major international courier companies have been able to adequately adapt to this change. Part of the structure of the enterprise has its own logistics services, while companies like Alibaba extend the C2C model to delivery services.

Authentication: Real-name authentication is a gradual process of improvement in Internet governance. Although the state constantly requires the implementation of real-name authentication at all levels of the Internet in accordance with the logic of political governance, structuring enterprises to bind and identify fixed producers and consumers through the account system is important for timely prediction and balancing of the unstable new economy. In particular, the merging of financial accounts and user behavioral accounts in the Internet era facilitates the analysis of users' daily behavior and consumer behavior together and deepens the understanding of users.[49]

Credit and finance: Traditional credit services cannot satisfy the sharing economy in which the public participates; after grasping a large amount of users' transaction/consumption data, architectural enterprises have the ability to conduct predictive analysis and reconstruct a new type of credit system with algorithms to provide loans or other financial services (such as insurance) for many individuals, which in turn further promotes the transactions of the real economy, forming a positive cycle and easing the problem of inclusive financial services that cannot be solved by commercial banks.[50] After the state allowed private enterprise credit services to carry out pilot projects, various types of credit algorithms not only used noncredit personal data but are also applied to more online services, often functioning as promotions or discounts, which deviate from the credit intent of credit services.[51]

2.4.4 Synthesis of above perspectives

If the aforementioned basic and derived architectures are combined, the "account-data-score" framework can be further enriched to reconceptualize the ecosystems of architecture enterprises around the theme of what forces can influence the behavior of subjects. This perspective is more akin to "platform governance" in a general

48 The delivery industry, along with online vehicle renting and bike sharing (and driverless cars in the future), who have occupied quite a portion of public road, is exploring transportation planning and urban planning that shape new smart cities for new kinds of rights of road, which are essentially driven by the Internet's mode of production.

49 Accounts are an important linking point for the Internet's incorporation of free/libre users into the production process of digital economy.

50 Liu Xinhai, *Credit Collection and Big Data: How to Reshape the Credit System in the Era of Mobile Internet*, CITIC Publishing House, 2016, pp. 146–169.

51 In early 2015, the central bank issued the *Notice on Preparation of Personal Credit Business*, which required eight institutions to make preparations for personal credit business, but for various reasons it has not yet been officially licensed.

sense, highlighting both the means of production in a scenario and the many elements that have the ability to regulate it. In addition to the user, the architecture consists of at least nine basic elements, and the forces that influence the behavior of subjects within the architecture include, in addition to the default rigid scenario design, the more flexible platform rules (and their dispute resolution mechanisms) and credit scoring mechanisms. Here it is highlighted that there is both coordination and competition between architecture and other norms with different levels of effectiveness.

It is worth noting the production and transaction management functions of architecture enterprises. This includes, at a minimum level, (1) transaction processes that can be enforced through code design;[52] (2) the development of transaction rules and guidelines for large numbers of traders, and coercive penalties for violators; (3) the use of social norms, such as reputation evaluation mechanisms, to score and sort out the subjects on both sides of the transaction through what is essentially a labor-management process; (4) the use of technological means for the detection of counterfeit and substandard commodities, online pushers, and illegal content, and other activities are screened and discovered;[53] and (5) standardizing and typifying users' dispute behaviors, with categories selected by users for easy handling in resolving future disputes, which is the core of online dispute resolution. Platform management rights arise from management rights established through user agreements, as well as from administrative obligations under certain administrative regulations.[54]

2.5 Concluding remarks

Architecture/Code Theory attempts to draw a map showing the extent to which the architecture of cyberspace influences user behavior and the visible/invisible pathways through which its power acts, depending on how the relationship between user and architecture is imagined. This chapter focuses on the consumer perspective, showing the legal and technological boundaries required by architecture enterprises, which form the basic sample of cyberspace familiar to us today.

52 Yochai Benkler has long found that the architecture of online platforms that rely on mass contributions must be designed explicitly, see Yochai Benkler, "Sharing Nicely: On Shareable Goods and the Emergence of Sharing as a Modality of Economic Production", *Yale Law Journal* 114 (2004), 273.

53 For instance, online pushing hands' behavior is quite a headache. Platform company will keep an eye on such behaviors by technical means, and those who make and sell counterfeit goods will be blocked and punished or sued for compensation.

54 Similar to the bylaws and internal management norms of traditional organizations, platform rules related to trading activities cannot be completely covered by agreements, and their formulation process requires a more open and transparent procedure.

3 Collaborative networks in digital commons

3.1 Introduction

"Network" has a long history in human life, especially in the form of social relationships among people, which subtly influence our daily behavior.[1] Traditionally, however, the law has focused more on individual behavior, keeping silent about the unseen forces behind individual behavior (subordinating them to political ethics, market forces, or social norms), and assuming that individuals act autonomously, mostly on the basis of free will. When we enter the "network society"[2] or cyberspace, not only social relationships between acquaintances, but also connections between strangers, between people and things/services, and between things/services, can be transformed into data that can be tracked, recorded, measured, analyzed, and predicted.[3] Networks are no longer hidden behind the scenes, but gradually become visible or intuitively perceived, and through ever-increasing connections become a dynamic "architecture" that influences individual social behavior.[4] In this process of change, the law has begun to pay attention to the power of networks in certain areas and has introduced networks or connectivity into its analysis when judging the nature and consequences of behavior. In particular, the network is not only a spontaneous social relationship between social subjects, but also a productive relationship consciously shaped and facilitated by the platform company, and the social capital thus formed and accumulated has become an important medium and asset for the platform to exert control and matching power over the actors in the network, and can even be described as a kind of "infrastructure". The creation, protection, and distribution of this intangible asset have become an important issue in the law and economics of digital commons.

1 Networks have become central to complexity studies and extend into more disciplinary areas, for instance, Eric D. Beinhocker, *Origin of Wealth: Evolution, Complexity, and the Radical Remaking of Economics*, Harvard Business Review Press, 2006; Matthew O. Jackson, *The Human Network: How Your Social Position Determines Your Power, Beliefs, and Behaviors*, Pantheon, 2019.

2 Manuel Castells, *The Rise of the Network Society*, 2nd edition, Wiley-Blackwell, 2009.

3 For a general discussion, see Steffen Mau, *The Metric Society: On the Quantification of the Social*, Polity, 2019; Lee Rainie, *Networked: The New Social Operating System*, MIT Press, 2014.

4 On architecture, see Lawrence Lessig, *Code: And Other Laws of Cyberspace, Version 2.0*, Basic Books, 2006.

DOI: 10.4324/9781003566243-4

For a long time, the study of cyberlaw has focused on the regulatory nodes of the Internet,[5] user behaviors, and their architectural design (horizontal and vertical) through information intermediaries (platforms), and attempted to apply traditional jurisprudential concepts to cyberspace, with less attention paid to the "network" itself. Even when networks are discussed, it is only at the level of physical infrastructure and data transmission (such as "net neutrality"), not at the more abstract level of "connectivity" and "interoperability".[6] We need to answer the question of what it means legally when more and more resources are constantly connected to others, thus forming specific digital networks. This chapter attempts to explore this question and to discover the meaning and potential of the perspective of "network" in cyberlaw as well as in digital commons. Indeed, this concept, like other basic concepts of cyberlaw (for instance, architecture, platform, and data), can provide an explanation of how the Internet works and what kind of law is needed to form a common resource pool, as well as assimilate and integrate conceptual elements and regimes from existing sectoral laws. Meanwhile the strong "productive" character of architecture and law in the digital transformation of society can also be realized through the use of the concept of "network" in the digital transformation of Chinese society.

The chapter discusses the three dimensions of networks in the following order. Section II discusses the network as a dynamic architecture, showing how networks enter into legal analysis through the emergence of business models and technologies, affecting the behavior of social agents and, over time, a number of core legal concepts, such as property, privacy, and speech, and then linking this concept to other more analytical legal concepts. Section III argues that the current digital network can be designed and shaped by platform companies, and embodies the typical features of "commercialization" and "platformization", thus changing the productive process of the digital economy. This changes the relations in the productive process of the digital economy, which itself becomes part of the mode of production, and "control" is an important factor behind this process. Section IV turns to the private and public attributes of networks, arguing that the offline distributed social functions originally carried by networks have also been massively transformed online (for instance, reputation, identity, social capital, and cooperative capacity) to meet the needs of a new mode of production, but that their public attributes as a kind of infrastructure are being obscured by the property interests of platform companies, and that unfair competition and monopolization laws are moving toward helping to contribute to this goal. As a conclusion, Section V briefly reflects on the productive orientation of law and how traditional sociality is being reshaped and mutated through its role as a network of mode of production/relationships.

5 For instance, Jonathan Zittrain, "Internet Points of Control", *Boston College Law Review* 44 (2003), 653.

6 For a discussion of these two concepts, see Jose van Dijck, *The Culture of Connectivity: A Critical History of Social Media*, Oxford University Press, 2013.

3.2 Networks as dynamic architecture

As Chapter 1 argues, Internet architecture and design undoubtedly affects the online behavioral expectations of social subjects. While in the abstract, doctrinal analysis of legal behavior is not much affected by changes in the surrounding environment (e.g., defamation's concept remains the same, whether online or offline, and therefore the legal provisions remain unchanged), expectations about the consequences of a subject's behavior, as well as the possibility of identification (for instance, real name), the process of proof (for instance, blockchain), and the cost and probability of entering into a legal proceeding (an online trial) are all subject to change. The ubiquitous connectivity enabled by information technology means that we are constantly in a state of being associated with and exchanging information with particular subjects/objects, namely, in a variety of intersecting and overlapping digital networks. This state is dynamic and fluid enough to have a potential impact on human behavior, and can be viewed as a digital architecture that transcends the layering and construction of the Internet. Early architecture/code theories viewed "code" as one of the regulatory instruments, emphasizing the regulatory effects of the static architecture of the Internet and the design impact of particular Internet layers on behavior,[7] while the dynamic network perspective helps us understand how particular legal relationships may change over time as a result of the existence of a network.

Since the invention of the Internet, behaviors and interests in cyberspace have been consistently defined as "networked" and almost ideological.[8] But this is not merely rhetorical, but rather suggests that abstract, yet perceptible, networked relationships can influence the way in which the law understands and applies particular concepts in traditional physical space. The following briefly illustrates how "networks" are embedded in the established legal system from different perspectives, including privacy, speech, property, identity, and risk regulation.

Privacy. While traditional notions of spatial privacy have led researchers to focus on the intrusion of technology into the physical architecture, when the notion shifts to informational privacy, the physical architecture no longer seems to be important as a space for protecting privacy. People are more concerned with how private activities are accessed and used without permission in an informational way, so that the protection of privacy becomes about controlling the flow of private information.[9] The expanding range of human interactions made possible by information technology completely breaks down the limits of physical architecture and space, and blurs the traditional boundaries between private and public space, with more connectivity between subjects highlighting "networked privacy". It further suggests that privacy is in fact situated in context-specific relationships between subjects, rather than being controlled by a single subject, and that private

7 Lawrence Lessig, *Code: And Other Laws of Cyberspace, Version 2.0*, Basic Books, 2006.

8 Mike Ananny, *Networked Press Freedom: Creating Infrastructures for a Public Right to Hear*, The MIT Press, 2018.

9 Daniel J. Solove, *Understanding Privacy*, Harvard University Press, 2008.

information flows along specific networks. It is important to recognize the different nature of such network relationships in order to identify and explain the limits of the dissemination of private information, and thus to integrate it with context theory.[10] For instance, in cooperative networks, privacy belongs to the information shared by the participants and is embodied in binding explicit/implicit contractual relationships or social norms; in productive networks, consumer behavioral privacy is simultaneously accessed by the merchant and used to improve the service, even if the activity occurs in a closed physical space. In this sense, cyberspace bridges the gap, where traditional privacy does not exist because users are in a constant process of information production and sharing, and have little control over the dynamic flow of information about themselves.[11] "Space" is thus transformed from an objective state of physicality into a political claim to resist the endless process of "datafication".

Speech and expression: The Internet has enhanced the ability of ordinary people to express themselves, which also highlights the network and dissemination orientation of expression, especially on social networks, where private expression can easily have a public impact through networked dissemination (for instance, WeChat and Microblog are two different architectural designs, with the former emphasizing private communication and the latter emphasizing public expression), spreading from one circle or group to another, which implies that a certain larger network will continue to absorb all kinds of small and medium-sized networks together, forming a "small world network" paradigm, [12] which will also contribute to the prosperity of the networked public sphere and public opinion to a certain extent.[13] Early Internet design and ideology tend to give people the impression that the Internet is a process of accessing the network by equal nodes, but as a matter of fact, both search engines and social networks clearly show that the evolution of the Internet is constantly replacing "commoner" networks with "aristocratic" networks, that is, the relationship between nodes on the network constitutes a power law of "the rich get richer".[14] This means that a few aristocratic nodes still have more speech power than ordinary users, and their speech content flows and spreads along the social network, and can be tracked and measured, so the power of dissemination and connectivity becomes very critical.[15] "Networked speech" offers a number of insights into the exercise and regulation of free speech: First, core nodes in networks are increasingly called upon to take on the role of gatekeepers

10 Helen Nissenbaum, *Privacy in Context: Technology, Policy, and the Integrity of Social Life*, Stanford Law Books, 2009.

11 This is why privacy by design was once a hot topic, for instance, Woodrow Hartzog, *Privacy's Blueprint: The Battle to Control the Design of New Technologies*, Harvard University Press, 2018.

12 Also known as "six degrees of separation". Empirical studies have also shown that on Facebook and Weibo, no two users are connected by more than six people.

13 Hu Yong, *Crowd Voices: Individual Expression and Public Discussion in the Age of Networks*, Guangxi Normal University Press, 2008.

14 Albert Laszlo Barabasi, *Linked: The New Science of Networks*, Perseus Books, 2002.

15 Manuel Castells, *Communication Power*, Oxford University Press, 2013.

because they are in a good position to control the spread of information. Second, the effects of speech can be measured by the amount of network connections and transmissions, thus facilitating the quantification of possible social impacts and the identification of violations. Third, due to the reduced cost of speech expression, users face the new problem of effectively distinguishing information from noise in a large amount of content, and the ability of AI technologies to set up default information streams to be pushed according to the user's own preferences, although it can serve as an information matching and filtering function, and can go to the other extreme, leading to a potential echo chamber effect, causing the public sphere divided, and rendering effective online communication in name only. Finally, the state and platform companies also have greater technological capacity to directly intervene and monitor private speech, particularly as platform companies can regulate speech subjects for violating state law by exercising their private power, which essentially blocks social networks, particularly large-scale social relationships and communication capabilities.

Property: As far as property relations are concerned, we are witnessing more and more offline resources being incorporated into a network and uniformly matched and managed by centralized algorithms. In the early days of the Internet, users had the ability to share and distribute digital works or virtual goods on a large scale, but this was prone to problems such as copyright disputes. For the first time, "free flow of information" as an ideology contributed to the illegal rise of the Internet. Subsequently, the safe harbor rule in digital copyright law regulated "link" as an important means of online communication.[16] The question of how to ensure that users share in an orderly manner while transforming the vast amount of virtual goods into value-creating services is at the heart of digital commons. Through business models and cloud technology, content service providers are increasingly able to make virtual goods stored on local terminals or hard disks available through streaming media or software, which can effectively avoid piracy, thus transforming "purchase" into "rent" and "commodity" into "service".[17] The shape of the property relationship has thus changed: Users no longer possess any controllable virtual property, nor can they effectively control and share the services they enjoy, which are entirely personalized and available only through a fixed account, and whose quality is not guaranteed by the quality of the initial product (which can be constantly updated and patched). Accordingly, physical property has become increasingly unstable with the rise of the sharing economy, and is more easily mobilized and rented out through networks shaped by central platforms.[18] Networked property/services further imply that the ethics and autonomy of

16 According to the safe harbor rules, if the Internet service provider receives a valid notice from the right holder, it must delete the link pointing to the infringing materials. This takes on a new meaning in the era of mini programs on WeChat, as analyzed later.

17 Aaron Perzanowski and Jason Schultz, *The End of Ownership: Personal Property in the Digital Economy*, MIT Press, 2014.

18 Shelly Kreiczer-Levy, *Destabilized Property: Property Law in the Sharing Economy*, Cambridge University Press, 2019.

interactions shaped by sharing are limited by both the platform's commercial contracts and its technological means, and replaced by vertical networks from the platform to the user and conditional sharing permission that cannot be accessed outside of the platform. According to this logic, in the Internet of Things environment, the "service-consumption-data" network formed between humans and machines may be more commercially valuable than the social network between humans. The logic of commercialization absorbs, overrides, and replaces sociality gradually.

Identity: Human social identity is in fact defined, recognized, and shaped by social relations (networks). In addition to citizenship, modern professions, religions, and social groups give us different social identities and strengthen the self-identification of their members through corresponding specialized networks. Identity then becomes an important means for organizations to ensure solidarity and provide limited services. Platform companies try to break down traditional identity mechanisms (thus breaking down the boundaries of tangible closed organizations and enabling the flow of resources) to provide services to a large number of users with unspecified identities, as well as to provide new work and consumption opportunities through networked information matching. But users no longer have traditional identities, and there is no fixed and unchanging unique citizenship in cyberspace—only unstable accounts provided by platform companies. Early cyberspace promised that through network anonymity users were free to change their identities from their physical space; but ultimately it is social networks or other service platforms that redefine digital identities through continuous connectivity, which are no longer endorsed and validated by a single subject in the form of certificates, but rather are multifarious and variable. Digital identity may be derived from labels from other users, or from analytical predictions made by the platforms based on behavioral data, and ultimately for commercial advertisements and recommendations (thus reproducing networks and connections). User-generated information/data are all interconnected and can directly/indirectly be used to identify individuals. The infinite possibilities of identities that are constantly generated through networks of strangers may not imply a free choice of the person, but are more likely to be shaped by algorithms and intrusive attempts to innovate through innovative services. Any innovation is nothing more than the development of new types of services generating new connections/networks to discover the "nature" of the user. Networked digital identities thus also imply discovery, recognition, and resistance at the same time.[19]

Risk and regulation: Summarizing the above discussion, the continuous generation of network connections means that the probability of unpredictable risks increases and may be transmitted geometrically through the network, bringing about uncontrollable order turbulence, including, say, the frequent emergence of cyber collective actions, unfair competition, botnet attacks, and P2P illegal

19 Julie E. Cohen, *Configuring the Networked Self*, Yale University Press, 2012.

fundraising, which have become normal in the network society.[20] The rationale behind this remains that the Internet creates a network effect through rapid connectivity, rapidly accumulating unregulated wealth, data traffic, and action, but without secure infrastructure and related systems as safeguards, interconnected networks will be very vulnerable.[21] The vulnerability of networks requires a balance between continued large-scale decentralized open connectivity (implying some kind of innovation) and a degree of centralized regulation and firewalls, placing greater demands on social governance and regulation. Possible measures include (1) the platformization of government and public services, (2) the strengthening of administrative responsibility of network platforms as intermediaries, (3) the establishment of early warning mechanisms and the enhancement of pre-emptive prevention through the monitoring of user behavioral data, (4) the reinforcement of credible identity authentication of incoming resources, and (5) encouragement of platforms to adopt technological measures to ensure the ordering of competition in the marketplace, among others.

3.3 Networks as mode of production

The previous section has briefly sketched out how the network, as an external architecture and default setting, has manifested itself in several fundamental legal sectors and issues, thereby changing our understanding of core legal concepts. Among the key questions that remain unanswered are why and how the networks arise and function. Unlike the formation of networks in specific scenarios in the physical world, digital networks cannot be separated from the targeted efforts and investments of platform companies. In other words, in the offline world and in the early days of the Internet, network connections might still have been seen as randomly generated and accidental; however, as platforms uncover their proven business models, firms innovate more and more consciously to exploit new resources (such as the ongoing "creative destruction" of traditional industries, the creative use of established mode of production), providing new services, absorbing all kinds of productive resources into the network, and thus having the ability to establish connections among users and between users and new service providers, solidifying connections through basic services that allow social capital to be tracked and shaped into a mode of production of economic value. In this sense, the digital network in cyberspace is to a large extent generated for the creation of economic value, capable of flexibly adjusting the "nodes" and "edges" of the network according to supply and demand, and thus guiding the flow and exchange of information, data, and productive resources along the network.

20 For instance, Niall Ferguson, *The Square and the Tower: Networks and Power, from the Freemasons to Facebook*, Penguin Press, 2018.

21 John Palfrey and Urs Gasser, *Interop: The Promise and Perils of Highly Interconnected Systems*, Basic Books, 2012.

It is necessary to carefully identify how networks are created in the productive process of the new economy in order to understand how they are accompanied by the rise of platforms and other forces that are transforming traditional offline networks. First, the free services provided by specific entities through low-cost information technology create connections that transcend spatial and temporal relations, and have the ability to gradually subsume various online and offline sub-networks and their elements, which together form a large network.[22] The whole society thus becomes flatter, and the traditional organizational, spatial, and geographical boundaries are gradually broken. Cyberspace and the physical world originally followed different logics, but the former gradually had a tendency to expand to cover the latter, so that online and offline activities are carried out according to the same logic of governance and production. Second, platforms play an important role in creating, enabling, and stabilizing all types of connections to form powerful infrastructure services. The core of this is that the platform has the ability to assign a unique machine-readable virtual identity to every node in the network, through which it continues to accumulate the data of all kinds of subjects/objects, and promotes the formation of the two-sided market to create more high-quality resources cross-subsidization. In this productive process, the platform not only replaces the traditional market, strengthens and expands the commercial network among market subjects, but also absorbs the traditional unproductive social network, using the social network to accumulate free labor and attract more users.

As a result, digital networks are increasingly characterized by "commodification" and "platformization". The digital services of platforms first transfer offline social relations to online world, and at the same time further abstract them into production relations that can directly or indirectly create value for the platforms. Such a productive relationship is characterized by the following: First, it is embodied between users (e.g., C2C model of sharing economy) and between users and platforms (B2C model). No matter which model, the platforms play the basic function of orderly allocation of liquidity resources in it. Second, the productive process of digital networks relies heavily on and takes advantages of noncommodified social norms and cooperative ethics (for instance, sharing, cooperation, reputation), thus turning social networks into the service of economic networks (rather than the other way around[23]). Third, the digital network itself represents the productive process, and it is in this process that users are transformed into digital laborers with flexibility, constantly adding value to the platform through their online activities. The network also exhibits a more sophisticated process of organizing labor through algorithmic allocation and manipulation. The relationship between users and platform companies is transformed from a simple consumer–merchant intermediary, buyer–seller relationship to a subtle labor relationship.

22 Similar to the Internet TCP/IP protocol gradually replaced other early network protocols, and eventually became a common protocol, the Internet is also called the "network of networks".

23 Mark Granovetter argues that it is economic activity that is embedded in social relations, see Mark Granovetter, *Society and Economy: Framework and Principles*, Belknap Press, 2017.

Aggregating networked labor, analyzing its behavioral data, and capturing its nuanced surplus value is the mystery of rise of new economy. Relationships of production, in turn, demand to rise to be recognized and protected as legal relationships. How the law can recognize in a substantive sense the labor invested and control exercised by platform companies in shaping the architecture, but meanwhile recognize in a formal sense that the labor created by the masses cannot be regarded as a typical labor relationship is a key question.

Judicial practice has also further clarified its attitude toward digital labor rights in recent years, notably in the following ways: First, in cases where platform labor is recognized, courts generally tend to find that user agreements are not labor contracts, and thus are not labor relationships, and that workplace injuries are only recognized in a few occasions like takeaways and couriers, and that the nature of the platform is thus still viewed as a marketplace based on the control of the platform company, which merely help coordinate and manage (rather than employ) market actors. Second, in cases where platform companies have been infringed by competitors, the argument of platform labor to collect and process data is often raised to argue that its virtual resources are private property, even if that kind of labor relies on a common pool of resources. Platform labor is reflected not only in shaping the underlying service, but also in processing specific data products. On the contrary, users cannot acquire any ownership of virtual property through their own labor; everything is subordinate to technical settings and terms of service. In other words, the labor and investment in building the digital architecture is much higher in value than the labor of an ordinary user, and therefore the platform can profit from its data with full legitimacy. Third, the court still only protects personal information from misuse from the perspective of personality rights, but does not address the issue of distribution in the sense of any property rights. Courts in similar cases have largely agreed with the internal regulatory norms and distribution rules of the platform companies without interfering.

In such circumstances, it is understandable that the concept of "control" exercised by platform companies through the Internet has not yet been well explored and discussed under Chinese law. This criterion can in fact be used to characterize the physical and economic subordination between flexible digital workers and platforms, and thus to understand the roots of platform value creation in the digital economy. Established cases show that the traditional labor law rule of subordination is beginning to be recognized by the courts, but has not yet given a more actionable standard for control. The control that traditional employers have over their employees is mainly reflected in some kind of subordination standard, but it is easier to ignore the abstract incentives for people to join the firm, namely, the ability of the firm to reduce the transaction and organizational costs of individual participation in the market, which allows employees to leave their jobs, but only to move from one firm to another, not to start up a business by their own (due to the high costs involved). This "informational control" of traditional firms in the abstract is often hidden behind the legal elements of labor relations. In such a perspective, the criteria of "physical/economic subordination" and "informational control" can also be reinterpreted for platform companies: Open networks appear to have the ability to separate the two types of control completely. Instead of issuing orders to network actors as an employer, the platform companies are able to divest and amplify the firms' original function of reducing transaction costs, and indirectly discipline network actors through the production and matching of information. This is the key to the often-underappreciated control of information, namely, the ability of platforms to consistently track users and to benefit directly or indirectly from a large number of recommendations and matches, while claiming to have nothing to do with transactional behavior. Even so, in terms of the criterion of subordination, in addition to traditional measures such as designing transaction structures and processes, setting norms of behavior and rules of trading on the platform, and controlling the level of transaction prices and the way in which they are paid, new measures like networked reputations, scoring mechanisms, monitoring of platform labors, authentication, and data tracking all reflect the true nature of the real control that networked laborers are enduring.[24] Thus, similar to the reasoning in the previous section, while the power of networks in cyberspace is already evident, continuing to obscure the benefits of productive networks for platforms (for instance, lowering traditional regulatory compliance costs) by applying traditional offline rules in a similar way online through legal interpretation may be a key tactic for platforms as they engage in legislative lobbying and litigation claims.

3.4 Networks as infrastructure and (private) property

Networks are abstract public good, and can be expanded at low cost to create opportunities for cooperation and transaction for a larger amount of people, and therefore a form of digital infrastructure.[25] The fragility of networks also suggests that arbitrary and unstructured connections may not be sustainable in the long run, always encountering trust and security problems, which in turn are not conducive to stable cooperation and production. These problems are less frequent in traditional offline societies, mainly because social networks of acquaintances themselves carry unseen trust and cooperative relationships, and are characterized by implicit mechanisms such as "facial recognition", "real identity authentication", "transactional security", and "reputation". However, when the network takes place in a cyberspace that is capable of transcending time and space, connecting any unspecified subject/object, these implicit institutions need to become visible in order to adapt to the mass connectivity in a stranger environment, connecting to more productive resources while ensuring security and trust beyond its vulnerability. In this sense, the network itself needs to become a modern underlying infrastructure that is not only capable of generating value in its own right, but also implies that the various functions and elements traditionally carried by the network need to be

24 Shoshana Zuboff, *The Age of Surveillance Capitalism: The Fight for a Human Future at the New Frontier of Power*, PublicAffairs, 2019.

25 Brett M. Frischmann, *Infrastructure: The Social Value of Shared Resources*, Oxford University Press, 2012.

reshaped and integrated. For instance, informal reputational system becomes formal rating system; private trust in specific scenarios becomes cross-context social credit; facial recognition by people becomes abstract identity authentication by machine; and new multiple identities continue to be generated through identification. Data accumulation changes from repeated games between a few to repeated games between a majority of unspecified people, and even blockchain applications collectively contribute to the process of reshaping trust in the cyberspace, which ultimately satisfies a kind of trust in an abstract society and reduces overall society-wide transaction costs.[26] All these explain the social function of private platforms to create infrastructure and its scalability and boundaries.

Networks and connections as infrastructure do not form spontaneously, but are designed and recommended by platform companies, and the process of their formation is guided and developed by the economic theory of a two-sided (or multi-sided) market.[27] For instance, attracting users through free services can help form a network of user groups (on one side of the market), followed by the gradual development of more free services (on the other side of the market) in response to user's demand, resulting in the formation of a new network of transactions. Platforms that are able to integrate a large number of services also expand the cyberspace by enabling more networks and connections through the continuous addition of services, cross-subsidization, or the merging of accounts for different services.

The problem, however, is that private infrastructure can be strongly influenced by private interests. As noted above, networks and connectivity can be seen as a dynamic and flexible figurative architectural design, and it is through the precise connection of productive resources that value can continue to be generated. Thus, the flow of productive resources is in a sense the generation and alteration of networks. The labor-input process of shaping the network can be seen as a public resource under platform control, and the virtual value the network generated needs to be protected by the law, especially the law against unfair competition. Interestingly, networks have begun to be recognized and protected by the law as a private, virtual, collective property right, as reflected in a number of Unfair Competition Law disputes. Courts have essentially developed and explored along three lines of thought: The first line of thought asks to what extent the business model of a two-sided market (and thus the connection itself) can be recognized, which has been starkly demonstrated in unfair competition and monopoly disputes; the second line of thought asks who is entitled to the social network and the social capital it brings with it, and how it can be protected as an abstract aggregative right. The third line of thought asks, in turn, how to reinterpret the figurative "link" after "connecting everything together" is realized through technological means, and to

26 Similar to Luhmann's dichotomy between concrete and abstract trust, see Niklas Luhmann, *Trust and Power*, Polity, 2017.

27 Jean-Charles Rochet and Jean Tirole, "Platform Competition in Two-Sided Markets", *Journal of the European Economic Association* 1, no. 4 (2003), 990–1029; David S. Evans and Richard Schmalensee, *Matchmakers: the New Economics of Multisided Platforms*, Harvard Business Review Press, 2016.

distinguish link from connection, so as to treat the former as an act of assuming the responsibility of a safe harbor and the latter as a kind of "basic service" to avoid regulation, thereby avoiding the duty of scrutiny and care while strengthening control over mobilized resources. These three lines of thought are briefly discussed next.

First, the two-sided market model can be seen as a morphing of network shaping in the field of economics. Although it is beginning to be widely recognized as a doctrine, the two-sided market is more in need of judicial confirmation so that the Internet platform business model can truly be left unchallenged. In a large amount of unfair competition cases revolving around data ownership, ad blocking, service interference and so on, this issue has received a very fortuitous broad consensus. This is mainly due to the fact that, according to the general logic of reasoning in unfair competition disputes, the court first needs to confirm whether there is a competitive relationship between the plaintiff and defendant as a prerequisite for the determination of unfair competition behavior. In the view of traditional competition law, only if both parties belong to the same competing market can they constitute a competitive relationship. The Internet industry happens to be through the cross-border way to constantly incorporate new resources, with the purpose of attracting the scarce attention of users. Then the two-sided market model is unavoidable, even if the two sides seem to be engaged in the business that is not quite the same. The court's recognition of a broadly competitive relationship has in effect sanctioned the legitimacy of production over the Internet. Paradoxically, however, in a number of Internet antitrust cases, courts have been reluctant to recognize the existence of a two-sided market, and have devoted a great deal of judgments to arguing how to find a suitable unilateral market. A single specific market has long been unable to explain the network effect and control of platform companies, and if this becomes standard, it will inevitably obscure the true source of market control—multilateral markets and networks—and thus indirectly provide shelter for giant platforms from unbundling. The apparently conflicting grounds for judgment actually reflect the different legal requirements of platform companies in different cases, but essentially, they are all about upholding the legitimacy of new mode of production. On the one hand, platforms do not want to challenge the function of their multilateral market services and the associated complex connections in antitrust cases; on the other hand, they want to use this ground to confirm their competitors' misconduct and to build a wall for their ever-expanding networks and connections.

Second, as social networks and connections continue to be transformed into data to be analyzed, who is entitled to such abstract relationships? The general idea may be to dismantle the network and bring a judicial claim on unfair competition grounds by protecting users' personal information as network nodes and network analysis results as data products, respectively. Social networks are further abstracted into "nodes" and "edges", with users as producers being part of the network and relationships between users being edges of the network. They are essential elements of the network and belong to the platform assets, rather than owned by all or specific users. In one sense, the network is still flowing and changing, and connections can be made and broken at any time, but platforms need to visualize it as an aggregate resource with property interests that are constantly generated only within the scope of the architecture. Although there is no law that explicitly provides for such rights, utilizing Article 2 of the *Anti-Unfair Competition Law* can currently be effective in protecting such network flows.[28] Even if users wished to extend new networks in competitors' platform out of existing architecture, this would require prior authorization by the dominating platform through terms of service, which is often unlikely to agree upon.[29]

Finally, platform companies want to "connect everything together", to shape and enjoy connectivity and the abstract control that comes with it, but have little desire to be responsible for connectivity (even if it is a safe harbor). This claim is fully reflected in WeChat's recent attitude toward content infringement on its mini program. WeChat does not want to be responsible for infringement on certain mini program, and thus tries to change the specific conditions of safe harbor liability under copyright law. The logic of the argument is that, first, WeChat wants to distinguish between "web links", which were displayed as URLs in a browser in PC Internet era, and "abstract connections", so that other ways of connecting cannot be covered by copyright law, such as APP jumping or going directly to other webpages. As a result, the former may continue to be interpreted as a form of technology subject to liability under the safe harbor rule, while the latter is not equally liable. Second, WeChat emphasizes that it views the mini program technology as a kind of underlying infrastructure, thus separating the technology from the business model and further avoiding possible bilateral market issues. Third, WeChat emphasizes that it lacks sufficient control (using the "with actual knowledge" criterion) to locate and remove infringing servers, but this is technologically impossible, but also ignores the issue of user perception, whereby the mini program appears to be integrated with the main WeChat interface. Finally, WeChat emphasizes the neutrality of connectivity rather than the proactive nature of creating connectivity driven by business models. The ultimate goal of this set of claims is to recognize the legitimacy of the continuous creation of new connections and networks through technological innovation, but not to increase the legal liability costs that come with it.

Technological formations have been shifting as platform companies innovate, but their core logic is becoming clearer, namely, to seize the network as an abstract medium for mobilizing organizational production, to absorb all productive resources into one networked flow, to ensure platform control over the flows through the network, and to seek to reduce the level of unnecessary responsibility for the behavior of nodes.

28 Similar to the litigations surrounding "data traffic", platforms and courts have attempted to define such abstractions as a competing interest.

29 The discussion in Sina v. Maimai (2016) of the three-tiered normative authorization structure for accessing users' personal information, while instructive, still obscures the control and influence that platform companies have over the contracting process.

3.5 Conclusion

This chapter briefly discusses the use and significance of "networks" in cyberlaw and digital commons. The central concern is in fact how legal relations change (or remain formally unchanged) alongside productive relations, and hence underlying social relations, and how networks can be manifested both in concrete changes of legal system and productive relations. Reclaiming networks implies a rethinking of the properties and functions of law itself. The study in this chapter has shown that to understand the spirit of legal rules in cyberspace, it is first necessary to understand what problems the law was created to solve and what are the essential attributes of the objects of governance. Law is not only regarded as controlling power, but also as productive power. In the four-factor framework of traditional architecture/code theory, the four regulatory elements (law, social norms, market, and code) are relatively static and are even thought to be able to be abstracted in a vacuum for study and analysis, but this is not the case in reality.[30] If architecture is seen not simply as an element of regulability, parallel to law, but as a mode of production and underlying infrastructure that encompasses resources, then each of the four elements in fact reflects, to a greater or lesser extent, the new mode of production, and thus transforms itself into part of a superstructure that reflects the economic foundation. The productive network approach is thus essentially a recognition of the architecture as a mode of production, embodied in everything from productive tools to process.[31]

This chapter has amply demonstrated what the law needs for networks, as the dynamic architecture at the top and the productive infrastructure at the bottom, that is, it needs to recognize the process of their continuous expansion and absorption of resources, and to acknowledge the requirements of vertical and horizontal integration, and thus to demand legal protection. It is a kind of "architectural right" that needs to be reflected in the law of today, and this abstract claim and concept of interest should be gradually realized in rules at different levels. It is in this sense that we can identify a specific body of rules and knowledge called "cyberlaw". One of the goals of the study of productive cyberlaw is to explain how cyberlaw is formed, but also to propose a methodology that reinterprets specific legal concepts in the context of the productive process, where traditional concepts such as property and privacy are not able to explain the current situation because the digital network redefines these concepts, centering them around and aligning them with the process of production. Methodologically, our perspective on the Internet can thus be shifted from political economy to the more specific economics and sociology of law. This chapter exemplifies what cyberlaw means by demonstrating the significance of the object of the Internet in laws related to privacy, property, speech, labor, and competition.

30 Ratings (not simply reputation) as a new type of regulatory element should also be highlighted based on the Chinese experience.

31 For United States, see Julie E. Cohen, *Between Truth and Power: The Legal Constructions of Informational Capitalism*, Yale University Press, 2019.

Rethinking the nature of networks and cyberlaw ultimately leads us back to the primary and fundamental question of "sociality and cooperation". Information technology has undoubtedly helped to enhance sociality to a certain extent, with the proliferation of interactions between acquaintances on social networks such as WeChat, and open networks facilitating large-scale cooperation and cultural production between strangers.[32] However, from another perspective, once social networks are transformed toward production networks or subordinated to the profit-making goals of economic production, the emergence and extension of social networks is no longer a sign of domains and systems with autonomy, but more likely a temporary phenomenon in the process of mass production. Just as the emergence of the sharing economy has its background in the decline of the traditional economy and its eventual replacement by smarter, low-cost machines, so the networks of relationships among members of society are likely to be squeezed by the economic interests of the platforms, and nonpecuniary online communities will decline. As a result, social networks and commercially driven networks are not exactly equivalent, and in the trend toward connectivity centered on machine production, authentic collaboration and sharing become less common. Users have to become more attached to centralized platforms because they are subjected to the unequal mode of production, and increased interaction with machines (which can be personalized AI), while immersing themselves in free labor and endless consumption for the platforms, yet less interaction with other members in society.[33]

32 Yochai Benkler, *Wealth of Networks: How Social Production Transforms Markets and Freedom*, Yale University Press, 2006.

33 Sherry Turkle, *Alone Together: Why We Expect More from Technology and Less from Each Other*, Basic Books, 2011.

4 Building information infrastructures in digital commons

4.1 Introduction

At an abstract level, the commercialization of the Internet in China over the past two decades has itself led to the reshaping of markets and societies by redrawing productive resources from different productive organizations and networks, and redeploying them on a larger scale to form solid new networks of transactions and cooperation. In this process, the productive resources are removed from their established environment and realize their value in a platform with mobility, requiring a set of digital infrastructures and information systems to enable such flows. Digital markets do not emerge naturally in a vacuum, but rather evolve in concert with established production networks and infrastructures, and need to be supported by a variety of complementary mechanisms. Infrastructure in the usual sense serves to confirm the true and unique identities of market participants, match resources efficiently, and ensure the orderly and secure flow of resources. In order to realize these functions, it is necessary to integrate the information of the subjects entering the market network and make use of it, otherwise the digital market will not be able to mature and stabilize. For instance, if the real identity of market participants cannot be confirmed, fraud, counterfeiting, copyright infringement, and other misbehaviors may occur, while the real identity authentication in the behavioral structure to achieve the most basic behavioral constraints, providing stable expectations for the actors. Another example is that if there is a lack of evaluation of the historical behavior of market participants, opportunists in one-off transactions may appear in the future, which does not help to improve the behavioral standards of actors as a whole, while scoring is actually an evaluation of the past behavior and history of actors, which helps to accurately match the productive resources toward the future.

From a historical perspective, new digital infrastructures in China include at least systemic powers such as payments, logistics, authentication, finance, dispute resolution, and credit, and have developed institutional norms. Unlike traditional infrastructures, they are more gradually developed by private digital platforms and help to create scale and network effects, but while reaching a certain market scale they may also create anti-mobility mechanisms that restrict the flow of resources across platforms, and thus need to be recognized and regulated by the state. In this chapter, publicness is mainly reflected in these infrastructures around the market and society, that is, how the state provides systematic support for the effective

DOI: 10.4324/9781003566243-5

flow of market resources. As will be shown specifically later, personal information plays a key role in the development of the digital economy and can fulfill its infrastructural functions through display, data products, and backend analysis. As these functions are needed to sustain the growth and expansion of a mature digital marketplace, they need to be included in the scope of mandatory collection and use, and not simply determined by individual consent, lest the tragedy of the anti-commons arise. While user agreements and usage practices in their current form can still ensure the continued production of personal information as a whole, there is still a need to clarify the sources of legitimacy beyond informed consent at the normative level so that such information can be better utilized for the public good.

The theoretical framework of this book asserts the need to see how changes in the new mode of production brought about by technology and business models drive changes in the overlying legal relations and related institutions. The formation of digital markets and societies further facilitates the generation of liquidity and aggregated value, but there is a need for specific governance processes to ensure that this market can operate smoothly, and the gradual formation of digital infrastructures helps us to better understand what the digital economy wants and how to promote the realization of the effective use of personal information through the law to serve the public interest. This theoretical framework argues that the expansion of digital markets and societies occurs within specific architectures, and that digital architectures shape the cyberspace and function as micro-power mechanisms through the three main mechanisms of account–data–ratings, which form constraints on actors and a complete set of production/control processes. It is not difficult to see that the three informational functions of the digital infrastructure mentioned above actually correspond one to one with the three resources of architectural power. Resource mobility and digital infrastructure in architecture are core concepts in Internet governance in China, in which not only the demonstrative data resources need to flow, but also assistant resource information can continuously flow and become part of the digital commons, which can link the wider digital market and open up the digital platforms that are closed to each other, which makes the public nature of such personal information more significant.

This chapter begins with an analysis of why certain infrastructural services are needed in the platform economy process, starting with the nature of platform companies, followed by a brief analysis of the types and functions of infrastructural services, and then an analysis of how information (including personal information) can be transformed into important infrastructural services through the production mechanism that facilitates cooperation and resource mobility in the digital economy.

4.2 Nature of platform companies

The background to the emergence of platforms is the further socialization of production, which is predicated on a well-developed infrastructure; otherwise, transaction costs and innovation costs would be higher and the scale of the economy would not grow rapidly. The platform economy is a product of the development of the Internet in China and Western countries almost at the same time, but the particularity of the Chinese market since the reform and opening up is that the offline infrastructure used to support large-scale market transactions is underdeveloped, especially the infrastructural services serving small-scale groups or even individuals have considerable room for expansion. Privately led Internet companies have the motivation and ability to recreate, and even surpass, the infrastructural services that have traditionally served large-scale enterprises and business activities and are often run by state-owned enterprises which are less sensitive to the changes brought about by information technology.

Information technology provides space and tools for mass innovation and entrepreneurship, and platforms are the intermediaries and promoters of all this. In terms of formality, a platform can be a hardware, an operating system[1], an APP, a client software,[2] a browser, a search engine,[3] or a website. What matters is not the external form, but what is common to all of them, namely, the underlying architecture of technology and business services that allows for the realization of a large number of innovations and services. The traditional underlying architecture includes industry standards, basic communication facilities, financial institutions, exchanges, and so on, with numerous intermediaries serving the function of communicating information about transactions and facilitating their completion.[4] On Internet platforms, the many intermediaries from production to consumption are dissolved, and platform companies are unified to provide powerful transaction infrastructural services, which are technology services at their core and later extended to more areas (see Section III for details). These IT-enabled, low-cost infrastructural services have obvious value for platform companies: (1) making the link between production and consumption shorter and faster, with value production rapidly outpacing traditional organizations; (2) organizing "unorganized" and fragmented market resources as much as possible into continuous and stable production activities;[5] (3) providing a platform company with the ability to offer more and more value to its customers; and (4) providing a platform company with the ability to offer more and more value to its customers. It is a competitive advantage for platforms that have the ability to provide more infrastructural services, so that small enterprises without such ability can only rely on large platforms and rent their services, and at the same time carry out different forms of value exchange.

1 Annabelle Gawer and Michael A. Cusumano, *Platform Leadership: How Intel, Microsoft, and Cisco Drive Industry Innovation*, Harvard Business Review Press, 2002.

2 David S. Evans, Andrei Hagiu, and Richard Schmalensee, *Invisible Engines: How Software Platforms Drive Innovation and Transform Industries*, MIT Press, 2006.

3 Stefan Weitz, *Search: How the Data Explosion Makes Us Smarter*, Routledge, 2014.

4 Marina Krakovsky, *The Middleman Economy: How Brokers, Agents, Dealers, and Everyday Matchmakers Create Value and Profit*, Palgrave Macmillan, 2015.

5 This process is rather overshadowed by writings that emphasize individual power and empowerment, such as Clay Shirky, *Here Comes Everybody: The Power of Organizing Without Organizations*, Penguin Press, 2008.

Empirically, the core components of the platform economy include the following:

- *The growing pool of productive resources,* made possible by the reduction of transaction costs through information technology, is integrated into various trading *networks*, creating cross-subsidized bilateral markets.
- The large amount of *data* generated by the activities accompanying the former.
- Use *algorithms* to dynamically analyze data for predictions to help improve trading efficiency.
- *Infrastructural services* provided and continuously improved by the platform companies.

According to this perspective, platforms can encompass essentially all Internet-based business practices, and more and more entrepreneurs and start-ups are clearly recognizing the advantages and costs of platform-based businesses. Platforms are not just oligopolies, but are embodied in all types of Internet services, such as search engines, social media, e-commerce, and the broader "sharing economy". Volume and market share are not the main criteria for judging platform companies, although we can typify them according to volume and model, and only companies that have all four of these resources can be discussed under the framework of a "platform", whereas a service-specialized company that is weak or missing in one of the resources can hardly be considered as a platform for the purposes of this chapter. This chapter also wishes to highlight platforms as an organic whole of productive processes and underlying capabilities, rather than a static goal. In this sense, there are firms that are more "normative" platforms, raising the bar in the market for platform companies and internalizing their core competencies.

The definition of platform in the current Chinese law is "an information network system that provides web space, virtual business premises, trading rules, transaction matching, information dissemination and other services for trading parties or multiple parties to carry out trading activities independently in network trading activities", which is mainly based on its function in the process of trading.[6] With further development of the Internet, it is increasingly difficult for this definition to reflect the complexity of the platform economy. First of all, the platform transcends the traditional enterprise organization, enabling enterprises to manage the production and market transaction behaviors outside the boundary of traditional enterprises at low cost, and to use all kinds of activities on the platform to obtain economic value, externalizing the cost of internal management of production resources into the cost of transactions on the platform, which is a new type of industrial organization form. As a matter of fact, even if the Internet reduces the cost of information within the society, if it leaves many infrastructures that support the operation of modern market, it will still remain at the level of "media" that relies on earning advertisement revenue. The Internet seamlessly connects the production and sales

6 Article 9 of the *E-Commerce Law*.

processes together, enabling information about goods/services to reach consumers directly, but the costs of sales, payment, and distribution still exist, and for a period of time there is still a need for a certain market entity to provide such public goods within a specific geographic area, which is an important reason for the existence of the platform company. From this perspective, platforms are but a further extension of the information revolution initiated by the Internet, providing strong support for the socialization of production.

Second, platforms also have property of market.[7] A two-sided market theory better explains how productive resources are microscopically attracted to platforms through cross-subsidization. Platforms expand their value through technology that integrates multiple services in a single client software or application in a one-stop portal, continuously expanding the range of services and the amount of markets, with different markets interacting with each other to form a rather complex market system. The emergence of platforms helps us to re-understand markets. Traditional markets appear in bazaars, shopping malls, supermarket chains and exchanges, which themselves are formed as a result of various social forces constantly influencing and aggregating transactions.[8] Internet platforms mobilize resources in a much more visible way, exerting a much wider and deeper influence on the market than traditional businesses. The power of platforms does not lie in the simple possession and control of market shares, but rather in the substantive inputs that facilitate and rationalize market transactions, make information more symmetrical, and enable innovation.[9]

Third, control over transactions. Platforms in fact have a degree of control and management over online production and transactions (partly from administrative obligations), and giant platforms are even strong enough to influence entire specific markets or a significant share of them. If platforms mobilize idle resources that traditional economic organizations cannot effectively utilize in the early stages of development, they have the ability to reorganize the production chain based on fuller information and complete the integration of upstream and downstream industries as the platform matures. On a platform driven by intelligent algorithms, production and sales will become more process-oriented and modernized, creating competitive advantages that traditional enterprises and offline markets cannot match. At the same time, some platforms have a significant impact on the pricing of market resources and have even been questioned for exploiting information

7 Arun Sundararajan points out that platforms have a mixture of both corporate sectionalism and marketplace characteristics, which also confuses traditional antitrust investigations. See Arun Sundararajan, *The Sharing Economy: The End of Employment and the Rise of Crowd-Based Capitalism*, MIT Press, 2017.

8 Ray Fisman and Tim Sullivan, *The Inner Lives of Markets: How People Shape Them-And They Shape Us*, PublicAffairs, 2016.

9 In this sense, the platform economy continues the process of "rationalization" of social life in the Weberian sense, so that bits, atoms, finance, and labor all flow at the same pace, a process that is ultimately unified by smart algorithms/artificial intelligence in a more automated way.

asymmetry to extract consumer and producer surplus.[10] Such a form of private power transcends traditional businesses and is increasingly becoming an important theme in Internet governance.

In addition, platforms have been referred to as "infrastructures" in different senses, such as the commercial infrastructure advocated by Alibaba, or the considerable amount of Internet platform companies that can be recognized as critical information infrastructures under *Cybersecurity Law* and subject to special regulation and protection.[11] This chapter argues that many of the functions that currently constitute platform infrastructural services are not special or natural monopolies, and can be used in modular arrangements and combinations, competing to the extent permitted by law and technology. Treating platforms as infrastructure with a heavy emphasis on raising security standards and ensuring continuity of services does not mean ignoring the dynamic competition in the platform's primary and secondary markets, let alone entrenching the market position of giant firms, which is a prerequisite for the market-oriented regulatory policies.

The production process of platform leads to a relationship between the platform and the resources on it, which requires a set of legal structures appropriate to the platform's production to ensure its legitimacy. For platforms, the inherent legal structure should also include how to organize and service production and trading activities in an efficient and orderly manner, which is an important function of infrastructural services.

4.3 Digital foundations for platform shaping facilities

4.3.1 Evolution of platform infrastructural services

This section attempts to show that the emergence of platform infrastructural services to deal with large amounts of "unorganized" productive resources is an endogenous consequence of the evolution of the digital economy. Certain infrastructural services that would otherwise fall into the usual category of inclusive infrastructure or utilities (for instance, payments, logistics, finance, and credit service) cannot be adapted to meet the needs of the digital economy, while public services that are not traditionally considered infrastructure (for instance, authentication and dispute resolution) can also be provided by platforms. This chapter collectively refers to these two types of services as platform infrastructural services. Economic studies have long shown that efficient infrastructural services that can be shared with members of society at low cost are conducive to lowering transaction costs for society

10 This is because the platform itself becomes the only intermediary after the elimination of other industrial chain intermediaries. For a critique, see Anna Bernasek and D. T. Mongan, *All You Can Pay: How Companies Use Our Data to Empty Our Wallets*, Nation Books, 2015. Depending on different industry practices there will still be new intermediaries, such as guilds on live streaming platforms which act as brokers and have the ability to negotiate with platforms.

11 Chapter 3, Section 2 of the *Cybersecurity Law*.

as a whole.[12] This has become a reality in digital era, and this chapter focuses more on how new types of infrastructures and universal services can be established under the leadership of private platform companies and elevated to the level of laws embodying the will of the Chinese state.

Empirically, core infrastructural services can be broadly categorized into nine types (technology services, data storage/analysis, payment/settlement, logistics, authentication, credit evaluation, financial services, dispute resolution, and behavioral management/regulation), which do not appear at the same time in time, and which vary widely across platforms.[13] Usually the more developed a platform's transactions are, and the more sophisticated the market is, the more infrastructural services are needed to services to intervene in transactions and reduce transaction costs.

Infrastructure of a natural monopoly is usually considered to require a large one-time upfront investment, which fails to cover the complex process of public goods services in the era of the platform economy. In contrast, the cost of infrastructural services is not necessarily provided by the platform company itself, but can be outsourced or C2C model, giving users more choice. Whether a platform company chooses to adopt a C2C model for a particular infrastructure service is related to the following resources: (1) path dependence; (2) lack of relevant license qualification; (3) less likely to carry out in its own advantageous area in order to enhance its control and highlight the characteristics of the platform service;[14] (4) switching from C2C to B2C (or vice versa) due to the reduction of technological costs; and (5) avoidance of direct infringement liabilities for the cost trade-offs. By outsourcing, a platform's particular infrastructural service creates a new secondary market outside of its core services. However, the platform still needs to master control (especially over data) and coordination on the basis of outsourcing in order to provide uninterrupted support for its core transactional services. Platform infrastructural services evolve dynamically through the interaction of complex secondary markets, which suggests that the basic resources of a platform can be reduced to interconnected multi-sided markets (rather than simply a patchwork of "modules" bound together). In this sense, platform companies are a collection of infrastructural services, and regulation needs to be reduced to different parts, targeting different service characteristics. Meanwhile, regulation of a single part will undoubtedly have an incalculable impact on other parts.

12 Brett M. Frischmann, *Infrastructure: The Social Value of Shared Resources*, Oxford University Press, 2013.

13 The selection of these nine functions is only with respect to platforms in general, and will vary in different scenarios. For instance, geolocation and navigation services are more critical for platforms mobilizing offline resources (for instance, dedicated vehicles).

14 Infrastructural services like payments, express delivery, and credit look to be dependent businesses that revolve around core transactional behaviors, and also have the ability to facilitate the integration of upstream and downstream businesses once they have formed a scale and an entry point to become a core link in the transactional chain and a new platform.

To summarize, platform infrastructural services underpin the socialization of production, distinguishing it from traditional firms and markets. On the one hand, these infrastructural services, with increasing marginal utility and near-zero marginal cost, are able to support an ever-expanding range of market transactions across different domains or geographies, far beyond the capacity of cost-constrained bounded firms. On the other hand, platform companies remain loosely connected to market resources, providing substantive services to the latter, and regulating productive processes within a larger social context, with an orienting power that goes beyond that of traditional monopolies. In this sense, platform infrastructural services are an important part of the digital economy, serving the deployment and organization of productive resources, which goes beyond the simple platform strategy of the earlier IT industry and is a production organization strategy with a broader vision.

Existing laws in China have established some infrastructural services (e.g., technology, data, and certification services) and even regulated them by licensing (e.g., payments, logistics, and credit), giving a competitive advantage to those who are the first to enter a particular market.[15] Platforms that are qualified and capable of providing such infrastructural services become more attractive and capable of integrating resources and data, creating a situation where the rich get richer. Platform infrastructure service investments are expensive, and emerging companies will need to pay greater costs (for instance, acquisitions) to obtain licenses, or directly attach themselves to large platforms. At the same time, it is also important to see that technological innovation and portal changes leading to infrastructure service iteration will make the market more competitive and unpredictable.[16]

4.3.2 Platform responsibility and neutrality

A significant amount of research has focused on the type and extent of civil and administrative liability of platform companies. Although platforms are not liable as employers for the productive resources they mobilize to match,[17] they still should be subject to a higher duty of care or duty of security for some types of online infringement or illegal conduct, and a lower duty of care or safe harbor duty in other cases. The problem is that it is difficult to link the discussion of liability to

15 This is the norm in China's Internet legislation, that is, the regulator first allows Internet companies and capital to engage in some kind of commercial innovation, and then after a period of time (usually one to two years) when the market stabilizes and unicorn companies emerge and become market oligarchs, then proceeds with more regulatory measures based on the existing issues in terms of technical standards, market access, and behavioral norms. See Angela Huyue Zhang, *High Wire: How China Regulates Big Tech and Governs Its Economy*, Oxford University Press, 2024.

16 Christopher S. Yoo, *The Dynamic Internet: How Technology, Users, and Businesses are Transforming the Network*, AEI Press, 2012; Larry Downes and Paul Nunes, *Big Bang Disruption: Strategy in the Age of Devastating Innovation*, Portfolio, 2014.

17 For instance, Wang Tianyu, "The Determination of Labor Relationship Based on the Provision of Labor Services on the Internet Platform", *Jurisprudence,* no. 6 (2016).

the nature of the platform company, and the relevant thinking either continues the discussion of the liability of ISPs from the *Sony-Napster* case onward, failing to see the change in the substantive function of the platform, or overall wants to label it as a "quasi-public utility", and simply calls for the creation of new legislation.[18]

Network neutrality, or technology neutrality, is a major argument in favor of mitigating platform liability. While traditional net neutrality theory discusses the responsibility of telecom operators as transmission conduits, the platform economy is quite different.[19] If neutrality is understood from the perspective of market resource management, it becomes clear that a significant number of platforms have long since deviated from neutrality, with incentives to organize the production of resources and profit from them, or conversely to exclude competitors' services. Net neutrality theory seeks to separate platforms from resource activities as much as possible, ignoring the direct source of the platform's value and its autonomy in choosing its resources, while the other extreme view would see the platform and its flowing open resources as a whole, requiring as much scrutiny as possible of the activities on it and increasing the cost of management. Almost any provision for platform liability could fall (even randomly) at different places on this spectrum.

Platform infrastructural services provide a new perspective to such discussions. Platforms, as forms of productive organization, are already deeply involved in the transaction process, unlike a simple software tool that allows information to be published and leaves resources to be matched. In the abstract way, therefore, the allocation of responsibility should match the extent and capacity of the platform to intervene in the transaction process, but in practice it is difficult to draw boundaries. Platform liability is essentially the cost to the platform of handling and managing unanticipated risks (from unorganized market resources in the first place), while infrastructural services (especially regulations and dispute resolution mechanisms) can help minimize the same kind of risks and keep the cost of liability. Managing costs that are not invested in infrastructural services *ex ante* can lead to reputational and financial damage by taking on pressures and liabilities from various parties after the risk has occurred ex post. An important regulatory idea thus is how to promote a shift from external to internal platform responsibilities, and improve the platform's ability to handle disputes and achieve an orderly flow of resources. Empirical studies have found that platform companies are better able to adapt to the production and trading of massive amounts of information content and services by adopting self-regulatory means. This implicitly requires strong platform infrastructural services to maintain market order, establish basic databases and credit systems, and enhance monitoring capabilities, authentication, and dispute resolution,

18 In particular, the overlap between platform infrastructural services and traditional public infrastructure has led to arguments in favor of regulating and restraining platforms as quasi-public services, modeled on the essential facility theory of European and American antitrust law.

19 Despite the fact that telecom infrastructure is monopolized by state-owned enterprises, one-way cooperation with large platform companies (for instance, free traffic for monthly services) has existed, which also involves the traditional topic of net neutrality.

so as to keep the flow of online activities smooth and efficient, especially when the capacity of regulators is insufficient.[20]

Tort liability/administrative obligation studies alone fail to see the dynamic market implications of imposing platform liability.[21] Large platforms can afford to impose higher *ex ante* review obligations and ex post tort liabilities (or even provide insurance and *ex ante* payments), while for smaller platforms, the same statutory obligations become costly in terms of competitive disadvantages. While it is legally difficult to make a sweeping judgment about which firms bear what level of duty of care (and the associated resource investment behind it), we can still judge the impact of legal liability adjustments on market structure. All else being equal, if the general level of liability is set or raised at a standard that is affordable to large platforms, it will drive more entrepreneurs in different areas to collaborate on large platforms, to use the latter's free infrastructural services, or to leave these specific high-cost areas, which is one of the reasons why some large platforms are successively adopting an open-door strategy.[22] Whereas if the level of platform liability is lowered in accordance with the many small platforms and start-ups' volume to reduce the level of platform liability, then more entrepreneurs can be expected to emerge, raising the level of competition, but increasing the regulatory burden. This chapter is not simply arguing that the level of platform liability should be increased or decreased, but rather that it is intended to link specific liability rules to market structure, to compare the externalities that different levels of liability impose on the market, and then to continually adjust and optimize them in the context of the rapid development of digital markets. Indeed, large platforms that call for a reduction in platform liability are likely to potentially benefit from an increase in liability, namely, by gaining access to more corporate resources that would otherwise be free to start their own businesses, and which would otherwise be invested in smaller platforms with which they compete.[23]

20 Compared with situations a decade ago, large platforms have become the competitors they destroyed through "illegal rise", that is, interest groups with large amounts of licensed film, television, and music resources, with incentives to strengthen intellectual property protection and firmly control the pivot of the cultural industry through distribution. They are also more technologically capable of monitoring and cracking down on piracy, forcing it to change from deep link to blocking advertisements.

21 Indeed, the rhetoric of platform companies (both large and small) against high levels of accountability also implies that if platforms were to increase censorship, they would not only increase their internal management costs, but would also raise the barriers to participation and exclude some users. This fails to see the flow of resources between different platforms (with varying impacts on size), and fails to show that there is no contradiction between better management by platforms and higher standards of user behavior.

22 Large platforms with huge resources and data did not adopt the strategy of cooperating with third parties right from the start, either because of the competitive pressure to mobilize more technical forces to mine data and make the pie bigger together, or because of social pressure, as Tencent realized after the 3Q war.

23 Specific analysis is still needed here. If the product of general level of liability and the probability of being regulated/claimed for is much lower than the pecuniary gain that can be obtained by letting the risk occur, platforms will let it go, rendering the *ex ante* deterrence of liability requirements

4.4 Personal information, digital infrastructure, and publicness

If in terms of the characteristics of the information itself, personal information can be roughly categorized into demonstrative information and assistant information: The former is produced by the subject of the information and assembled and used by the digital platform, and can be associated with the subject of the information through an account; the latter is functionally differentiated into the core system of identity authentication, connection matching, and reputation evaluation, which is important for helping to maintain the effective functioning of the digital economy and society. It is crucial to note that these three types of information with different functions existed widely in the offline world before the creation of the Internet, but only in the era of the digital economy have they been rediscovered and have value in a wider context. At the same time, as personal information becomes available in large quantities, it becomes questionable whether the emphasis on personal information protection will impact established functions and practices. For instance, traditional authentication information may be more creative in a broader digital marketplace, but meanwhile new demands are being placed on the use and protection of the personal information in question, and the question becomes how best to design rules for handling personal information while continuing to emphasize this authentication function. Another example is that the evaluation of the reputation of social subjects has always existed in traditional societies, but it is only in highly mobilized societies and markets that we need large-scale social credit or reputation scoring mechanisms based on personal information, which can be transformed into data products in order to meet the needs of real production and control processes.

4.4.1 Creation and use of authentication information

Identification information is a very special kind of personal information that is characterized by universality, uniqueness, and stability, originating from the demand of modern countries for precise management of all kinds of resources of governance within the scope of sovereignty, created by sovereign power and not fully attributable to individuals. For the state, there are two main types of operational identifiers: (1) the state issues a unique token or number for all citizens in a unified manner, which can be done for one person;[24] (2) biometric information, such as face, fingerprints. and DNA. However, the two have slightly different meanings for identity authentication. For the former, state-issued numbers represent sovereign power and are the source of legitimacy for modern citizens' identity, as well as

ineffective. But in terms of nonpecuniary gains (such as social reputation, which is still ultimately reflected in share prices), such indulgence causes far more damage to large platforms than to small ones. This is why "catching the big and letting go of the small" is efficient.

24 The identity card is an important embodiment of the authentication power of the modern state, embodying the registration and categorization of the population on its territory. For a similar document for passports, see John C. Torpey, *The Invention of the Passport: Surveillance, Citizenship and the State*, Cambridge University Press, 2018.

the authoritative identity credentials for their rights and obligations. For the latter, biometrics merely indicate that the subject is the same natural person in a physical and biological sense, although technical criteria may also need to be authoritatively determined by the state to be empowered and recognized. Authentication not only contributes to the day-to-day management of the state, but also helps equal subjects to confirm and demonstrate their true identities to each other, and even assists in identity and behavioral tracking based on security concerns.[25] Authentication information becomes functionally critical. In traditional trading and social cooperation processes, it is often the default network of acquaintances that helps to verify the true identity and background of participants to ensure security, but in a highly mobile society, as social subjects continue to trade and cooperate with other strangers, it is necessary to continually confirm each other's identities in order to enhance the degree of trustworthiness. This process often involves the use of state-created identifiers, which are constantly evolving as technology changes. For instance, early identity cards were primarily displayed offline, but gradually became machine-readable in the background in online environments; as technology changed, cellphone numbers, faces, and QR codes were gradually developed and incorporated into this framework as part of the authentication infrastructure.

In addition, authentication information includes other licenses, industry qualifications, and other broadly defined authentication information in addition to general basic personal identifiers, which plays an important role in strengthening state regulation of market subjects, especially in the area of e-commerce. In other words, as digital platforms integrate subjects previously dispersed in different organizations, networks and environments into the broader system by means of registered accounts, the original secondary identities of social subjects become relatively unimportant, while universal and uniform identity information becomes increasingly valuable and must be utilized in some legal and technical way. Once a particular account has been verified by means of a real-name system, it not only ensures that the user of that account is real and unique, but also ensures a level of trustworthiness in the transaction process that facilitates digital platforms to continue to recognize the preferences and multiple identities of their users, thus making transactions secure and predictable.

Traditionally, personal information is broadly categorized into sensitive and nonsensitive, with the former being enumerated and subject to stricter restrictions in handling procedures. For instance, the *Personal Information Protection Law* stipulates that a personal information processor has a specific purpose and

25 Article 13 of the *Resident Identity Card Law* stipulates that citizens who need to prove their identity in order to engage in relevant activities have the right to use their resident identity cards to prove their identity, and that the units concerned and their staff may not refuse to do so; and Article 6 of the Measures for the Administration of Public Security in the Hotel Industry stipulates that hotels must register to receive travelers for lodging. At the time of registration, the identity documents of travelers shall be checked, and the registration shall be made truthfully in accordance with the prescribed items. When receiving overseas travelers for accommodation, they should also submit an accommodation registration form to the local public security authorities within 24 hours.

sufficient necessity before handling sensitive personal information. By definition, sensitive personal information is personal information that, once leaked or illegally used, may lead to discrimination against an individual or serious harm to the safety of a person or property, including information such as race, ethnicity, religious beliefs, personal biometrics, medical and health care, financial accounts, personal whereabouts, and other information (Article 29). Where the handling of sensitive personal information is based on an individual's consent, the processor shall obtain the individual consent in advance (Article 30). In particular, with regard to facial information as a specific kind of biological information, it needs to be subject to special constraints in the process of use; the installation of image collection and personal identification equipment in public places shall be necessary for the maintenance of public security, comply with the relevant state regulations, and be equipped with conspicuous reminder markings; the collected personal images and personal identification information shall only be used for the purpose of maintaining public security, and shall not be disclosed or provided to others, except for obtaining the individual's separate consent (Article 27). In some industry norms for personal information protection and local social credit rules, there has actually been a shift from this traditional categorization to function-based regulations that specifically separate personal authentication information from other information. For instance, the *Specification for the Protection of Personal Financial Information* distinguishes the content of personal financial information into account information, identification information, financial transaction information, personal identification information, property information, and borrowing and lending information; the *Chongqing Municipal Regulations on Social Credit* stipulates that the aggregation of public credit information of natural persons shall be based on the citizenship number as the associated matching identification. If there is no citizen identification number available, the amount of other valid identification documents, such as passports, shall be used as the matching identification. Legal persons and unincorporated organizations' public credit information shall be aggregated using the unified social credit code as the matching identification.

This helps us to rethink the origins of specific sensitive personal information. The logic of this chapter suggests that the creation of authentication information has its origins in state governance. It is constantly used in the provision of public services by the state, and is expected to be enhanced along with the state's capacity to govern. If a certain kind of personal information can function as a quality identifier, it could be incorporated into the identity system. Specific personal sensitive information is of great value in the dimensions of universality, uniqueness, and authenticity and meets the requirements to become an identifier. In this sense, sensitive personal information is not only about the personality of the individual, but also arises from the power of authentication and the resulting technology of authentication. Authentication information requires special protection, not because it belongs to some kind of sensitive information but because the widespread use of authentication information enhances the value of that kind of information, which, if leaked or misused, can cause confusion and disruption to the normal proceeding of public services.[26] The fundamental identifier was first applied in the context of the state's provision of public services. If other social and market entities also begin to use it, it will dilute the effectiveness of the state's power and go beyond its original purpose of use, which is why there are advocates that the identification of bio-information should be set up in the key areas and adopt a license system. According to the logic of this chapter, the purpose of special protection is mainly to prevent dilution and to enhance rather than reduce the effectiveness of specific kinds of authentication information. As a result, the scope of sensitive personal information is constantly evolving and is often closely coupled with authentication mechanisms.

The creation of authentication information in the early days was mainly offline fundamental identification information, namely, identity card numbers or images of identity documents, which were created exclusively by the state and used in the course of public services. However, as technology changes, authentication information is again variable, meaning that the state needs to recreate a whole new set of identifiers in the digital environment, or generate and adapt them on the basis of other existing types of personal information.

As far as the former approach is concerned, eID, which the Third Research Institute of the Ministry of Public Security once tried to develop, is a good example. eID re-generates digital markers for users as citizenship identifiers by means of encryption technology on the basis of ID card numbers, and adopts a path of development at the hardware level, transforming the mobile phones/cards into a trusted intermediary. In terms of theoretical logic, eID puts more emphasis on the pre-procedure for the state to confer legal identifier on natural persons, and clearly constructs a set of technical standards for digital identity.[27]

As far as the latter approach is concerned, the state has recognized the practice of using information from telephone numbers to face information as a new type of basic identity identifier, and has been continuously improving it. In this process, the transformation of sensitive information like bio-information into authentication information needs to take into account a number of conditions, such as the cost of technology diffusion, the risk of data leakage, and the general uniqueness of information attributes, among others. Since authentication of a single type of personal information is risky anyway, multi-resource authentication is needed. This perspective helps us to look beyond the single perspective of personal information protection and try to think about the value of personal information in terms of other subjects of its production. The value of personal information in its creation and processing is multiple, involving both individual personalities and other subjects. This chapter argues that the discussion should first return to the basic

26 The existing discussion that the protection of face information deserves special attention simply because it is facial information may reflect a personality and social cybersecurity anxiety that face information represents personality and social cybersecurity stemming from the collective unconscious.

27 See Ministry of Public Security, Third Research Institute, *eID Digital Identity System White Paper* (2018).

authentication function for which certain personal information is used, and that it is possible to think about the design of systems to reduce the risk of utilizing it, as long as the associated benefits outweigh the costs of producing such information.

Currently, the *Cybersecurity Law* only stipulates that the state shall implement an online trusted identity strategy, support the research and development of secure and convenient electronic identity authentication technologies, and promote mutual recognition between different electronic identities (article 24). In the process of mutual recognition, the state is actually able to provide digital markets and society with authentication services that go beyond the platform itself, which facilitates the cross-platform flow of productive resources. However, it has not been articulated with the *Resident Identity Card Law*, nor has it systematically clarified the legal status of digital identity. Prior to this, China's digital identity only relied on the *Electronic Signature Law* and relevant online real-name regulations to get piecemeal provisions. It is necessary to start from the top-level design of the country and combine specific technical routes to determine a national universally applicable legal system of digital identity, so as to find legislative justification for biometrics and other new technologies in the future.

4.4.2 How personal information is embedded in digital networks

The transformation of personal information into some kind of abstract information in networks is the second approach to realize its public nature. From the perspective of digital production, resource connectivity and distribution networks have their origins in traditional production networks and organizations, and progressively disrupt and absorb these traditional networks.[28] The formation of traditional networks is directly related to individual behaviors and trajectories, constituting their life worlds, but social networks expanded by information technology can be generated more rapidly as a whole, connecting more productive resources, and undoubtedly have a public nature from an external perspective, as a kind of infrastructural service on a digital platform. This actually reflects the process of generating networked value, and digital platforms are able to generate value because of the network effect, where platforms accurately match and realize secure transactions based on connection information. With a stable connectivity in networks, platforms can better provide information, shorten the transaction process, provide high-quality information services, and steadily accumulate value. In this sense, the social network is an abstract aggregate interest that can help the use and flow of general productive resources to better realize value.

Traditionally, on application platforms such as social media, social network information is often considered to be private information. This is partly because private behaviors and information are often transmitted through chains of intimacy,

28 Theoretically, it is also a process by which the market absorbs society; for a similar historical process, see Karl Polanyi, *The Great Transformation: the Political and Economic Origins of Our Time*, Beacon Press, 2001.

in a relationship with others, and therefore specific norms are needed to identify the nature of such intimacy, and to prevent specific private information from being abused in an established information network once it is available. However, with the increasing activities of social subjects on crossing digital platforms, the network of connections with others goes beyond the behavioral trajectory of a single individual and becomes a relatively independent data product, thus departing from the scope of mere privacy.

Compliant personal information processing plays a critical role in the creation of connected networks. Personal information processing is itself a process of virtual identity re-creation, whereby platform companies distribute, match, and recommend content along the network through various types of labels set for accounts, and even make automated decisions to guide account's behavior. The *Personal Information Protection Law* initially provides two ways to address the issue of personal information not being accurately identified during processing but allowing the generation of connected networks. First, from the external perspective of the user, commercial marketing and information pushing through automated decision-making should be accompanied by the option not to target his or her personal characteristics or provide the individual with a way to refuse, where decisions are made through automated decision-making that have a significant impact on the rights and interests of the individual. If a decision is made through automated decision-making that has a significant impact on the rights and interests of an individual, the individual has the right to request clarification from the personal information processor and the right to reject the decision made by the personal information processor only through automated decision-making (Article 25). Second, from the internal perspective of the platform, the platform can adopt corresponding security technical measures such as encryption and de-identification to ensure that personal information processing activities comply with laws and administrative regulations, and to prevent unauthorized access as well as leakage of personal information or its theft, tampering, and deletion (Article 51). If combined with the aforementioned authentication information analysis, it is not difficult to find that in addition to the authentication information can be directly associated with the individual's unique true identity, in most cases personal information is in an identifiable state, that is to say, the absolute anonymization of the processing in the existing technical conditions is difficult to achieve, so the platform needs a specific legal ground for exemptions to ensure that it can handle to a certain extent personal information into the entire connectivity network. Currently, in addition to the linking and identification standard, a new standard is beginning to be discussed in the judicial sphere, namely, whether the technological cost of recombining specific information for identification is prohibitive in order to assess the platform's ability to use that information to identify an individual.[29] In addition, de-identification may also be carried out if (third-party) information processor can demonstrate that technical

29 Guangzhou Internet Court Civil Judgment (2021)(Guangdong 0192 Minchu 928).

means of de-identification make re-identification less risky and do not have the ability to identify a specific individual.

The way in which information networks really work is through connectivity, namely, through access and transactional cooperation between accounts, linking different social agents and users. "To Connect everything together" used to be the quintessential platform economic ideology and the root of the argument for technological neutrality and algorithmic black box non-interference. While the productive resources on digital platforms appear to be highly mobile, they actually flow along networks and architectures, and as platforms become capable of tracking and analyzing user behavior through accounts, they increasingly expect users to be able to transact on a continuous and stable basis, thus making established networks of connections more stable, and in fact serving an important infrastructural function. Similar to information commons, the generation of such networks is characterized by a certain publicness, with any participant entering the network potentially gaining access to more trading opportunities, and the network improving along with the profile and quality of the participant's activity. This is why the real value of digital platforms that master the connected networks actually comes from distributing and predicting them. In this process, the infrastructure is created more by private platforms investing the relevant resources to transform all types of relationships among users into valuable commodities, which ultimately become valuable assets and do not allow competitors to trespass illegally. In this sense, unlike authentication information, distribution networks are characterized by a certain dependency, relying on changes in account behavior and resource flows. Thus, as long as the production resources continue to flow through a given platform architecture, the platform can keep using that network for automated recommendations and matching. This also means that such infrastructures are less susceptible to cross-platform scaling, and that anti-flow mechanisms emerge when the connected network reaches a certain size, restricting resource flows across platforms and making the boundaries of digital platforms more and more closed.

Considerable research has argued that China should introduce a data portability provision derived from the EU's *General Data Protection Regulation* (GDPR), arguing that this could help promote the flow of data resources based on user-led choices. This chapter argues that a proven way to promote data flows is not necessarily user-led portability and transfer, because once the law allows individuals the right to make specific kinds of cross-platform data transfers, not only is it prone to third-party developers vaguely obtaining users' consent and engaging in large-scale personal information grabbing, thereby disrupting the market order, but it also means that the transferred data is easily detached from the established value network and needs to be revalued, and increases social costs. The consequences are therefore not necessarily conducive to a healthy and orderly flow of data resources and value-adding. In fact, based on current experience, the opening up of new types of service development or mutual access based on API interfaces stipulated in the cooperation agreements of digital platforms is a concrete form of opening up the connectivity network. At the same time, it implies some kind of flow and transfer of data. This not only avoids market disruption brought about by unorganized crawling of data, but also avoids separate pricing for data as a by-product of making the pie bigger. In this sense, a safer option may be to allow productive resources belonging to different digital platforms to open up to each other into their respective connectivity-matching networks.

4.4.3 Mandatory disclosure of reputational information

The third type of information that personal information can be converted into infrastructural functions is reputation information, that is, the reputation of a particular subject in a social network as a result of specific behaviors. This approach has been widely adopted since the commercialization of digital platforms, such as e-commerce platforms and sharing economy platforms, where rating systems can not only partially solve the "lemon market" problem of traditional economics, but also help promote resource mobility, and even serve as a tool for the management and control of flexible labor processes. If viewed in the framework of the classic "code theory" in cyberlaw, this process also means that social norms are gradually rationalized by social credit and scoring mechanisms, turning them into a new type of social discipline and regulatory power, which is reflected in the social level of the social credit mechanism being implemented by the state. The goal of both the platform scoring mechanism and the social credit mechanism is to discipline the behavior of social subjects through flexible information and to assign specific values and meanings to their past historical behaviors which are measured and evaluated by some uniform standards. These historical behaviors are constantly occurring in the process of continuous interaction, cooperation, and transaction with others through the connecting network, which ultimately influences the subject's behavior in a subtle way and helps to gradually improve the overall behavioral order. Reputation information undoubtedly reduces the cost of resource flows and transactions, and together with authentication and connectivity information becomes a solid digital infrastructure.

Not surprisingly, such reputational information mechanisms are closely linked to the production of personal information and require mandatory disclosure in specific ways. These ways include at least the following: (1) Direct disclosure and display, such as traffic departments taking images of people violating traffic regulations at intersections for public display, which is more of a "shaming" behavior in traditional law enforcement; publishing the basic personal information of deadbeat individuals on a unified platform for relevant interests to inquire about; blocking the violating artists or anchors from the entire network, and so on. (2) Indirect disclosure, such as the establishment of various types of specialized databases (for instance, domestic violence, academic misconduct, violation of teacher ethics) for specific subjects or industry groups to query with certain procedures. (3) Data products, such as the formation of data products such as individual credit reports or social credit scores, which allow social subjects to query and inform the individual, but do not disclose specific behaviors, and so on. In accordance with traditional thinking, according to the principle of informed consent to the use of personal information between equal subjects, no one will be willing to voluntarily disclose the information that affects his/her reputation to his/her detriment, and it is necessary for a specific public entity to transform it into an information public resource through a legal relationship to require mandatory disclosure, in order to realize flexible governance based on information.

Reputational information amounts to a complementary and supportive institutional arrangement to the connectivity network, as the connectivity network itself cannot help people to judge the authenticity of the information transmission process. Traditionally, when people receive information through networks, they need to verify the real identity of the other party, or varying degrees of relevance, before deciding whether or not to continue to cooperate or interact, and the basis for judging whether or not the other party is trustworthy often lies in the accumulation of external reputations. The efficacy of the connectivity network itself also depends on extrinsic dynamics such as the number and quality of people's past dealings and their willingness to engage the first time around. Without such publicly disclosed public information, many new trading networks based on risk aversion could not be established. Therefore, this public information must be produced in some mandatory way, rather than voluntarily, and applied through certain harmonized channels and standards. As with authentication information, what kind of personal information can be transformed into reputational information is also subject to frequent change, and can be added to specific lists or databases after certain legal procedures have determined that it can influence specific social behaviors. For instance, the *National Public Credit Information Base Catalog* (2024 Edition) lists 11 items of information that should be included in the scope of public credit information and four categories of information that should be included with caution in accordance with the law. The main considerations affecting the ability of specific personal information to be transformed into reputational information include (1) the cost of production and technological diffusion of such information; (2) whether such information has a certain degree of universality; and (3) whether such information can serve a reputational function and potentially influence human behavior, among others.

Reputation information, like connectivity information, is strongly dependent on specific interaction, cooperation, and transaction scenarios and is generated in connectivity networks. Specific reputation information generated on a particular platform will therefore be strongly geographically colored. It is entirely possible for different platforms to develop incompatible rating scales and guide users to adjust their behavior, which means that certain reputations or ratings lose their value once they are removed from a particular platform network. When combined with the right to data portability discussed above, it is easy to see that even if the choice of data transfer based on individual users is safe and orderly, there is still no way to ensure that the same data will gain its original value on another competing platform, which inhibits the willingness and motivation of social subjects to transfer personal information, because it means that the data will most likely be of less value after the transfer. At the very least, it will not be able to reflect the historical behavior and value of the social subject, or even bring potential risks of cooperation in the new environment due to information asymmetry. Therefore, if a large number of productive resources are to be transferred across platforms, it is necessary to standardize the relevant evaluation criteria, and in the process of resource transfer, it is also necessary to transfer specific types of personal information and the reputational information of its evaluation, in order to provide sufficient incentives to promote the flow of resources, and not simply a matter of empowerment. This idea can also be guided by neutral public institutions outside of digital platforms, integrating specific types of reputation data products based on big data analysis at the technical and application levels through the establishment of joint ventures, and guiding the fusion of data between the ecosystems of different platforms, so that mobility on a wider scale can be gradually realized.[30]

4.5 Conclusion

Legal rules for the protection of personal information, including the *Personal Information Protection Law*, do not focus specifically on the production of information, but history has shown that the core issues dealt with by cyberlaw as a whole have always been those relating to the legitimacy and efficiency of the production of information and the rating of resources. This chapter attempts to think about personal information from a more fundamental perspective, namely, that a considerable amount of personal information needs to be transformed into infrastructural services that enable markets to function efficiently in the digital commons. It is only from a functional perspective that it is possible to understand why personal information is created in one way or another, and to understand how a certain kind of personal information can be protected and better utilized within a given function. Only once the mechanisms to ensure stable production are in place can further thought be given to how the public functions of such personal information can be better utilized. The premise of the discussion in this chapter is that personal information is produced in large quantities at low cost, anywhere, anytime, as a result of the ubiquity of information technology and the resulting resource mobility. If resource mobility is taken as a given variable, the next question is how the personal information that comes with mobility needs to be best utilized.

The discussion in this chapter is multilayered and focuses on three nonexhaustive scenarios that analyze how personal information can move from merely satisfying private interests to realizing the public interest. As an illustration, these three scenarios actually embody specific functions of infrastructural information, all aimed at ensuring the safe and orderly flow of productive resources and increasing the number and overall value of transactions. Existing discussions around the attribution of personal information or corporate data tend to ignore the public interest dimension. In order to ensure the efficient functioning of this broader market and

30 The most direct example is the establishment of the Baihang Credit, a joint venture to share personal credit information generated by large digital platforms and to harmonize credit standards and scores to facilitate mobility. Although the operation of the "credit union" is not perfect, in the long term it is a path that retains the autonomous status of large platform companies while strengthening infrastructure through centralized authority.

society, there is a need to continually transform information produced by individuals into public information, helping to keep the productive resources moving, to the benefit of the participating subjects and productive resources in the commons. The productive dimension of personal information can thus be brought back into the academic discourse and, on this basis, emphasize the public nature of personal information, which also involves a great deal of public and private institutional cooperation.

To some extent, this chapter also revisits the abstract connotations of publicness in China. Following the creation of digital platforms, the complete separation of public and private institutions and the behavior of public institutions as the only kernel of publicness may not fully reflect the changing reality. In fact, private subject-led publicity exists as well, as a process of publicity realization, because the digital infrastructure it builds facilitates the flow of resources in the digital marketplace and assumes a considerable public function, which is difficult to fully distinguish from public institution-led publicity. As a result, it may be important not to continue to differentiate and solidify public–private boundaries at the legal level, but rather to look at the consequences of how public–private cooperation can help transform personal information as a private resource of production into one that is conducive to a broader public environment, and thus to further explore how to connect the existing specific closed digital markets in a coherent and connected way. In this sense, what may be important is not so much the rights to the productive resources, but rather a systemic approach to enabling the productive resources to serve better market mechanisms. Explorations around publicness also help us to understand how rights and interests are distributed in particular information functions. While traditional scenario theory cannot provide further guidance on how to grant digital rights and interests to be allocated in a given context, the process of production of personal information implicitly requires consideration of the purposes and functions for which particular personal information is produced. If individuals are allowed to have greater control over the information associated with them, a common pool of resources cannot be formed for effective utilization.

5 Two types of property rights in digital commons

5.1 Introduction

Since information technology has continued to expand in Chinese society, there have been many legal claims for new types of rights in the digital environment to go beyond traditional types of rights and keep pace with the times, such as the right to personal information, the right to virtual property, the right to be forgotten, the right to data portability, and even the right of the subject of artificial intelligence. Some of these claims have already entered into the legislation of different jurisdictions. Among the more influential ones are the property rights claims typified by the right to data. As data is widely recognized as a productive resource like oil,[1] the *Civil Code* in China only provides for data-related property rights and interests or other virtual properties in principle.[2] Thus, refined claims for the establishment of rights and interests in large-scale collections of data have begun to emerge, in particular the question of how property rights and interests can be effectively distributed among relevant stakeholders. If not a simple extension of traditional doctrinal thinking, this kind of broad-based discussion of rights discourse may be the result of new economic forms' demands for the legal establishment of rights as they change modes of production and relations of production. The common problem with such demands for empowerment is that they fail to adequately demonstrate what policy goals are served by empowerment per se, as if all that is required is to reason along existing legal principles, and that the rest of the systemic problems can be solved by having a noble name. Regardless of whether this touches on the so-called generalization of rights, the key lies in whether the assertion of rights is able to effectively embed and explain the vein and governance trajectory of China's Internet growth over the past two decades.

This chapter refers to the claim to ownership of productive resources, represented by data rights, as "resource property rights", and argues that in order to promote the high-quality development of the digital economy, it is necessary to

1 Opinions of the Central Committee of the Communist Party of China and the State Council on Constructing a More Perfect Institutional Mechanism for the Market-based Allocation of Resources (2020).

2 Article 127 of the *Civil Code* provides that where the law provides for the protection of data and virtual property on the Internet, it shall do so in accordance with its provisions.

DOI: 10.4324/9781003566243-6

establish rights with clear boundaries; otherwise, it is difficult to carry out the relevant transactions, which hinders the flow of data.[3] The principle of determining rights can be based on labor inputs, user agreements, and different kinds of rights (especially property rights). This idea is now accepted by more and more academic studies and is constantly being refined. The central problem with this framework is that it appears to be a new type of right evidenced by policy objectives outside the legal system, if not by rights, and it is impossible to respond empirically to the question of whether data rights contribute to the production of value, to the mobility of resources, and to a more equitable distribution. Answers to these points help us to understand the nature of the digital commons and data resources, and what the Internet wants.[4]

This chapter is more concerned with experience in China, namely, the boundaries of property rights and their effects that have actually occurred and been shaped, than with assertions of rights to data (or other digital resources). This chapter argues that after more than two decades of development in Internet industry, through technology, competition law, and business practices, platform companies have shaped a new type of property right in cyberspace that is organized around "architecture", which I called "architectural property rights", even though this term has not been reflected in statutory law. Architectural property rights are more flexible than resource property rights in adapting to the development of the digital economy, helping to integrate the fragmented cyberspace, ensuring the progressive realization of relevant market order and security, and better responding to the production, mobility, and distribution of value. More importantly, digital architecture absorbs data with specific functions in the process of continuous improvement and becomes infrastructure, providing a stable environment for the flexible deployment of productive resources.

However, in the process of extension of architectural property rights, it is easy to go to the opposite direction, forming a data monopoly for giant platforms, especially constituting a kind of anti-mobility mechanism that restricts the free flow of productive resources across platforms. Therefore, there is a need to reconceptualize how data as a resource can support the extension of architectures, and explore how to use the infrastructural function of data as a breakthrough that leads to the consolidation of architectures and the realization of the public interest. In this sense, this chapter argues that data resource entitlement itself is limited in its functionality and still relies on external institutional design, and that there is a need to look beyond entitlement thinking to the operational logic of more fundamental market mechanisms. It is important to understand how digital markets function well, and how this

3 For instance, Zeng Zheng and Wang Lei, *Data Market Governance: Theories and Policies for Constructing a Foundational System*, Social Science Literature Press, 2021, pp. 15–18. This way of thinking is more popular in civil law countries.

4 Xin Dai, "Dimension Expansion and Issue Transformation of Data Privacy Issues: a Legal Economics Perspective", *Jiao Tong University Law* 1, no. 1 (2019), pp. 35–50.

has reshaped property rights in China, which also provides a useful perspective for reconceptualizing value generation and establishment of its legal rights.[5]

The discussion in this chapter is centered on the two property rights mentioned above. Section II takes data rights as an example and analyzes in detail the basic claim of resource property rights and its consequences, arguing that such a claim actually fails to fully comply with the characteristics of data, and that its realization has little impact on the value of the new economy, but may increase social costs. The data rights required by digital economy are actually an integrated right to data commons related to architecture. Section III analyzes the property rights in digital architecture that have in fact already been established. The protection of architecture by legal and technical measures helps the flow of resources in digital market as well as help the platforms build up their own private infrastructures, but it also has certain negative externalities for the public interest. Section IV further discusses the different legal mindsets represented by the two divisions of property rights, and explores a compromise solution from the perspective of continuing to promote the safe and orderly flow of resources, and thus bridging the architectures created by different platforms to allow the cross-platform flow of productive resources. The basis thereafter is not to establish or empower rights at the resource level, but rather to make full use of digital infrastructures formed by data, and to progressively realize equitable distribution within the wider society and publicity.

5.2 Resource property right and its consequence

5.2.1 The right to resource property

The term "resource property right" is used in this chapter to loosely refer to a notion that advocates the granting and delineation of property rights over productive resources that enter digital markets, especially since the recent official recognition of data as a new type of resource. The promotion of data exchanges around the world has further spawned such a discourse. Without repeating the extensive discussion of data property that has already taken place, this chapter summarizes the main idea that data is not a special item (such as "the oil of the twenty-first century"), but may well be formulated or imagined as intangible property or open bundles of rights in the context of property law. So, the boundaries of data property can be clearly defined in the existing civil law framework of property rights or intellectual property rights, especially if a specific data carries a number of different kinds of rights (such as privacy and other personality rights).

Another intellectual source of such attitude is traditional economics that deals with transactional behavior in the physical world, that is, the idea that market resources can be contractually commoditized and facilitated to flow and trade securely as long as the boundaries of resources as property are sufficiently clear. It is therefore inconceivable to imagine the use of an ambiguous resource of production,

5 See Carl Shapiro and Hal R. Varian, *Information Rules: A Strategic Guide to the Network Economy*, Harvard Business Review Press, 1998.

which would bring about a "tragedy of the commons". The cause of large amount of data infringement disputes that have arisen on the Internet is believed to lie in the failure to effectively define the ownership of data.[6] As long as data is imagined as oil, from which the core value of the Internet is derived, it is definitely important to provide sufficient property rights incentives, as is the case with intellectual property rights. In addition, not unimportantly, the practical consideration is legality, namely, the ability to clear illegally obtained data for continued circulation through the process of rightsizing and trading.

The judicial way of thinking embodied in resource property rights will be reflected upon in Section IV, and the response here is limited to economic thinking. First, the analogy of intangible data to an object that requires the determination of the boundaries of rights actually perpetuates our intuitive perceptions and imaginings of static property in the physical world, whereas it is difficult to delineate the fixed boundaries of a dynamic object such as data, which is continually generated in large quantities and is extremely mobilized, or it is costly to make the careful distinctions. Second, it is a mistake (and misleading even in a rhetorical sense) to analogize data to oil. Unlike physical resources, data analytics has only statistical value and cannot steadily generate visible returns. So not only is it necessary to categorize and discuss data according to its market function, but also the value of the data itself is only meaningful when coupled with the platform architecture, and to attribute all the sources of value in the digital economy to the data itself is biased. Third, data property rights do not provide sufficient incentives for data controllers or data subjects to trade or flow. The market for personal data has failed to establish over the years. This is not because the property rights are not in place but because of insufficient supply of high-quality data as well as the imperfections of the market infrastructure.Where the data available for trading is useful, even if the boundaries of data rights are not clear, there still will be trading activitis (typically in the black market). Finally, even if the right to confirm on paper is realized, or the existence of data exchanges to help black and gray industry whitewashing, data trading through informal channels (including data unfair competition behavior) will not stop.

5.2.2 Functions and values of data

From the point of view of scientific understanding, it is necessary to return to the discussion of what data actually are. However, use of the term "data" is still too broad, and is likely to invite completely different imaginations from different commentators, not to mention the fact that data and information overlap in reality and cannot be delineated, and that data serve very different functions. In order to get rid of the semantics, this chapter attempts to discuss data according to its functions throughout the digital economy. Broadly speaking, data generated through

6 He Bo: "The Problematic Dilemma Facing the Definition of Data Ownership and Cracking Ideas", *Big Data* 7 (2021), pp. 3–13.

platforms and end hardware/software can be generally categorized into data that is mainly used for its information content (Type I) and data that is mainly used for assisting market behavior (Type II).[7] Type I data is the type of data that is most often talked about in the context of data rights enforcement. Legal cases of unfair competition around data are usually related to this type of data, which refers mainly to a collection of information such as videos, images, texts, interfaces, and so on, available for consumption by users. Existing research has largely been able to reach a consensus on this type of data rights, recognizing the property interests (even competing interests) embedded and its value to digital platforms (say, by attracting data traffic for free). Type II data is less well-discussed, and serves different functions at different points in the formation and expansion of a digital marketplace, the absence of which would reduce the steady production of Type I data and its value. Type II data is not intended for user consumption, but rather fulfills ancillary functions of a market infrastructure, such as authentication, behavioral analytics, connecting and matching, and reputational function. Authentication data can be used to verify user uniqueness and authenticity of identity information (for instance, ID card, phone number, face, and QR code) to help establish an account. Analytics data, also known as metadata, can be used to automatically record and track the user's behavior at the bottom layer, forming a dynamic and multiple digital identities in cyberspace. Connectivity data is used to automate decision-making and summarize matches based on an existing transaction network, which is manifested in the form of intra-account recommendations, dispatching, and search services. Reputation data is the cumulative assessment of the platform or third party on the historical mobility of productive resources, which often manifests itself in quantifiable data products such as scores. These data functions can effectively enhance the credibility of unfamiliar resources or subjects entering the digital marketplace, ensure traceability after the fact, maintain transaction security, and continuously accelerate economic cycles and production efficiency.

Not surprisingly, tracking and data accumulation begins when a user authenticates to an account via an identifier. Even if the user does not engage in direct Type I data production (for instance, shooting short videos or tweeting), Type II data is still used and useful. In this sense, Type II data is a dependent resource that cannot exist separately from other productive resources. Effective data utilization inevitably requires a continuous acceleration of the closed loop from behavioral data production to analysis to feedback, which in turn promotes resource mobility.

Mobility on the Internet is manifested in various types: (1) first type is the "illegal rise" of the early Internet as mentioned in previous chapters, which actually facilitated the transfer of information content from traditional to digital media, completing the digital transformation; (2) second type is the sharing economy, in which online cars and riders in the physical space are mobilized by digital platforms,

7 This is roughly analogous to Hart's distinction between rules of the first nature and rules of the second nature, whereby the latter confirm and underpin the former. See H. L. A. Hart, *The Concept of Law*, Oxford University Press, 2012.

generating dynamic mobility during the service process; (3) third type is the mobilization of mass production through low-cost information systems, completing the temporal segmentation and recombination of specific production activities. The new inter-temporal production processes are accompanied by digital platforms that offer a wider variety of services, continuously covering different aspects of the user and enabling transactions to be constantly precise and predictable. Thus, the strength and value of Type II data lies in tracking it dynamically rather than analyzing it statically in a vacuum; there is no essentialist data value, and it loses its significance for independent corroboration.

In summary, when we talk about data ownership, we first need to distinguish between Type I and Type II data. Type II ancillary data actually functions as market infrastructure. Regardless of whether it may initially be associated with individual users or other market players, it needs to be processed in some de-identified way and transformed into public information so that all participants on the platform have equal access to that information service. As Chapter 4 shows, historically, digital platforms have facilitated the building of private digital infrastructure in a variety of ways with the support or acquiescence of the state, shaping the limited public nature of such platforms above all. Therefore, if the issue of corroboration is involved, it should be said that Type II data together constitute part of commons, serving the platform company and the whole mobile resources.

Therefore, if we confine the object of data ownership to Type I data, does that mean the boundaries can be effectively identified and delineated? Not necessarily. From the point of view of the object and cost of inventing rights, a large amount of data is produced by various types of subjects, some of which could be protected under copyright law, and more of which are too fragmented or homogeneous to be original. Theoretically, a digital market could recognize the property rights of individual pieces of information based on labor and price them separately, but it is often too trivial and socially costly. Due to the high volume and speed of information production, the value of Type I data remains strongly dependent on the design of the profit model and the functionality of Type II data. First, empirical approaches to pricing large amounts of fragmented data content tend to either use long time period subscriptive pricing (for instance, monthly billing rentals) rather than individual billing. Second, from the perspective of the data producer, it is important to accurately push the information content to those who need it through an effective distribution network as well as to benefit from systems, such as instantaneous bounties, that drive reproduction. Third, the analytical value of individual data can only be realized by placing it in a larger collection of data for computation and disaggregated statistics. Lastly, reputation scoring can effectively help to confirm the value of fragmented labor over a long period of time and accumulate credit. All of these benefit from infrastructure such as distribution networks and third-party payments as public goods, while the confirmation of rights is less critical.

This further illustrates that Type I data value is not exclusively embodied through the process of creation of the resources themselves, but is realized on digital platforms through the ever-accelerating and shortening cycle from production to circulation to consumption feedback, namely, the process and mode of transaction itself shapes relevant property rights and perceptions.[8] Both the pro-network peer production economics[9] and the critical political economy of communication[10] attribute aggregate value in the platform economy to the fragmented labor creation of individual flexible workers and the collective contribution of surplus value, differing only in the distributive orientation of mass production. Data rights claims can also use these theories to justify property rights for platforms or users. However, the aforementioned analysis points out that in addition to mass contribution, it is also necessary to see the key function that Type II data plays in the value integration process. The scale effects and behavioral surplus from Type I data actually constitute a small part of the value production. More critically, Type II data shapes the safe environment by connecting, aggregating, scoring, and accumulating value in the flow. The strength of the productive chain in which data is steadily produced, distributed, consumed, and reproduced determines the shape of data property rights. In economies with weakly mobile chain of production, property rights function as an institutional guarantee of labor inputs because of the uncertainty of value realization and the need to protect the productive resources with property rights to ensure adequate control, incentives, and expectations for participants at each stage of production. But in economies of scale where circular chains are shortened and mobility is increased, and producers do not need property rights protection as incentives (production and distribution costs are low), the security, speed, and effectiveness of production and transactions become even more important.[11] This is now made possible by a network of automated platforms. This theory helps us to understand that the engine of aggregated value often lies in the flow of data traffic as well as in a well-developed infrastructure, and that corroboration only solidifies what would otherwise be a modest amount of fragmented value, but instead raises the cost of transaction and utilization. Valuable commoditized resources do not necessarily need legal rights to be realized and protected, as long as the market mechanisms provide sufficient alternative functions. If there is a genuine need for legalization, then digital platforms need only maintain the rights to data commons in their current state and address the distribution among internal producers through other market mechanisms.

8 It has been argued that this can be attributed to the centralization of algorithms in the data processing process.

9 Yochai Benkler, *The Wealth of Networks: How Social Production Transforms Markets and Freedom*, Yale University Press, 2006, pp. 14–19; Clay Shirky, *Cognitive Surplus: Creativity and Generosity in a Connected Age*, Penguin Press, 2010, pp. 27–35.

10 Shoshana Zuboff, *The Age of Surveillance Capitalism: The Fight for a Human Future at the New Frontier of Power*, PublicAffairs, 2019, pp. 36–37.

11 For an example of the speed for innovation in some industries that outpaces copyright protection, see Kal Raustiala and Christopher Sprigman, *The Knockoff Economy: How Imitation Sparks Innovation*, Oxford University Press, 2012, pp. 105–105.

5.2.3 The paradox of data ownership

The foregoing provides a theoretical reflection on the issue of resource property rights as a normative legal claim, and sees it primarily as a state of fact based on the practices of the digital economy. The possible consequences of a normative claim are unsatisfactory: Allowing the generation of ownership in data based on labor inputs or contractual authorizations is intended to facilitate transactions, but in practice the possibility of "tragedy of the anti-commons" in extreme cases where users do not authorize aggregated usage of their data also creates great uncertainty for the entire productive order of the digital economy. The theoretical framework of property rights proposed above has already explained that data rights do not contribute to the overall production of value, do not provide institutional incentives for low-cost resource mobility, and do not even contribute to a more equitable distribution among workers. The right to portability of personal data, already enshrined in Chinese *Personal Information Protection Law* and derived from the EU's *General Data Protection Regulation*, attempts to construct a data flow system around individual choice, but it is difficult to create a systematic orientation for data scaling, which not only poses a security risk, but is also prone to impacting the existing order of market services.

The digital economy has demonstrated the need for some kind of exclusive control over the abstract collection of data generated in platforms, whether it is Type I or Type II data, which is an aggregated entitlement that transcends specific resource. We have already seen that the development of the platform economy in the past, where there was no claim to resource rights, has still maintained a steady growth in data production, and that de facto data transactions have not diminished at all. In practice, data transactions between digital platforms are not strictly based on the valuation of data for a consideration, but rather view Type I and Type II data as a whole, allowing each service to compete for data traffic into the other's architecture and to exchange derived information, jointly increasing the total common pool. Similarly, a wide range of practices suggests that the primary concern of digital platforms is not the rights to specific resources, but rather the right to regulate the productive process through data aggregation.

Abstract aggregated data rights do not concern themselves with the ownership of specific data, but rather with the cost-benefit of data exclusivity. On the surface, digital platforms will fully respect the information self-determination of individual users and allow them to transfer a limited amount of their data on their own, but oppose their use of third-party tools for bulk transfers on market order grounds, and at the same time stipulate their choice of authorization for the transfer of personal information as subordinate in the user agreement. The current emphasis on the security of personal information is also conducive to the formation of a more closed data exclusivity environment for large platforms to a certain extent. In addition, because digital platforms have a legally loose relationship with other productive resources, generalized control over data commons (especially Type II data) actually facilitates platforms to increase their control over the flow of productive resources through accounts and data analytics. This all reminds us that to understand the generative mechanisms of data, we need to go back to basic digital mode of production.

5.3 Digital architecture as property

5.3.1 Rise of architectural property rights

As noted earlier, the digital infrastructure function of Type II data facilitates the flow and production of value from Type I data, and the aggregated rights and interests constituted by the two types of data need to be recognized and protected by a solid "shell" or an architecture. As previous chapters have shown, architecture is a proposed abstract spatial concept, shaped and controlled by digital platforms through technology and private norms, which allow productive resources to flow and generate value through accounts, but account access cannot exceed the tangible or intangible boundaries of the architecture. The digital platform expands its architecture continuously through practices like space creation, corporate mergers, and third-party account logins, expanding the space for resource activity. They are inherently open to absorbing more productive resources, but at the same time tend to become closed due to the extension of digital infrastructure.

In a sense, the architecture is the digital mode of production itself, which defines how cyberspace is created according to a logic of control/production that requires covering hardware, servers, transmission pipelines, and so on, packaged into a continuous whole. The foregoing discussion has shown that legal involvement in the real rights of specific productive resources is of little significance, but it does not mean that the law has completely abandoned its involvement in the productive process. In the first stage of the "illegal rise" of the Internet, the law is less involved in the digitization of the productive resources in the field of cultural media, contributing to the establishment of the legitimacy of the business model of digital platforms. However, in the second phase, with the discovery of the value of flexible labor, large platform companies began to demand legal protection of the right to exclusively deploy the resources that circulate within their own structures, in an effort to clarify the boundaries of their legal structures, which has been manifested in a large number of disputes (as well as in criminal case disputes) over unfair competition.[12]

Crawlers, plug-ins, ad-blocking plug-ins, and malicious browser URL jump hijacking, all of these seemingly unrelated unfair competition behaviors essentially point to the complexity of competition for productive resources space. The rules of (unfair) competition first originated from the protection rules of the technical protection measures of software in copyright law[13] and the rules of protecting the normal operation of software from being interfered with.[14] But with the gradual

12 When the law doesn't work, digital platforms are more likely to use technical means to compensate, such as traffic monitoring, anti-crawling, setting access rights, and closing interfaces.

13 Article 4 of the *Regulation on the Protection of the Right to Information Network Dissemination.*

14 Article 12 of the *Anti-Unfair Competition Act.*

evolution of the terminal software into the platform portal, the platform competition has actually become the process of space creation/expansion and the competition for the right to organize and control the production of flexible resources. The function of law has been adjusted accordingly to the protection of architecture (but not the actual competition) of resources and spatial shells as a result of this competition. The function of the law is correspondingly adjusted to protect the architecture as resources and spatial shells (but actually embodied in computer systems, servers, software, pipelines, and other bounded spaces that can be understood as forms of property).[15] Interestingly, although most of these cases have been adjudicated according to unfair competition disputes and have given rise to many doctrinal interpretations of the Principle Clause of Article 2 in *Anti-Unfair Competition Law*, the regulation of specific unfair competition behaviors in fact protects the resources within the architecture from being violated at will, and serves the de facto function of elastic and flexible property law.[16] It has been argued that it is precisely because of the failure to establish the resources rights that competition law has inappropriately taken over the status of property or tort law, and the inability to form a logically coherent doctrinal system of such pocket clauses, that the rules of competition law should be humbled, and should preferably give way to clear rules of civil law rules. But this misalignment makes sense when viewed from the perspective of digital platforms. First, the courts' finding that behavior in the architecture occurs in a relevant market with competitive relationships coincides with the efforts of digital platforms to construct a unified market and its infrastructure. Second, given the architecture's ever-increasing control over the resources, most of the time the platforms do not need to maintain a close legal relationship with the resources, meaning that the resource flows, and transactions and collaborations remain quite autonomous.[17] Third, as long as digital platforms maintain exclusive control over data collections and are not infringed upon, they can ensure a steady growth of value within the architecture and reduce the costs of internalization, which is not conducive to the accumulation of value if the resources are constantly flowing up across platforms.

The rise of architectural property rights and China's positioning of platform companies in Internet governance also fit with each other. As Chapter 8 argues, the subjective responsibility of platform companies has been strengthened in recent

15 The latest shape of this process is the 2021 State Market Supervision and Administration of China's Provisions on Prohibiting Unfair Competition on the Internet (Public Draft) and the Supreme People's Court's Interpretation of Certain Issues on the Application of the Law of the People's Republic of China against Unfair Competition (Public Draft).

16 The number of damages for unfair competition around data has been increasing in recent years and can provide some deterrence to infringers. Another parallel phenomenon is that property law can also partially function as competition law, especially in the gaming, video, and literary fields, where parties are not really concerned with the determination of rights in a particular work, but rather with the loss of data traffic as a result of infringement.

17 This is particularly evident in the zero-work economy discourse, see Jeremias Prassl, *Humans as a Service: the Promise and Perils of Work in the Gig Economy*, New York: Oxford University Press, 2018, pp. 59–65.

years, and they have become state agents in the governance of online activities to certain extent. By formulating and enforcing online rules, platform companies have assumed the functions of developing digital economy and public administration. Protecting their interests in the virtual space, which they have constructed through significant investment, can have an incentive-compatible effect.[18] This forms the subjective and normative basis for structuring property rights. While traditional economic law focuses on regulating the externalities of private property, the emergence of architectural property rights is itself a confirmation of the legitimacy of the value of the resources and the order of distribution within the architecture, that is, it recognizes the exclusive right of the platform companies to organize production and distribution, to regulate by themselves the property rights of the resources within the architecture and to reduce the intervention of the law, which in turn contributes to the generation of the communal value of the market within the platform.

5.3.2 Institutional support and limitations in architectural property rights

Resource property rights can only be better understood on the basis of an understanding of architectural property rights. First, resource property rights are only one of the many new types of rights and interests that digital platforms wish to legally utilize and require legal protection. Limited to the high social costs of legislation, enforcement, consensus building, etc., dynamic and important rights and interests such as virtual goods, data traffic, attention, social networks cannot be fully recognized and precisely defined by statute law, but they keep being invented (and suddenly disappearing) with the expansion of architectures and the change of business models, and can only be relied upon to be mitigated by the competition law in single cases through the regulation of conduct. The proliferation of unfair competition is not a matter of competition law or property law, but inherent in the digital economy. It is precisely the protection of the platform architecture that can ensure its stable expansion and allow for more new types of interests to be formed and developed.

Second, one of the unspoken assumptions of resource property rights claim is that the establishment of rights to new types of resources occurs in the context of stable and static market transactions and can help further form a market order. This assumption is not accurate for digital markets (nor indeed for traditional markets), where not only is there a lot of unfair competition outside of the architecture, but even the digital platforms themselves are constantly entering and driving change in established traditional industries (which is then called disruptive innovation rather than unfair competition). Given the original nonexistence of smooth and coherent market forces, the interaction and creation of a large amount of service providers

18 See, for instance, Zhou Hanhua, "Exploring an Incentive-Compatible Approach to Personal Data Governance", *Legal Studies* 2, no. 2 (2018), 3–23. In many cases, the interests of platform companies appear through the vague claim of "enterprise data", but the two are not exactly the same, and what platform companies acquire and control is actually the data of market subjects.

populating the different levels of the Internet has in fact resulted in the fragmentation rather than the integration of cyberspace, and the inability of resources to flow across platforms. The force that led the architectural property from fragmentation to integration was not legal empowerment, but rather the gradual formation of infringement and whitewashing, negotiation and cooperation, merger and absorption. Once the integration and legitimacy of the architecture is established, there is room for a broad single market to accommodate the free flow of more resources, as well as room to legitimize the process of illicit emergence.

Third, an effective property rights system is not only about external defenses and remedies, but also about synergistic and complementary mechanisms for internal effectiveness. Architecture as a holistic property interest is already comprehensively requiring a shift in the legal system and concepts to focus on clear relationships of interest. For instance, architecture requires that users only obtain a limited right of use rather than an absolute ownership through formal terms and conditions; conversely, they authorize platforms to license the content of the information they produce in the open areas of the architecture with a nonexclusive, perpetual, and free right of use. All of the user's behavior within the architecture is recorded and analyzed to satisfy specific business model (such as targeted advertising) or to improve services (like personalized recommendations). The relationship between user and platform is agreed to be one of use and cooperation, not employment.

It is not difficult to see that the emphasis on the collective rights of resources and the protection of their boundaries in the digital economy actually reflects the upgrading rather than the downgrading of the capitalist production process.[19] This means that the ability of digital platforms to control the entire market system has exceeded the control of simple production resources or upstream and downstream industrial chains, and the independent and orderly production of resources can be realized without legal intervention in the property rights of specific resources through the creation of infrastructure, the release of trading rules, and the formation of a flexible reputation mechanism. The intervention of law in empowerment may instead increase the cost of production. On the contrary, it may increase the production cost. It is in this dimension of empowerment that architecture perfectly replaces the law, or the law itself.[20] However, the function of external law is still indispensable for digital platforms. The goal of early cyberlaw was to confirm the legitimacy of the production methods of the digital economy as well as to alleviate the conflict of interests between old and new, and to ensure a continuous and stable supply of productive resources. With the maturity of the digital economy, contemporary cyberlaw has begun to be called upon to help break down the barriers to

19 Shoshana Zuboff, *The Age of Surveillance Capitalism: The Fight for a Human Future at the New Frontier of Power*, PublicAffairs, 2019, pp. 25–28.

20 This helps us to rethink the assertion that "code is law", the original meaning of which can be found in Lawrence Lessig, *Code Version 2.0*, Basic Books, 2006, pp. 16–19.

resource flow within the platform, to promote the construction of digital infrastructure, and to address the issues of architectural security and order.

Architecture as private property, despite helping to digitalize productive resources and bringing efficiency, undoubtedly has negative externalities. First, the expansion of architecture means not only the creation of new spaces, but also the absorption of traditional physical space, not only traditional private space, but also traditional public space, which raises questions about the power and legal status of the private platform itself. Second, although Type II data as digital infrastructure contributes to the security and stability of the market order, once it is extended on a cyclical scale, it creates a sort of counter-flow mechanism that continuously absorbs resources. Digital platforms often restrict the flow on the grounds of information security, contributing to the closure and self-preferentiality of especially large platforms and reducing interoperability with other platforms, which raises concerns about data monopolization.[21] Third, we have recently seen new types of labor disputes around the legal nature of flexible work and labor rights, suggesting that architectural property rights does not necessarily guarantee that digital labors will be able to participate in a more equitable distribution.[22] We need to rethink the mindset behind the two types of property rights and how to mitigate their respective negative externalities and move beyond them.

5.3.3 Judicial application of the doctrine

Like resource property rights, architectural property rights currently remain at the level of descriptive theoretical explanations and claims, that is, envisioning an integrative spatial interest to be acquired or exercised exclusively by controllers of the space, rather than a preexisting civil law claim.[23] Nonetheless, architectural property rights are capable of flexibly allocating the value of resource and functioning externally to prevent others from obstructing, destroying, or intruding into the architecture without permission or lawful authorization, and both of these rights are capable of solving the real-world problem better than data ownership.

Specifically, from an internal perspective, architectural property rights provide default rules on how to use resource resources more efficiently through. For instance, users' authorization to transfer data also requires the prior platform's consent.[24] From an external perspective, when it comes to a large number of illegal behaviors that are not yet explicitly prohibited by law, they need to be regulated by court through application of unfair competition. These illegal behaviors

21 Han Wenlong and Wang Kaijun, "A Political Economy Analysis of Data Control and Monopoly Issues in the Platform Economy", *Contemporary Economic Research*, 7, no. 7 (2021), 5–15.

22 Ministry of Human Resources and Social Security and other Guidelines on Safeguarding the Rights and Interests of Workers in New Employment Patterns (2021).

23 Some study calls this as "rights of code space", see Wu Weiguang, "Constructing New Civil Rights in the Network Economy: Code Space Rights".

24 Sina Weibo v. Pulse Unfair Competition, (2016) Beijing 73min final 588.

could include (1) crawling competitors' information content such as images[25] and user-created text,[26] (2) competing for traffic space on other people's architectures[27] or adding plug-ins,[28] (3) setting up deep links to syndicate pirated content[29] and blocking online advertisements,[30] and (4) obtaining competitors' information through cookies.[31] In these cases, if we follow the idea of resource property rights, it requires detailed theoretical explanations of how pieces of information and data can be recognized as property or works in copyright law. It also requires more costs to prove the possible damaging consequences, which are often abstract and uncertain. The court's protection of architectural property rights reduces such costs. By simply confirming that the two parties constitute a competitive relationship and interpreting the damaged interests as "competitive interests", it can objectively make it clear that it is not permitted to illegally enter the platform's servers through crawler technology or other unauthorized means to decrypt the content or simply crawl the publicly available information content.

The practical consequences of the application of architecture theory are clear. The local courts are able to resolve disputes quickly at the margins, but have also resulted in the unsystematic application of principled standards in Article 2 of the *Anti-Unfair Competition Law*, the lack of a coherent explanation of what constitutes business ethics, market order, and the failure to explore the connotation of architectural property rights in depth. *The Provisions on the Prohibition of Unfair Competition on the Internet* issued by the State Administration of Market Supervision in 2024 still follows the idea of behavioral regulation, listing many novel unfair competition behaviors, so that the market order can be maintained more efficiently by the administrative law enforcement forces, but the principles of the property law behind them still need to be more systematically formulated.

5.4 Between market and society

Resource and architectural property rights co-occur in the evolution of the digital economy, where aggregated data interests effectively interoperate with architectural extensions and ensure the efficient stabilization of the digital marketplace through the infrastructural function of Type II data. This section attempts to further apply and extend the theoretical framework that distinguishes the two types of property rights in digital economy. First, two types of property rights actually represent two different ways of thinking in law and economics, which can help

25 Mass Dianping v. Baidu Unfair Competition, (2015) Pu Min San (Zhi) Chu Zi No. 528.

26 Volkswagen Dianping v. LoveHelp.com Unfair Competition, (2011) No. 7512 of the First Intermediate People's Court.

27 Baidu v. Sogou Unfair Competition, (2015) Hai Min (Zhi) Chu Zi No. 4135.

28 Tencent v. external hangings "airplane group" with large unfair competition case, (2019) Jin 0116 Minchu 697.

29 Unity v. Baidu Video Copyright Infringement, (2013) Hai Min Chu Zi No. 27286.

30 Tencent v. World Starlight Unfair Competition, (2017) Beijing 0105 Minchu 70786.

31 Tencent v. Doflash Unfair Competition (2019).

us understand the operation of the rules of the digital economy at different levels. Second, seeing from the goals that the two types of property rights want to achieve, it is necessary to overcome the negative externality of the resources and the architecture. Third, from the perspective of distribution, this framework also helps to reflect on the social function of property rights, which requires both the promotion of value production and the promotion of fair distribution in a wider context, ultimately realizing the organic integration of the market and society.

5.4.1 Two types of mindsets

As mentioned repeatedly, it is more common to focus on the claim of property rights at the level of specific resources. This approach starts from a single resource as the object of study for the normative analysis of legal doctrine, in particular the characterization, validation, or empowerment of a system of established rules from statutory law. If data can be discussed independently out of its function and the resources to which it is attached, and independently of the architecture through which it flows, and finally identified in a vacuum, then lots of discussions that have arisen on the attributes of virtual property could be fully understandable. Because such arguments do not need to take into account the real situation and the possible consequences of the logical reasoning along the specific concepts can be justified with some universal answers. This kind of thinking not only tends to fixate the resources, but also fails to see the connection between resources and their external environment. In particular, it fails to understand the generation and flow of the resource from the perspective of mode of production, and fails to grasp the characteristics of the dynamic generation of data resources. It only sees the trees without forest.

Due to the rapid changes in the target of rights protection, a model of competition law adjudication and enforcement that concentrates on behavioral regulation is more desirable for resolving disputes. Chinese legislators and judges have found that, with the rapid and massive increase in disputes over unfair competition, statutory law cannot exhaust the enumeration of all new types of market order violations that have arisen, and have had to turn to Principle Clause. What is needed, however, is not simply to typify behaviors for legal recognition, but to go beyond the superficial ways of illegal trespass, to see the political and economic motivations behind them, and to understand what the digital economy wants before returning to the rhetoric of market order, business ethics, and consumer welfare to weigh the cost and benefit.

Instead, the mindset along architectural property rights goes beyond the model of single resource rights and is concerned not only with the production and mobility of resources, but also with the realization of the infrastructural mechanisms required for such mobility, and thus empirically asks what kind of legal rights are required for the new economic formations in the context of the entire modes of production and the market order, rather than simply applying the concepts. This line of thought sees both the solidity of architecture as a shell and the mobility of internal resources. Viewing architecture as property means not focusing on the outcome of rights to particular resources, but rather situating them within the productive relationship, seeing that the many interests in the cyberspace are intertwined and underpinned by a holistic legal mechanism that works together to ensure rights to data commons.

Both the resource property right and the architectural property right ideas are flawed under their respective logics: The former tries to empower the resources and promote mobility at the level of individual resources, but ignores the environment and institutional support in which it is located, which in turn increases the overall social costs and fails to achieve good results; the latter, although it establishes a digital infrastructure, is also prone to go to the opposite side of the mobility, so that the open Internet at early age is gradually closed and feudalized, which is not in line with the original goal of the digital economy policy for safe and orderly flow of resources across platforms. To a certain extent, both attempt to respond to fundamental questions of how to enhance mobility in a stable environment, but each has its own focus. So how to combine greater resource mobility with an infrastructure that ensures security and order will be a core issue of future market economy and social policy in China.

5.4.2 Regaining control of the market

Markets never form spontaneously, but rather external forces help shape the mechanisms that make them work effectively.[32] Their expansion is often characterized by a single logic of commodity exchange that continuously absorbs established production and social networks.[33] The specificity of the digital era is that markets are shaped more by digital platforms, and once the architecture is recognized and protected as private property rights, it is inevitable to encounter the problem of neglecting the public interest by emphasizing the autonomous management of markets on the basis of the operational autonomy of platform companies. In order to limit digital platforms from becoming closed, the idea should be to further strengthen the competitive environment, and reregulate the various core mechanisms of the market through the external power of public institutions. We also need to think about how to start from the perspective of promoting sharing of Type I and Type II data, especially how to utilize public power to guide the effective use of social data resources, with the eventual goal of promoting flow of productive resources across platforms and further increasing the use of social data resources under the prerequisite of extending the infrastructure. The current policy in work is to promote cross-platform flow of production resources under the premise of extending infrastructure, further increase the overall social value of data, and gradually realize distributive justice in the market mechanism. The following will

32 Yongnian Zheng and Yanjie Huang, *Market in State: The Political Economy of Domination in China*, Cambridge University Press, 2018; Steven K. Vogel, *Marketcraft: How Governments Make Markets Work*, Oxford University Press, 2018.

33 Karl Polanyi, *The Great Transformation: the Political and Economic Origins of Our Time*, Beacon Press, 2001.

briefly discuss two kinds of practices and designs in China: (1) open public data, and (2) extension of data infrastructure.

5.4.2.1 Driving data resource exchange through public data

The traditional Big Data Exchange in many cities follows a market model, although it adopts the system of modern exchanges such as the membership system. However, because the data exchange itself does not own any data and relies solely on a third party to provide data for collocation and matching, it makes it less motivating for social subjects to enter the platform. The key therefore is to provide the first impetus to enter the trading platform, namely, using better quality data to attract social subjects. In this sense, Big Data Centers/Bureaus of local government that are responsible for the collection and cleansing of public data have a natural advantage over ordinarily data exchanges, and if they can be transformed into a specific type of exchange or enter into the trading process, they can avoid many of the problems in the existing practices of opening up public data: (1) there is no need to define public data as a state-owned asset because data is not meant to be clearly demarcated but rather to be continuously integrate and flow; (2) it solves the problem of information matching, as the platform can understand the respective needs of society and government departments, thus targeting requirements for matching and production; (3) it enables the assessment of the social value of specific kinds of data, thus exploring general data pricing standards and mechanisms; and (4) it also prevents data leakage and security risks, and can be tested and regulated in closed environments.

Therefore, the Big Data Center/Bureau can improve on the premise of the current system of public data openness by exploring the authorized operation of public data, maintaining the unconditional openness of data types, while implementing conditional openness of data with special value, and operating and managing the data through a semi-closed trading platform, which has the right to formulate trading rules, the access and withdrawal mechanism, provide data products, and carry out sandbox supervision.

5.4.2.2 Extended data infrastructure

In the process of market operation, relying on data ownership cannot automatically realize the order of transactions, and public power needs to intervene to make the infrastructure more perfect and regain control of market construction. The experience of Internet development in China shows that digital platforms are more inclined to build their own infrastructures, but use them as a means of competition without opening them up to competitors, gradually moving toward closedness. Type II data sharing is more crucial, helping to link up the architectures of different platforms, and enhancing resource capabilities, so as to realize the orderly flow of Type I data in a wider scope. For instance, the sharing of authentication information through public institutions, which in turn promotes the mutual access of large platforms to share data traffic; the promotion of the standardization of platform workers' reputation information and evaluation, and the realization of the sharing and utilization of credit and social credit information can further promote the exchange of data value in different digital markets.

5.4.3 From production to distribution

A complete theory of property rights should encompass the entire spectrum from production to distribution. This chapter cannot fully discuss distributive mechanisms in the digital economy, but it has been shown that neither type of digital property rights is best solution to the problem of users benefiting from their own activities or the fair distribution of aggregated value between platforms and users. Traditional property rights theory does not mainly involve the distribution issues: Whether it is the empowerment of resource property or the protection of architectural property, they essentially hope to reduce transaction costs and promote the safe and effective realization of transactions, thereby promoting the production of value in the digital economy. This idea still belongs to the primary distribution through the market mechanism, that is, to effectively promote various types of market infrastructure to make the pie bigger, so that more productive resources are available to participate in the benefit production. The two measures mentioned above can be seen as specific applications of this idea, with the aim of guiding the use of data pools formed in the architecture of specific platforms, facilitating cooperation, promoting the interconnection and interconnection of infrastructure between different platforms, and facilitating the further mobility of resources on a wider scale.

At the same time, it should be noted that in order to ensure data security and the stability of the order of transactions, it is still necessary to facilitate cooperation within a specific architecture and to respect the basic control and distributional power of the dominant platform companies, which means that the above-mentioned initiatives still need to be carried out from within the architecture of the market. In addition, market logic cannot fully address the mechanisms by which resources can be rationally distributed, especially when markets can be systematically created and controlled by digital platforms, because the productive process itself needs to be underpinned by various types of social mechanisms, and the digital economy will be unsustainable if social mechanisms are not fed and strengthened. For instance, flexible labor in the sharing economy relies in part on workers' access to other incomes or security channels outside of the digital platform, even if the data is interpreted as a form of labor that cannot be made more profitable within the existing loosely defined non-employment relationship. It is therefore not possible to simply imagine a market and property rights operating in a vacuum, but it is necessary to return to specific social contexts to understand and strengthen the protection of workers and to realize effective secondary and even tertiary distribution. For instance, there is much room for exploration of anti-discrimination in employment access, minimum wages and payment guarantees, rest systems, responsibility for occupational safety and health, basic pension and medical insurance, occupational injury protection, and trade unions or workers' representative systems.[34] The aim is to consolidate the corresponding social security system on the basis of maintaining the market mechanism. The theoretical significance of these measures is that, in an era when structural property rights are becoming increasingly important, it may be necessary to go beyond the traditional initial distribution mechanism and focus more on guidance through external public institutions and strengthening the protection provided by the power of social organizations. This will not only connect the digital market together, but may also help to rediscover society, fully mobilize and explore the resources of governance, safeguard mechanisms in traditional social networks and practices, and break away from the simple government–market dichotomy, so that social actors can participate more actively in the process of building the digital society.

5.5 Conclusion

This chapter responds to the classic topic of property rights in jurisprudence in the digital age, that is, how property rights are created, exercised, and functionally realized, with particular attention to the effectiveness of new types of rights. As in the age of industrial capitalism, the central questions to which the Internet and cyberlaw respond have always been the stable access to the means of production, the security of the production process, and the formation of value cycles. Once a stable market order is formed within a closed architecture, digital platforms are more concerned with the clarity of the boundaries of the architecture and freedom from arbitrary interference than with the clear boundaries of the resources within the architecture. While (especially huge) digital platforms also form a market, platform companies only wish to maintain flexible and loose legal relationships with the productive resources and to strengthen their ability to match and control. Neither loosening control nor giving too many rights to the resources is in their fundamental interest, as long as the law is able to recognize property rights in the aggregated resources, which is mainly achieved by way of protecting the abstract boundaries of intangible asset flows. The emergence of architectural property rights implies an upgrading of the capitalist production process under the new technological conditions, that is, an extension of the control of a single instrument and mode of production to the control of a "system" of resource activities. As a result, the key to the prosperity of the digital economy lies not in the rights/empowerment of particular kinds of resources but in the improvement of digital markets and their infrastructure. Data as a resource still plays a key role in creating a robust infrastructure, but its function is much closer to serving the public interest in digital commons. This is why it has become so important to connect different markets through digital infrastructures that can help transform traditional productive resources into new digital

34 Ministry of Human Resources and Social Security and other Guiding Opinions on Safeguarding the Rights and Interests of Workers in New Employment Patterns (Ministry of Human Resources and Social Security [2021] No. 56).

resources and empower them in a way that enhances their mobility. Thus, in terms of property rights theory, if there is any contribution to be made, this chapter does not place special emphasis on resources affecting property rights, such as labor and other capital inputs, contract conclusion, and so on, but rather focuses on the analysis of how the formation of productive channels and trading markets shapes new types of property rights claims and boundaries. Further, it is not possible to make a hasty judgment as to whether or not resource property rights on digital platforms will disappear altogether in the twenty-first century with the rise of the intangible economy, and it remains to be seen how different stakeholders perceive and act in the social process in China.

6 Mobility and integration

Labor issue in digital commons

6.1 Introduction

Along with the continuous proliferation of information technology represented by the Internet, more and more new forms of business have emerged on the basis of new media, generating many incremental values. Generally speaking, these values originate from the mobility of various productive resources, and the generation, circulation, transaction, and consumption of resources have become more precise and efficient. Value production has become more and more integrated and cooperative. Specifically, digital labor has presented a number of new features—fragmentation of value production (which leads to the blurring of labor and non-labor behaviors, as both can generate value), greater reliance on information for integration and management (therefore privacy has become less important), and more flexible labor organization (which requires greater competence on the part of the organizing subject). In this process, disputes and controversies around "labor" have gradually increased, and have contributed to academic and social discussions on the legal protection of emerging labor rights.[1] Existing analyses of platform-flexible labor or new forms of labor have focused on issues such as the recognition of labor relations, the determination of work-related injuries, social insurance, and the regulatory system, and has focused more on the future design of the system or the judicial judgment standards, but less on how this flexible and loose process actually occurs in conjunction with the changes in the mode of social production.

This chapter attempts a more theoretical distillation of the changes in the labor process and its legal response in the digital era. Labor issue has a very close relationship with the formation of digital commons. While the current legal system of labor has continued to respond to the changes brought about by the digital economy at the margin, the characteristics and consensus of the digital labor process need to be further refined in the context of the fact that the mode of production on which the new forms of labor are based has not yet been fully fixed and recognized. This

1 While new forms of labor have become commonplace at least since the sharing economy, the trigger for widespread social and policy attention originated in a 2020 online article "Takeaway Riders, Stuck in the System". The public debate over the new form of labor has been a major issue in the past few years. This discussion then triggered the central ministry of labor management to focus on a number of related policies.

DOI: 10.4324/9781003566243-7

chapter will argue that, in terms of the historical evolution of labor law in China, the central concern is how to promote the development of advanced productive forces and how to continuously adjust the legal norms and institutional structure to facilitate the flow of various types of resources at a low cost, so as to give full play to their maximum economic and social value through the function of integration.

As Chapter 5 argues, mode of digital production, which utilizes low-cost information technologies to accelerate mobility of productive resources, offers multiple possibilities for transactions and cooperation in an expanded spatial and temporal context, thereby generating more value, but also tend to lead to further fragmentation of those resources. There is thus a need to reintegrate the flowing fragments through innovative organizational processes, functional design of platforms, or property regimes, in order to prevent an overemphasis on the value of fragmentation per se and to reduce the likelihood of a tragedy of anti-commons. The essence of "integration" is that fragmented rights or interests need to be protected only at the margins, but not in a way that affects the shaping of new mode of production and overall policy expectations.

Although the current labor law system in China is planning to move toward codification,[2] the real-world labor order is not formed solely by a set of written rules, but must be premised on some relatively stable and widely accepted mode of production. In case of traditional industries encountering the creative destruction of new technologies, and even new industries constantly subverting themselves, a solid business model has not yet been formed, and it is unlikely to shape the reasonable expectations of the behavior and rights of the workers concerned. Only when the profit model of a particular platform is relatively clear and the supply–demand chain tends to be stable can the benchmarks of workers' behavior be fixed to form a locking effect on them, become part of the new mode, and even become the competitive advantage of the head of the labor platform companies.

In this sense, observing the evolution of labor law in the digital age not only has practical significance for a specific legal sector, but also has general theoretical value that radiates to other legal sectors. This chapter actually takes labor law as an example, following the trace of previous chapters, discusses how the relevant legal mechanism responds to and affects the changes in the mode of production, and explains how the "productivity" of labor law is embodied in the two core elements of "mobility" and "integration", and at what institutional level it needs to be solved. This chapter further realizes that the mobility and integration of productive resources is a problem that the whole legal system needs to face constantly in the digital commons, so as to think about the institutional structure for the existence and effective exercise of specific legal rights, and try to answer the question of whether we need to solidify certain (even constitutional) rights, or whether we

2 Legislation on basic labor standards has been included in the legislative plan of the National People's Congress, and the relevant departments are actively carrying out research and demonstration work to form a draft law as soon as possible.

need to promote a constant change in their content, waiting for the new form to be restabilized.

The chapter proceeds in the following order: Section II restates the mode of production of the digital economy, analyzing from the level of productive organization, how this mode of production promotes the flow and integration of labor and its value, and how the corresponding changes have raised different controversial issues in labor law through different discourses. Section III provides an in-depth analysis of how the law responds to these disputes, both at the margins and as a whole, from the judicial dimension, proposing, in particular, a more theoretical model of judicial decision-making that differs from traditional adjudicative thinking. Such thinking is oriented toward the promotion of value production, identifies the normative structure in which labor rights and behaviors are situated, helps to differentiate the kinds of value-producing behaviors that fall within the scope of labor law protection, and offers a solution to the controversial issues that exist in the utilization of other productive resources. It also provides ideas for resolving the controversial issues that exist in the utilization of other productive resources. Section IV concludes by summarizing the findings of this chapter.

Following previous chapters, the rest of this chapter tells the labor law version of the story of "illegal rise": Similarly to the copyright and competition areas, labor law has in effect given the green light to the development of the digital commons by inaction, acquiescing to the emergence of new forms of labor organizations like platforms for a considerable period of time rather than forcing new forms of labor into the established labor system and regulating them. We are far from reaching a stage where we can identify stable new forms of labor, even though some large platform organizations such as logistics, takeout, transportation, and performing industries have already reached a considerable scale. The gradual emergence of labor disputes makes it necessary for the judiciary to consider how to shape predictable adjudicative standards to promote the change of a new mode of production at the margins as well.

6.2 Mode of production and labor law

6.2.1 Restatement of mode of production in digital commons

This section begins with a discussion of changes in the mode of production and how it desires the law to adapt accordingly. Following the logic above, if one is to understand the productive dimension of labor law, one needs to understand its nested productive process. Changes in mode of production are not a black-and-white process, but parallel, complementary, and gradually absorbing and replacing each other. The mode of production, which consists of a number of elements such as the organization of production, tools, relations, sources of labor, forms of ownership, and so on, tends to change itself gradually at first by adopting a new technology that changes certain elements of the established production process. Taking information technology as an example, the smart end device carrying the operating system is not a single technology, but a universal technology, which is not only able to be embedded in the existing production process, but also able to be continuously adapted and applied to more new scenarios and forms of business, and is therefore a generative technology.[3] This kind of generative technology can be applied in industrial productive organizations as well as in consumer-level software and end device, thus facilitating the mobilization and matching of productive resources on a wider scale, and forming a kind of economic process and organizational form in the process of utilization.[4] Therefore, it can also be said that, similar to the phenomenon of "phase change" in physics (where molecules change in relation to each other to form different forms of matter), the mode of production is a subtle art of reintegrating various resources under different technological and institutional constraints, constantly adjusting the constituent elements for the purpose of reproducing and readapting them for a relatively stable organizational goal, which is, in fact, a form of economic process of Schumpeterian innovation. The process of changing mode of production in history is cognitively very similar to the paradigm shift in scientific knowledge, which implies a whole set of changes from technology and interests to institutions and knowledge.[5]

This process has been demonstrated in its entirety throughout history. Economic historians since Karl Marx have continually shown that change in the mode of production is the process of human history itself. At the beginning of any new mode of production, it may be only a new technological invention or a marginal modification of an existing production process; with the use and diffusion of such technological tools, the organization of production adjusts itself once it has improved efficiency and expanded the economy, further increasing capital accumulation and changing the human relationship in such process, which are eventually confirmed and fixed by law. Historically, capitalism's industrialized mode of production overcame the agrarian mode of production globally over a long period of time, especially politically driven by bourgeois revolutions, colonial activities, and wars, and finally created a whole set of modern legal systems and their ideologies that are constantly reinforced and maintained.[6] The labor system and the protection of rights in this process is not at all a precursor issue, but rather a systemic adjunct, because systemic labor disputes involve a fair division of the whole economic pie, and in the process of making the pie bigger, there are many marginal disputes that may be absorbed and obscured by the fast-growing economic model. It is only when it is firmly established that the groups concerned have the incentive to draw the boundaries of their rights and obligations. This explains why disputes over flexible labor only began to emerge about 20 years after the introduction of the Internet in China, during which time the traditional labor organization system was further entrenched and the emerging digital labor organizations grew larger.

3 Jonathan Zittrain, "The Generative Internet", *Harvard Law* Review 119 (2006), 1974.

4 W. Brian Arthur, *The Nature of Technology: What It Is and How It Evolves*, Free Press, 2009.

5 Thomas Kuhn, *The Structure of Scientific Revolutions*, University of Chicago Press, 2012.

6 Katharina Pistor, *The Code of Capital: How the Law Creates Wealth and Inequality*, Princeton University Press, 2020.

Whether it is the interpretation of the history of the past two decades or the perception of the current economic policy, it is necessary to seriously answer this question: Does the digital economy really mean the emergence of a completely new mode of production? In the early years of reform and opening up in China, there was also a process of enhanced mobility and even privatization of productive resources controlled by state-owned enterprises, and the mobility problems brought about by information technology seem to have more similarities than differences (such as whether it is resource mobility that creates a two-track system of prices, or governments at all levels that support it through the administrative contracting system[7]). Even if one goes back to the text of the Constitution, the institutional foundations of the industrial mode of production can be found in the text of the Constitution of 1982, so it is not too much of a stretch to think that the digital economy is merely an artificially constructed, but deceptively ideological term (like the popular term "metaverse").[8] It appears to be just a further extension of the productive activities in market,[9] all coordinating non-personal labor activities in a society of strangers, where labor-controlling processes exist,[10] and even have an inherently coherent structure of capital accumulation.[11]

The answer to this theoretical question is considered both in an epistemological sense and as a result of the division of interests and public policy choices, involving the legitimacy of legal policies and affecting the adjustment of labor policies and institutions. If the answer is yes, stakeholder groups in the digital economy can use this discourse to assert their own advantages and uniqueness compared to traditional industries and demand deregulation from the government, arguing that they are more capable of harnessing resource mobility and making the pie bigger.[12] Traditional stakeholder groups, on the other hand, will try to deny it, hoping to protect their competitive position from challenge, accusing their emerging industry rivals of unfair competition, hoping to bring them back into the regulatory framework of the existing productive organization, and hoping to absorb the IT dividend

7 Zhou Li'an, *Local Government in Transition*, Gezhi Publishing House, 2017.

8 Legal research also noticed this problem early on and raised the question of "law of the horse"; see Frank H. Easterbrook, "Cyberspace and the Law of the Horse", *University of Chicago Legal Forum* (1996), 207. The legal academia in China has been discussing the construction of new disciplines (such as digital jurisprudence and computational jurisprudence), but has not been able to find a unique object and theoretical basis that can unify the knowledge of the discipline, and can only broadly pile up many contents together.

9 Daniel Bell, *The Coming of Post-Industrial Society: A Venture in Social Forecasting*, Basic Books, 1976.

10 Chen Long, "Labor Order under 'Digital Control': A Study of Labor Control of Takeaway Riders", *Sociological Research* no. 6 (2020).

11 Shoshana Zuboff argues that the new capitalism is not fundamentally different and is still based on the machine process of extracting surplus value. See Shoshana Zuboff, *The Age of Surveillance Capitalism*, Profile Books, 2019.

12 Some researchers have argued that information technology not only represents a change in the mode of economic production, but even opens up a civilization. See Jiang Qiping, *An Introduction to the Theory of a New Civilization*, Commercial Press, 2012.

within the existing mode of production. These discursive competitions generate a lot of bubbles, and even if they succeed in attracting investment or lobbying regulators for a short period of time, they need to be able to demonstrate their potential to become a stabilizing mode.

The core changes brought about by information technology were not initially in an organizational sense, but mainly in terms of supply-side changes and the relationship between the supply and the demand side. First, resource mobility and market agents have become more diverse. The 2008 financial crisis[13] and the 2020 COVID-19 pandemic[14] have had a large impact on the traditional economic agents of wage labor, thus providing opportunities for more flexible platforms for gig labor, which have given rise to new industries such as online delivery workers and car drivers during this period. In addition to the above groups that are closer to the labor practices of traditional industries, digital labor forms have also expanded to include traceable mass cultural production activities that can generate value, and the boundaries between the two have become more blurred. Second, with production and consumption inextricably linked, consumer behavior has become more predictable, driving the production process to be more precise and the economic cycle to be accelerated. Consumers can be motivated and mobilized to become producers. This all means that the productive order is infinitely expanded in the digital economy (and can also be expanded to include machines and objects), with the narrow order of labor being gradually absorbed into a grander order of production. However, both of these aspects can be improved in the industrial production process, suggesting that resource mobility itself does not necessarily bring about a change in the mode of production, and that the organization of production and its relations can remain completely unchanged in the process of increased mobility, so that the adoption of digital technologies not only profits from it, but also strengthens the traditional production labor control (for instance, increased surveillance of employees). Conversely, control systems and organizations that coordinate production like digital platforms can actually adopt employment relationships in order to legally increase control over resources and employees, depending entirely on cost consideration and the need to ensure production stability.

As legitimacy argument, digital platforms of the day want a theory that can prove their superiority by tying the flexibility of work to the exclusivity of the new mode of production, while competitors in traditional industries rely on the association of that mode of production with control/subordination, thus proving that the use of labor in digital platforms is also a labor relationship. In the view of this chapter, neither of these opposing views fully captures the nature of the new mode of production, let alone the fact that the two sides are already rapidly converging

13 Nick Srnicek, *Platform Capitalism*, Polity, 2016. Interestingly, the country has largely copied the Western-style sharing economy ideology without mentioning the broader context of its financial crisis driving labor mobility.

14 Despite strict state regulation of digital platforms in the name of preventing capital expansion from 2020 onward, the instability during the COVID-19 pandemic since 2021 has made platform economy policies flexible again.

from the two extremes of the spectrum to the middle. For instance, the large-scale digital platforms that currently employ flexible workers are hybrid in their labor processes, with some directly oriented to individuals for matching, while others need to use secondary organizations to reduce their own costs, forming industrial chains at different levels and pluralistic production orders.

In any case, it is the new types of organization and channels on the Internet that make digital production orderly and predictable, which is the root of new types of legal issues. The meaningful research question then is not to dwell on discovering whether a completely new species is replacing the old one, the criteria for which may vary from person to person, but rather, while seeing the rhetoric behind it representing different interests, to focus on how the digital economic production using the platform as an organizational form is evolving and whether it is stable enough to create a relatively independent economic circular system dominated by platform companies. The fact that some fragmented workforces, with the help of information technology, are detached not only from traditional industry and occupational norms, but also from the mode of digital production, may be the original meaning of "flexible labor" and the result of market processes. But this chapter is more concerned with the mobility and flexible labor practices that are gradually being "captured" by the new mode of production, and that are entering into some kind of loosely flexible, yet powerfully controlled, production process. Perhaps in the middle of the twenty-first century, we could look back and establish some ideal type of theoretical paradigm, but for the time being we need to see the dynamics of a shifting paradigm and the expectations of sustainability.

6.2.2 The illegal rise of digital labor

Stable mode of production is continuously constructed through technology, institutions, and discourse, the more important external environment of which is the confirmation and fostering of law and policy. As far as the industrialized mode of production is concerned, it is necessary to guarantee that enterprises concentrate all kinds of market resources into a closed productive organization, with property rights as incentives, in order to carry out stable capital accumulation and form a stable and predictable production process, and the operation of hired workers and labor contracts also function mainly in this sense.[15] Before the breakthroughs produced by information technology, efficiency gains continued to be realized through increased research and development within the industrial system, as well as through competition in external markets. Since employers cannot calculate and control precisely, productive resources may be wasted in handling the processing, and employees may also slack off, but it is still efficient from the perspective of

15 The *Labor Contract Law* strictly limits the amount of labor dispatch employees to a certain percentage of the total amount of employees, with the intention of ensuring the stability of the traditional production process.

overall economic accounting.[16] As for the mode of production of the digital economy, its primary task in the early stage of development is still to obtain the means of production at low cost and reach a wide range of consumers, and to solve the effective cycle between the supply and demand sides, which is the great historical process of "illegal rise". The emergence of illegitimacy refers to a state in which specific productive resources, through low-cost technological innovation and other reasons, flow from industrialized productive organizations to be reused in the new space of digital production. This is a process that constantly violates the established legal rules that are in line with the industrialized mode of production, and gradually grows outside of the system, eventually succeeding in forming a new productive order that requires the formulation of new rules to establish its legitimacy and resolve conflicts of interest.

Clearly, not all technological innovations that have sought to challenge traditional mode of production in the past have finally succeeded, and apart from the availability of financial arrangements such as venture capital and the exploration of free business models (both of which are also not unique), the main external reason for the success of the digital economy is instead the disembodiment of traditional productive processes. The illegal rise not only shows revolution, but also reflects dependency and symbiosis. First, in the face of massive infringements, traditional mode of production has not been able to successfully use legal or policy weapons to limit the development of the digital economy, especially the unauthorized use of resources, which has provided ample space for digital platforms to explore business models on their own.[17] Labor laws have largely remained modest and have not been actively extended to the yet-to-be-formed digital economy, and labor authorities have continued to focus on how to deepen the protection of labor rights relying on traditional productive organizations, with no goals of shift to digital labor. Second, the digital economy needs to provide lucrative trading opportunities for resources displaced from the established production space, so as to further enhance mobility, and even tacitly allow some resources to profit from the "double-track", fearing that without the support of traditional systems and environments, more people are unlikely to be willing to take the risk of moving to a new productive space when mature business models have yet to emerge. For instance, many takeaway deliverers have moved from rural to urban areas for flexible employment, with their families retaining farmland as a guarantee that they can return to their jobs at any time if they encounter difficulties. Third, the lack of effective organization and management of productive resources after they have left the traditional industrial organization may give rise to a series of negative externalities, such as bringing

16 The Harberger Tax in economics designs an auction system that puts resources to good use and promotes turnover; see Eric A. Posner and E. Glen Weyl, *Radical Markets: Uprooting Capitalism and Democracy for a Just Society*, Princeton University Press, 2018.

17 This is very different from Europe and the United States, where the traditional economy is more developed, and where the rule of law is more mature and there are strong industry associations. But even this does not prevent the Internet industry from expanding beyond the established economic processes.

about disorder and chaos on the relevant digital platforms, fragmenting the dispersed production of value, making it difficult to carry out the stable accumulation of capital, and so on. Similarly, if flexible employment lacks effective constraints from employment platforms to ensure the most basic norms of behavior and management systems, it will not be able to form a stable model for attracting consumers in the long run.

It is this tense and close relationship between the old and the new mode of production that has led to a tendency to think in terms of traditional rules, which is reflected in the law by applying the rules of the traditional economic process to the new environment, rather than by simply creating new rules. If this must be done, the question needs to be asked to what extent the new rules reflect the particular interests of the new mode of production. During the illegal rise, different areas of law have responded to this problem by adopting different lines of thought: (1) special legislation to introduce new rules adapted to the emerging business, recognizing its legitimacy and regulating it through special rules (for instance, creating the right to disseminate information networks, or formulating a separate regulation for online car rental), which provides institutional facilities for the use of elements of mobility on digital platforms; (2) legislation that is completely modesty, and the judiciary converts all new disputes (such as the right to virtual property or new types of intellectual property infringement) into contractual issues or unfair competition disputes as far as possible, which also recognizes in fact the productive autonomy of the closed structure of digital platforms, and protects the internal and external autonomy of the platform companies from interference.

The theoretical significance of these lines of thought, which inform adjustments to labor policies and institutions, is that legal rights and obligations are not realized in a vacuum, but rather are identified and realized through legal relations within established mode of production. Specifically, the current labor rights are integrated into a whole set of traditional labor relations and production processes, and if one wishes to recognize the disputed behavioral status on digital platforms as a new type of labor relation, it is necessary to reimagine a whole new labor process, a theoretical project that is not only ambitious, but also difficult to reach a consensus in a short period of time, and more difficult to grasp in judicial process.

As detailed in Section III, the existing judicial decisions have actually made two extreme choices that are in opposition to each other: One choice is to completely let flexible workers choose their own status, and consider digital labor relations as mere contracts; the other choice is to simply apply the standards of control and subordination in the context of traditional industrial organization, without taking into account the special characteristics of digital platform. However, both options ignore the willingness and practical measures of the platforms themselves to shape the labor and production process, as well as the consensus that has evolved among flexible workers, and this new type of relationship is difficult to cover by simply proposing a type of "quasi-labor relationship" legislation. The driving force behind the real legal and institutional issues of labor in the digital economy is not the ideological attacks of the traditional economy and its competitors, nor the lawsuits filed at the margins by flexible workers, but rather the giant platforms that have evolved into a new form of labor process, which need an unchallenged position in the law, in order to continue to profit from mobility while maintaining a certain degree of control. Thus, we return to the assertion that the legitimacy of labor relations ultimately depends on the legitimacy of mode of production. For digital platform entrepreneurs, the key question is whether they can demonstrate to regulators that the technologies they employed represent advanced productivity and provide services different from those of traditional industries, even if this means that they have to provide a set of self-regulatory measures that are below national standards.

Digital platforms for flexible labor have attempted to construct several new organizational and management systems that take advantage of mobility, guided by the productivity clause of the Constitution (the so-called shift from Fordism to post-Fordism), forming an extended labor order that differs from the traditional labor process. This order unfolds through the following logic: (1) work is continuously designed into modular combinatorial states capable of fragmentation and deep segmentation; work progress is coordinated through low-cost information and algorithms; changes in the value of labor can be measured in real time; (2) on this basis, multiple productive subjects can enter the loose production process on a large scale, and do not need to be tied to digital platform by employment relationship, whereas the platform maintaining a certain degree of organizational integration can cope with possible negative externalities of mobility, both by issuing directives directly and through community synergy; (3) with a sufficiently large amount of mobile laborers, a hierarchical classification of laborers is needed for stable capital accumulation in order to identify those who are able to produce stable outputs, and then to take more incentives to keep them within the digital platform; (4) such organizational approach is realized through the establishment of various types of information infrastructures for the market and society on the platform, such as identity authentication, platform specification, analytical matching, and scoring management. Commercial insurance mechanisms can also be widely utilized in order to replace employer liability, and ultimately, a new controlling ecosystem can be formed.

Depending on the form of flexible labor, two types of labor platforms can be broadly distinguished in order to further understand how the structure of labor rights is internalized in the mode of production of digital economy. The first category is more labor-intensive platforms ("Type I platform") that focus on manual labor, with the nature of labor very similar to that of some traditional service industries (for instance, housekeeping, transportation, distribution). The labor processes emphasize more on localized, hierarchical management and a stable labor order. Under the Type I platform model, a considerable amount of manual work is repetitive labor that can be piece-rate accounted for and is more substitutable (either by other people or by machines), and although there is a certain degree of mobility of laborers, the lack of diversified jobs on the platforms leads to stronger inter-platform, rather than intra-platform, mobility. Further, these types of platforms are relatively useful complements to the insufficient marketization of existing related service industries, which more or less guarantees a certain income during economic downturns through odd jobs. In terms of market structure, Type I platforms provide more services in vertical areas, which tend to be functional rather than routine in nature, and the flow effect of multi-sided markets is not obvious. The purpose of the general digital platform multi-sided market model, in addition to constructing a competitive defensive wall, is to ensure that the labor force and consumers can stay within the flow of their own platforms, somewhat analogous to the process of transferring and exchanging jobs in a traditional productive organization. The function of transferring jobs within the system is definitely a proper part of the employment relationship, which allows for a better identification of the capabilities of the labor, and maintains a competitive dynamic against uncertainty flexibility in the face of uncertain competition. However, under Type I platform model, since functions such as management and organization have basically been replaced by automated algorithms, labor positions have become relatively homogeneous, and can only be promoted to a limited extent based on the working time limit. Help for the improvement of laborers' vocational skills is also very limited, which determines that the vocational outlook of Type I platforms can only be adjusted within a low level. If the platform does not improve remuneration or offer new job possibilities, it is unlikely to become a stable choice for workers.

The other type of platform focuses on "immaterial labor" centered on virtual content services[18] ("Type II platform"), with a greater emphasis on digital content and creation, and a labor culture that is more oriented toward nonpecuniary sharing and the gift economy, whose services themselves are not functional and are less likely to fluctuate much with economic downturns. Type II platform model relies heavily on fragmented cross-geographical participation in creation by the masses and is less in need of stable labor organizations to coordinate, and the fruits of their labor tend to be creative. Their incomes are difficult to quantify and are less likely to be replaced (even the avatar industry is still essentially reliant on real people) but prone to a situation where the rich get richer, so digital platforms will invest more traffic and other resources in head producers based on the distinction between laborers, as well as more means to prevent them from leaving at will. On Type II platforms, workers update their knowledge more quickly, easily learn new skills from the community, have more opportunities to develop job-switching skills for creative work, and are able to derive satisfaction from creative work and the fan economy even if they are not promoted in a significant rank sense, and are willing to remain working on the platform as long as the platform continues to develop new types of creative technology to keep things fresh, which instead leads to greater intra-platform rather than higher mobility between platforms.

The greater incentive that both types of platform laborers are able to derive from digital platforms seems to be the ability to choose and adjust their work patterns and hours as they wish, with sufficient autonomy and flexibility: If the industry is sufficiently competitive, the ability to continually move through low-cost mobility to gain access to more work and trading opportunities. But with the concentration

18 Lazzarato, Maurizio, "Immaterial Labor", in Paolo Virno and Michael Hardt (eds.), *Radical Thought in Italy: A Potential Politics*, University of Minnesota Press, 1996, pp. 142–157.

of industry-specific digital markets and the intensification of platform control, at least Type I platforms are no longer able to support this type of laborer's ideology of autonomy.[19] At the same time, flexible workers continue to lose traditional labor rights and protections due to changes in mode of production, such as the lack of occupational injury protection, intensified surveillance to ensure safety and other reasons,[20] the lack of minimum wage and payment guarantees, and the lack of powerful trade union organizations that can reflect their views.

6.3 How judiciary imagines mode of production

6.3.1 Criteria for labor relations test

An amount of studies have suggested that a compromise level could be added between existing labor and non-labor relations, which may not seem too difficult in terms of macro-legislative techniques, but the difficulty lies in recognizing when it is most appropriate to do so and how to define a relatively stable set of regimes as a result, with the implicit question of whether or not the new category of labor relations is fundamentally different. It is not a question of simply deregulating a particular emerging industry by lowering the level of labor production responsibility and attention, but rather answering the question of how the corresponding organizational forms and responsibilities can be designed so that all types of market players can participate in the economic cycle and reap the benefits. Until there is a systematic legislative response, it is often the courts that help to study and break through new issues at the margins. In the flexible labor context, disputes arise from workplace injuries or torts committed by (especially Type I platforms) flexible workers in the course of their work, and labor relations judgments are needed in order to hold the employing platforms liable for workers' compensation or employer liability, or to incentivize preventive inputs of ex ante workers' compensation insurance.

Generally speaking, judicial decisions do not have much impact on the mode of production in single cases; however, if similar disputes increase, judicial activities may have an impact on the creation of new rules. This is mainly because decisions involving new issues can enhance the reputation of the courts of first instance within the system, which will be exchanged and imitated by courts in other regions, and may be followed by the Supreme Court to issue relevant judicial interpretations to unify the adjudication standards. As a result, in response to the new problems in the process of illegal rise, the courts need to choose and explore between

19 Jeremias Prassl, *Humans as a Service: the Promise and Perils of Work in the Gig Economy*, Oxford University Press, 2018.

20 On July 21, 2022, the State Internet Information Office imposed a fine of RMB 8.026 billion on DDT Global Co. The main reasons included over-collecting 167 million pieces of precise location (latitude and longitude) information when passengers evaluated the chauffeur-driven service; over-collecting 142,900 pieces of information on drivers' academic qualifications, and storing drivers in clear-text format 57.8026 million pieces of ID card number information. It can be seen that DDT's monitoring of drivers and passengers has become the norm.

the established legislative framework and the assessment of possible social consequences, and have formed considerable adjudication rules in specific types of cases (for instance, disputes over unfair competition online). The problem is that when assessing the limits of legitimacy of online act, legislation provides only vague guidelines or no rules at all, and for risk-averse judges, who lack sufficient information to assess in depth the socio-spatial structure and the industrial consequences of the occurrence of the act, there is a tendency to adjudicate conservatively in terms of the doctrinal attributes of the act or the legal right itself.

Courts generally interpret and protect particular legal rights on the basis of identities and behaviors, setting standards for specific behaviors in specific contexts, which are derived from either rational human beings or more refined behavioral structures of certain norms, but do not take into account the structure of social production in which the right itself is embedded. This is mainly because the identity itself has been embedded in the established mode of production, and the structure is relatively fixed and able to reach consensus as a default setting; so when applying the relevant rules, it seems that only the interpretation and discernment of the meaning of the words in a vacuum is necessary. However, under conditions of transformed mode of production, it is difficult to continue to follow this approach without potentially misjudging or impeding the new mode of production.

Regarding the judgment of the nature of flexible labor, the existing cases have distilled completely different criteria from the different dimensions of the labor form: (1) the form criteria, holding that as long as the act of formally signing a labor contract, regardless of whether or not it produces value, can be recognized as a labor relationship; (2) the organization criteria, holding that as long as it is subordinate to a labor organization with a mature mode of production, it can be recognized as a substantive labor relationship, regardless of the contractual form; and (3) the value criteria, holding that an act is a labor behavior as long as it produces economic and social value, regardless of whether that value is fragmented or integrated. Many courts have previously held that the standard is mostly a formal one, viewing user behavior as an equal form of collaboration between equal subjects, for fear that the value standard is too generalized, with the result that flexible workers are excluded from the established labor protection system, without even being asked whether they are entering into another new type of productive relationship, which is undoubtedly advantageous for digital platforms. However, a few courts have adopted the organization criteria in support of injured parties seeking workers' compensation. This attitude simply applies the control and subordination rationale in traditional industrial organizations without considering the specificity of platform organizations. In addition, no court has adopted the value criteria, mainly because Type I platforms are more likely to generate understandable and referable labor disputes, while Type II platforms are not even considered labor forms in the judicial and public perception, although this is not logically well-thought-out and does not have much impact on the platforms in question.

In decisions supporting that the platform had established an employment relationship with the workers, the courts often resorted to the 2005 Ministry of Labor and Social Security's *Circular on Matters Relating to the Establishment of Labor*

Relationships, which was not problematic in terms of normative nature of its application, except that the courts were unable to conceive of a more complete productive structure in which digital labor operated in the context of a new mode of production. The judges had no choice but to use it, and as a result, such criteria have been perpetuated. Its effect has only been to help specific plaintiffs to obtain workers' compensation. The standard is not without controversy, such as the fact that control itself is not an a priori prerequisite for determining whether a labor relationship exists.[21] More importantly, the standard fails to further distill the particularities of digital mode of production; instead, it endorses its universality by reference to traditional industrial mode of production. If we want courts to be truly substantive in their review, we need a more persuasive test that screens labor activities that are subordinate to a new mode of production from labor detached from such a mode of production.[22]

This chapter tries to develop a three-step test for normative adjudication, which continues the way of thinking in the 2005 Ministry of Labor and Social Security's official document, but aims not just to properly resolve disputes, but to demonstrate a way of thinking that helps courts identify more deeply the kind of productive structural environment in which a particular labor behavior is situated, and also distinguishes Type I platform labor from Type II, thus making the logic of reasoning more circumscribed. This set of standards is inherently productive and requires understanding and imagining exactly what the environment associated with digital labor is. Labor that appears more flexible on the surface can also have negative externalities in reality. Once the labor relationship is required to be recognized with digital platforms, it may upend the normal mode of operation of established platforms due to cost. However, it does not mean that labor platforms can do whatever they want. We need to see the productive architecture in which the new type of labor rights is situated, namely, it facilitates the flow of productive resources and promotes the integration of production processes and values. If the relevant digital platforms lack such self-awareness, then such judicial decisions have the positive function of rallying social consensus.

A brief restatement of this three-step test is as follows. The first standard is the subjective intent of flexible workers' activities, which means that the reasonable expectation of workers about the nature of their actions should be taken as an important reference resource for the protection of legitimate labor rights and interests. For instance, how they subjectively perceive their online activities, whether they think they are working for the platforms, for themselves, or from non-commercial activities such as recreational and entertainment sharing, as well as whether they expect to be paid for their labor in the process. This standard can help distinguish two types of labor platforms and instead focus on disputes on Type

21 Yan Tian, "The Historical Logic of Platform Employment Regulation—Taking the Subordination Theory of Labor Relations as a Point of View", *China Law Review* no. 4 (2021).

22 A similar example is that the right to communication of information networks, although also specified as a function of copyright, is adapted to the mode of production of the Internet.

I platform. The second standard is to distill the external environment and structure in which flexible workers work, namely, the macro-market structure and the organizational nature of the platforms. The court needs to recognize that both the platforms and the marketplace are driving the development of distributional and value-exchange mechanisms adapted to the different business models, as well as to their labor-organizing processes. If these mechanisms already exist and work well, there is no need to forcefully intervene by confirming the labor relationship. The third standard is to judge the space of choice in which flexible workers can choose to join or leave on their own, that is, whether they can escape from the subordinate influence of the platform's productive process and are able to move to other spaces on their own. If it is difficult for them to escape, the digital platform is considered to have more market influence, and the recognition of a specific labor relationship can be considered at the margin.

This three-step test provides a fuller formal justification and more room for flexibility than the previous subordination/control test; the underlying spirit is to test what appears to be highly fragmented behavior in order to determine whether it is in some kind of mature mode of production, and to synthesize a judgment as to whether or not the party is in need of relief at the margin. However, its strength is also its weakness. The test is so complex that its cost of thought and proof will undoubtedly put some judges off. Once clearly demonstrated through certain typical cases, this kind of dynamic justice may have a demonstration effect for the whole judicial system. Of course, if we look at it from the later, whether we can draw a scientific conclusion that is not a labor relationship is not very important, the key is to create more specific exceptions to the rules of productive relations through single cases, in order to show how to do in practice is considered to be a better use of mobile productive resources for the integration of production. This criterion is therefore necessarily consequence-oriented. It requires a careful identification of mode of production that might otherwise imply a potential disruption of the digital economy model, creating a chilling effect.

6.3.2 Further applications

As a whole, courts of first instance have less incentive to break with established rules in the face of new types of Internet cases, with the aim of reducing the rate of appeals or following the ideological notion of political correctness in view of possible political gains, which is to some extent conducive to the emergence of digital mode of production in a more stable environment. For instance, as described in Chapter 5, the recognition of the illegality of a large number of acts of unfair competition has facilitated the emergence of de facto architectural property rights, freeing the architecture of digital platforms as spaces of production from arbitrary interference. Yet other types of cases still lack clear guidance in legal application; for instance, how to create property rights for data, whether privacy or personal information has been violated in reality, among others. These issues are similar to those in labor relations cases: Courts or regulators lack a productive perspective when determining the nature of the act or the nature of the right. They are unable to think about these productive resources in the context of production relations and processes.

Central to the idea of productive interpretation is the recognition that mobility, accompanied by low information costs, can add to the overall welfare and communal value of society, but that it needs to be shaped to take advantage of it in some new approach. Productive resources can flow within a controlled organization or outside it. Being able to flow means not only that the information costs and constraints on the external choices of productive resources are lowered, but also that the valuation of the transactions that can be realized on their own cannot be too high (for instance, by relying on some kind of entitlement to be knocked down). If digital platforms want to benefit from mobility at scale, the barriers at the institutional level need to be lowered as a whole, which means that the granularity of the rights granted cannot be too fine-grained. If viewed in the context of a cyclical process of mode of production, the question of whether or not to grant rights also needs to be recognized at the stage of a particular production activity: In the upswing of the digital economy, if the benefits that resources can derive from mobility outweigh the benefits of a fixed interest, there is no need for rights and special protection; whereas, in the maturity of the production method, there may be a need for rights to come from a fixed-interest group.

6.4 Conclusion

As this chapter has continually emphasized, the balance between mobility and integration of productive resources is a central issue to which the digital economy needs to continually respond. Market infrastructures on platforms first solve the problem of localized mobility, helping to establish a labor order within a controlled and larger scope, thus establishing solid production relations; while the cross-platform mobility of productive resources all the time allows giant platforms to continuously absorb more fresh market resources, helping to shape and enhance more uniform labor standards. The determination of labor behavioral benchmarks under discussion at the moment not only needs to take into account the form of wage labor in the traditional industrialized mode of production, but also needs to see the particularities of the two types of digital platforms in order to determine different behavioral standards in a more specific way. It is foreseeable that the extended labor order will be dominated by at least these three types of mode of production in the coming period and will profoundly influence changes in the body of knowledge of labor law.

A holistic production system can be developed in three main areas. The first area relates to the productive infrastructure regime. As mentioned earlier, head digital platforms begin by providing basic services in a market shaped by themselves and gradually evolve into more general digital infrastructures, which not only serve the functions of market authentication and matching, but may themselves also become important information security infrastructures (for instance, logistics, maps, and warehousing), which are relevant to the public interest and national security. In addition, from the perspective of market regulation, the head platform may also be classified as a giant platform in the relevant industry to be strictly regulated, thus strengthening the monopoly position of such platforms in disguise.[23] Although the antitrust movement for digital platforms initiated in 2020–2021 is an important measure to prevent disorderly expansion, it does not institutionally address the legitimacy of the platform's two-sided market model, and fully utilizing intra-platform mobility remains the basic mode of expansion for closed platforms. For Type I platforms, because they cannot provide an effective internal mobility mechanism, their monopoly effect will also be offset by high cross-platform liquidity; while Type II platforms are more likely to adopt non-compete measures due to the rich getting richer for headline laborers. The formation of platform market dominance may directly affect the platform's management of flexible workers, bringing them closer to Type I platforms and traditional productive organizations. If labor benchmarking is modeled after Type I platforms, it may also lead to further concentration of market share and resources, affecting the survival of small- and medium-sized platforms that adopt lower labor standards and raising the overall cost of labor compliance. In addition, the core regime of the production system also includes ownership of the means of production, and in particular, the emergence of new productive resources such as data resources are raising additional new issues. Current legal practice indirectly ensures the orderly flow of data within platforms by protecting the architectural property rights of platforms, but how to promote the safe flow of data elements between platforms still requires the state to develop an infrastructure for connecting platforms.

The second area is the construction of the digital platform and industry management system, which is mainly reflected in two aspects. The first is the gradual formation of industry and professional norms. At present, we see that various online industry associations are gradually strengthening self-regulation within the industry, reinforcing the normative discipline of flexible labor platforms and workers, including webcasting, and strengthening their professional identity. Therefore, in the future, professional ethics and discipline may also prioritize the search for mature management methods from the more stable new industry. Second, although platforms do not bear employer responsibility, it is entirely possible to further summarize and refine the existing main responsibilities and precedents, and to implement the relevant production responsibilities in different areas of employment, such as the platform's management of speech, personal information, intellectual property rights, and other elements.

Finally, there is the legal issue of distribution as well. At present, the distribution of income on digital platforms is still mainly in the form of primary distribution. Mobile workers receive flexible and diversified incomes from the market, but there is no guarantee of stability, and even the issue of legitimacy will affect

23 State Administration for Market Supervision: Guidelines for Categorizing and Grading Internet Platforms (Draft for Public Comments) (2021).

expectations.[24] Because the dividend brought by the Internet still exists, it is foreseeable that it will continue to absorb more laborers into the digital mode of production for some time to come.[25] Besides, the shape of income has also changed in the digital economy; for instance, on Type II platforms, laborers value traffic more than simple reward income, which means that the measurement of labor welfare is not simply to increase wages, but to increase the weight of traffic and trading opportunities, which furthermore implies the algorithms non-discriminatory distribution. The value of the data traffic will be transformed efficiently in the development of different tiers and different types of activities.[26]

In summary, this chapter discusses the following theoretical issues: First, labor law and the basic labor regime have a distinctly productive character, created, among other things, to promote or at least not to impede the development of productive forces, either by relying on and preserving the established mode of production or by becoming an institutional force for changing the mode of production when groundbreaking technologies come into widespread use. Over the past two decades, we have witnessed the labor regime since the 1982 Constitution begins to loosen around the adjustment of the mode of production and the emergence of new types of labor organizations centered on digital platforms outside the framework of standard labor law. As of today, labor law remains modest about the digital economy, depending on how legislators perceive the nature and function of the new employment form of labor. At the same time, the exploration of judicial decisions at the margins helps to understand the socioeconomic constraints that confirm rights or solidify particular interests in times of changes in mode of production, and the test for judicial decision-making formed by this line of thinking can be extended and applied to other informational constitutional rights or productive resources, making it more explanatory and operational in times of changes in mode of production.

Second, labor law is essentially a dimension of the production system, and cannot be observed and discussed separately from other platform rules or even infrastructure structures of productive significance; when faced with breakthrough technological shocks, they tend to change synergistically as a whole, and it is only as the emerging interests and production structures tend to stabilize that the relevant systems evolve along their respective logics and become more refined and deepened. This chapter does not attempt or have the ability to answer the question of what the organization of labor might look like in the future, other than to say that the state and social forces will need to continue to create the institutional conditions

24 For instance, the legal nature of the live streaming reward is actually a gift behavior or the consideration of the service contract has been in the judicial decision; there are different points of view, especially when it comes to minor's reward, the court for the consideration of the social consequences of the anchor and the platform is often found to return part of the money.

25 Chi, I. D., et al., "A Study of the Impact of Internet Use on the Wage Earnings of Flexibly Employed Persons in the Age of Digital Economy", *Social Science Series* 1, no. 1 (2022), 36–37.

26 Jia Kai, "Distributive Impacts and Governance Reforms of the Digital Platform Economy", *E-Government* 5, no. 5 (2022),69–78.

that will drive productivity forward, which means that the law will need to loosen the reins on new mode of production in due course.

Third, mobility and integration are the two core concepts around which the evolution of productive labor law revolves; mobility is a prerequisite for the production of value and an inevitable result of the widespread application of information technology, and in order to mitigate the risks of mobility and to organize production in an orderly manner, it is necessary to create new types of labor-organizing functions, including infrastructure, and to form a stable pool of labor-value resources. After confirming and consolidating the dominance of the new mode of production, the digital platform still requires a pluralistic system of labor rights and protections to maintain the stable mobility of flexible workers. In the spirit of the productivity clause of the Constitution, it is the dynamic adjustment in the stable labor model that promotes more innovative changes and competitive environments at the margins, while absorbing the productive resources into a relatively stable production system, which represents a further application and expansion of the social cybernetic thinking that has been in place since the 1980s in the era of the digital economy.

7 Subcontracting

Governance structure of digital commons

7.1 Introduction

Information technology, represented by the Internet, is rapidly spreading throughout society, expanding space and time, and absorbing more productive resources and resources into the production and circulation process regulated by digital platforms. This process is widely recognized as a new type of production that is different from traditional industrial mode of production, covering production, distribution of goods/services, and consumption, which are traditionally separated in space. This process started with information content services and was later extended to more physical resources to facilitate mobility. Previous chapters of this book have illustrated in details how the new mode of production is generated in China, including (1) resource production and mobility mechanisms, emphasizing the modular combination of different resources based on low-cost information technology into the networked productive process for modular combination of matching, and its rapid flow and circulation process is very critical to the generation of value, and the acceleration of technology brings about a huge scale effect; (2) platform companies as productive organization, seeing that the transformation of the mode of production is a process of productive organization adjustment, emphasizing that the platform company itself plays an important role in resource matching and control as an organizational force; (3) digital market infrastructure, emphasizing that in order to realize the orderly flow of resources, it needs a strong market infrastructure (such as payment, logistics, and credit) to provide effective support; (4) relevant law and public policy, recognizing that the survival and growth of the new mode of production is not as natural and smooth as they seem, emphasizing the need for the law to protect the interests of unique economic processes, confirm their legitimacy, and appropriately resolve conflicts between old and new interests. The above perspectives cover different aspects of digital mode of production, but these explanations do not yet allow one to visualize the dynamics of paradigm shift. What points further behind this is the interaction between platform companies and the state as regulator. Possible question might include: What is the proper place of the rapidly changing platform companies as mediating subjects when carrying new modes of production in the Chinese state's political, social, and legal system.

The current platform governance has been an interdisciplinary and comprehensive field, which is closely related to the mode of governance, regulatory means,

DOI: 10.4324/9781003566243-8

and legal status of the platform.[1] Relevant research topics mainly focus on (1) shifting from the liability in private law to responsibility in public law and even the more common subject responsibility in China at present.[2] Some studies are critical of subjective responsibility of the platform, arguing that it is ambiguous, underwriting, lacks expectations, tends to bring unlimited inputs, and needs to be more neutral. This type of thinking makes it difficult to explain why platform responsibility is constantly being strengthened, and does not allow for an in-depth understanding of the logic behind the formation and existence of platform subjective responsibility. (2) Summarizing various models of platform governance, such as advocating public–private partnership governance, or focusing on the behaviors of platform as agents.[3] This kind of thinking lacks a broader perspective of government–enterprise relations, fails to discuss in a framework of government–platform company interaction, and neglects the extended perspective of traditional governance thinking. (3) Arguing for platform "private power" and its source of legitimacy.[4] Similar phrases and relevant institutions scattered in different legal areas, such as the boundaries of private power, platform self-regulation, digital market gatekeepers, the doctrine of essential facilities, platform fiduciary obligations, as so on. All these concepts in fact point to the legal status of large-scale platform companies, but lack a unified discussion of the boundaries of such power, the conditions for its behaviors, and the process of its enforcement.

From Chinese experience in the development of the platform economy, the rapid and effective formation of a digital mode of production cannot be achieved without a fully developed productive organization and a coordinated external environment, a process that is in fact realized through a certain power "subcontracting" or "outsourcing" governance mechanism, meaning the state has consciously adopted an inclusive and prudent strategy in the process of the rise of the Internet, allowing platform companies to explore the process of development in line with their own mode of production, without restricting market and investment access, while at the same time requiring platform companies to adopt various types of self-regulatory means and assume responsibility for platform activities and risk management. Regulatory requirements on the subjective responsibility of platforms have become more pronounced in recent years and have been continuously refined. For instance, regulatory documents like the *Regulations on the Management of Network Data Security* (Draft for Opinion), *Guidelines for the Implementation of the Main Responsibility of Internet Platforms* (Draft for Opinion), and the *Opinions on Further Compacting the Main Responsibility for the Information Contents of*

1 For instance, Huang Yiping (ed.), *Platform Economy: Innovation, Governance and Prosperity*, CITIC Press 2022.

2 For instance, Liu Quan, "On the Main Responsibility of Internet Platforms", *Journal of East China University of Political Science and Law*, No. 5, 2022.

3 For instance, Zhao Peng, "Beyond Platform Liability: Rethinking the Regulatory Model of Online Food Transactions", *Journal of East China University of Political Science and Law*, No. 1, 2017.

4 For instance, Liu Wenjie, *From Haven of Responsibility to Obligation of Safety and Security: A Study on the Intermediary Liability of Network Service Providers*, China Social Science Press, 2016 edition.

Websites and Platforms all focus on subjective responsibility. Some of the regulatory documents, although not officially released, can adequately demonstrate the state's perception of the functioning of platforms.

The perspective of mode of production transformation suggests that we may not need to dwell so much on the pure nature of platforms (whether administrative, corporate, or marketplace), but rather we can try to switch perspectives and observe the relative positioning of platform companies from the viewpoint of the relationship between the state and the enterprise. That is to say, if it is not possible to simply fit platform companies into the framework of the established policy perceptions no matter what the perspective is, it is better to take a step backward based on recognizing their legitimacy, and observe the political–economic conditions and governance structures that shape and drive their emergence; and better to ask how the interactions between the state and platform companies can be understood, and whether they are in the middle of a stable structure resulting from multiple games; and to explore further if such a fixed structure exists, whether it is independently generated and evolved or is an inevitable result of the established state governance relationship.

7.2 Rationale for the platform subcontracting system

The term "platform subcontracting system" used in this chapter is mainly derived from existing research on administrative subcontracting and outsourcing systems in China. This theoretical framework suggests that, on the one hand, administrative subcontracting deals with subcontracting relationships between the upper and lower levels of government, and is characterized by complementarity and internal consistency in the three dimensions of administrative power allocation (central residual claims), incentives (both personnel and economic), and internal control (by outcome assessment), thus forming a consistent governance system that last for hundreds of years in China.[5] On the other hand, administrative outsourcing is a matter of internal decentralization of governmental organizations. Sometimes, due to the lack of state capacity, power outsourcing is also used, whereby a wide range of administrative affairs are outsourced to social organizations (such as clans and big families). Although they do not have nominal administrative legitimacy, these agencies in fact take on a wide range of public management responsibilities.[6] With the disappearance of social power in modern societies, such as that of the gentry and clans, the state and political party organizations have ostensibly moved into more social spheres without any power outsourced, but in fact there is still a de facto separation of power to various enterprises and non-commercial units outside the administrative system.

5 Zhou Li'an, "Administrative Subcontracting System", *Society*, No. 6, 2014.

6 Zhou Li'an, "One Body, Many Faces: Re-examining State-Society Relations during the Chinese Imperial Period", *Society*, No. 5, 2022.

Drawing on the two types of power division (subcontracting and outsourcing) within theoretical frameworks mentioned above can help us reconceptualize platform-subjective responsibility. It is not difficult to figure out that in the past five years, a platform outsourcing structure has gradually been formed against the background of central–local decentralization in China, with central institutions taking the lead in responding to the problems of market structure and governance in the digital economy, and that the subjective responsibility is just confirmation and manifestation of this dynamic structure. This chapter here is not simply applying the concept of "subcontracting" or "outsourcing" to seemingly new phenomenon today. Based on the practice of platform governance, we can gradually figure out the similar traditional process of outsourcing (externally) of public affairs. Governmental departments at all levels (mainly at the central level) require platform companies (especially giant national platforms) to implement a package of governance tasks as a whole for activities occurring on platforms. Sometimes platforms are viewed as a form of private law enforcement agents strictly following administrative orders, and other times certain affairs would be loosely outsourced to the platform's discretion. Platform would also be assessed on the basis of social results. At the same time, it is also possible to draw on the constitution of administrative outsourcing at the analytical level to describe in detail the effectiveness of governance by platform companies in a number of different areas, as well as government relations. Despite the fact that the aforementioned theoretical framework addresses both internal and external dimensions, this chapter is more interested in emphasizing the rationalization process of platform companies in their management and organization process, as well as their similarity in the sense of assuming the subjective responsibility rather than the legitimacy of public authority. Therefore, this chapter still uses the conceptual description of "subcontracting".

The brief operational logic of the platform subcontracting system is as follows: First, in terms of the distribution of governance power, the regulator (central/local) fully owns the legitimacy of governance in cyberspace (Internet sovereignty), and proposes specific governance tasks to be accomplished by platform companies, with a certain amount of discretionary space for the latter. Second, from the perspective of economic incentives, the illegal rise of the Internet means that the government is less likely to impose market and investment access restrictions, and platform companies tried to gain access to market by competing with each other, leading to a continuous concentration of expanding digital architecture. The regulator in turn allowed platform companies to expand but required them to control risks during the process. Third, in terms of governance assessment criteria, regulators look more at governance effectiveness and results but care less about the whole process. They can gradually add new and refined requirements in some key areas while let the platform companies to make discretion in other areas. Fourth, in terms of enforcement capacity, regulators are limited by information and enforcement capacity and are unable to discipline individual online behavior in depth, whereas platform companies have the technical capacity to do so, but they sometimes need regulators to assist them in enforcement. Finally, in order to shape nationally harmonized rules, central government authorities are more likely to impose requirements directly on large platform companies with national influence, rather than relying solely on regulation by different levels of government in their respective jurisdictions.

The platform subcontracting system has been embodied in almost all areas of Internet governance, with some areas (such as digital speech and content service) being subject to ever-increasing regulation from the top, while others have demonstrated an attitude of inclusiveness and prudence, even at the high cost of social experimentation (such as P2P lending). What this chapter would like to emphasize here is the historical significance of the system as it relates to mode of production transformation, namely, it allows platform companies to create an independent cyberspace for self-operation that transcends territorial boundaries and continues to expand, generates new types of values and interests, and requires legal and policy adjustments and protections, which ultimately contributes to the emergence of a new type of mode of production.[7] Another theoretical significance of this creative system is to observe how mode of production in a vast country like China, with huge geographical area, is rapidly transformed according to a structured process. The internal and external structure of the organization of social production has to be included in the discussion of the transformation of the mode of production.

The platform subcontracting system is also an extension of previous chapters of this book. First, the "illegal rise" of the Internet is closely related to the emergence of new mode of production. New modes of production need to appear at low cost by violating the established rules and eventually replacing traditional mode of production. Second, "architecture" as a spatial interest that hosts new mode of digital production needs to be recognized and protected by law, meaning network regulations are more endogenous within the digital economy. The architecture itself forms a micro-control/production mechanism, materialized in "account-data-algorithm-rating" system, which facilitates the value reproductive process. Third, new mode of production requires the secure and orderly flow of productive resources, which are integrated through infrastructures that exhibit different aspects of openness and closedness of digital commons. Following the above logic, further research questions could be as follows: (1) How this mode of production operates effectively and stably anyway within the existing state governance structure. (2) How the corresponding power relations are conducted. (3) Whether they demonstrate the uniqueness of governance relation in China? The position and function of the platform company as the subject and medium for subcontracting the task of public governance provide the institutional basis for the smooth extension of this process.

Of course, the formation of the platform subcontracting system is a continuous process, the idea is not clear at the beginning of creation of digital commons, but

7 While US Internet governance studies have often taken the creation of cyberspace triggered by anarchist ideology as a logical starting point, this chapter also attempts to make such a theoretical endeavor, that is, to find a logical starting point for Internet governance in China, and to explore what are the logical and supportive conditions for the emergence of a relatively independent space, both ideologically and realistically.

is a dynamic process of gradual adjustment along with the changes in the shape of Internet and its business models. New mode of production is also gradually explored accordingly. For instance, in the early days, the legal status of platform companies was merely that of a content service provider, with a safe harbor responsibility, and without the ability and qualification to get subcontracting for governance tasks. This dynamic process is the result of a series of continuous improvements from concept to practice. First, its theoretical premise is the Internet sovereignty that the state has been emphasizing all the time, which holds that the cyberspace is not illegal sphere. Part of the governance power, even if it can be subcontracted to platform companies, is not absolutely autonomous in cyberspace. Second, the Internet has been gradually stabilized from its illegal rise to mature mode of production, with little local regulations at first. As the logic of the platform economy has deepened from online to offline (such as the sharing economy, Internet plus policy), new problems have emerged, and the complexity and risks have been greatly intensified, resulting in changes to the platform liability regime. Third, the emergence of privately driven market infrastructures has facilitated the formation of national online markets across regions, with the national dominance and interests of giant platforms gradually becoming entrenched. On the basis of these experiences, there is an obvious need for systematic reflection on the extent to which it is necessary to continue to rely on the giant platforms to drive sustained change in mode of production and to realize functions that cannot be replaced by the traditional administrative subcontracting system.

7.3 Institutional effectiveness of platform subcontracting system

The subcontracting system implies not all areas of public affairs would the regulators step in. If we can set up a four-quadrant for the regulatory affairs based on the incentives of regulator and platforms, then we can conduct the following analysis accordingly and categorize various issues into those quadrants. Specifically, Quadrant I is the category of regulating market order, including competition issues, consumer and labor rights, etc. Since the effect of market competition among platforms is less obvious, more focused on maintaining the internal market order and the rights and interests of the participating subjects, the state has the incentive to outsource to the platform companies, but in general, respect for their autonomy, and acquiesce to their discretionary space. Thus, the main responsibility of such platforms is more consequence-oriented, and requires less intervention from the state. Quadrant II is the category of productive resources as well as information security. Its effect of competition among platforms is more obvious, but also could be further divided into two categories: The first category involves information and data security that state has the incentive to outsource but hopes to strengthen the detailed guidance. If the platform company lacks the incentive to implement, it will be supervised by way of special rectification; the second category involves a new type of future market that can be accessed and developed and the state encourages the platform company to develop continuously. After platform has transformed the market into a digital one, the state would strengthen regulation by license to limit the threshold of access. Platform-subjective responsibility implies that they not only bear the relevant consequences of digital governance, but also need to implement them in accordance with detailed state requirements beforehand. Quadrant III is the category for market and social infrastructure. Its competitive effects among platform companies are obvious, such as the establishment of in-platform authentication and credit services, but the inability of interconnection and the possible increase in risk could lead to a gradual decrease in the state's willingness to outsource. Quadrant IV is mostly utilities and pure public services. The public sector has low willingness to outsourcing and there is a lack of incentives for firms to operate as well.

As mentioned earlier, this chapter is concerned not only with the operational status of platform subcontracting in the governance process, but also with the impact it brings to the mode of production and the possible institutional effects that differ from traditional administrative subcontracting. In fact, when mobile Internet has not yet taken shape, the problems brought about by information technology are mainly governed through territorialized administrative subcontracting (such as regulation on cybercafes, website content, online games), and the attribution of local governance is not systematic. With the popularization of mobile terminals and 4G networks, the further strengthening of various types of resource flows, and the increasing systematization of governance after the establishment of the Cyberspace Administration of China in 2011, all of these have led the state to take seriously the governance status and public function of platform companies, namely, how to bring into full play the value of resource mobility, while at the same time lowering its own governance costs and promoting collaborative and cooperative governance between the state and giant platforms.

It is easy to see that the existence of two subcontracting system in the abstract reflects two different modes of production, digital and industrialized (or networked and gridded styles), which will coexist for a certain period of time, influencing and constraining each other, and serving different functions in different areas. While administrative territorial segregation and differences in governance standards are unavoidable on a large country scale, the platform economy proposes an alternative model of governance that facilitates resource mobility while harmonizing standards, which is a profound reflection of the differences in modes of production. The following is a brief comparative illustration of five examples of the institutional differences that platform subcontracting system can bring about and the challenges they pose for law and public policy across different modes of production.

7.3.1 Data policy

To promote the flow of data resources, in December 2022 the CPC Central Committee and the State Council issued the *Opinions on Building a Fundamental System to Better Utilize the Data Resources*, in an attempt to establish a normative and unified data order. However, data resources can be understood and applied in different senses if placed in two modes of production. One is traditionally generated by the organization's internal generation and improvement of services and data. This type of data is more in the localized productive process about the product or service development within the factory, and does not involve real-time feedback to the user or consumer. Data belonging to this category lies in areas of public data, data generated by the traditional industry associations, traditional enterprise data, and even the so-called data intellectual property rights. The other type is the data generated in the platform economic process, that is, the productive process led by platform companies, beyond the geographical boundaries of the cross-domain deployment of productive resources, which is more central to the behavioral data that occurs in different networked relationships, especially based on the real-time behavioral data to make production and consumption decisions, so as to promote the whole economic cycle. The two types of data orders have been formed and stabilized under two types of subcontracting system, but they have demonstrated significant differences in data ownership, pricing, transaction models, infrastructure, and other institutional aspects. The platform subcontracting system is more capable of stimulating the value and vitality of data resources based on the characteristics of its mode of production.

7.3.2 Property rights

Article 127 of the *Civil Code* states: "Where the law provides for the protection of data and online virtual property, it shall do so in accordance with its provisions". This sets the stage for changes in form and function of property under different modes of production. Under the traditional industrial organization-dominated mode of production, enterprises rely on basic machines, plants, land, intellectual property, and other means of production. A large amount of resources are incorporated and processed into the enterprise organization to form new commodities for sale to the outside world, while the production, distribution, and consumption segments are separated. Ownership is transferred when consumers buy goods on the market, and consumers can possess and dispose of their private property. In the digital mode of production, however, the streaming services provided by platform companies make consumer possession irrelevant. Producers are also consumers in the digital economic process, and people can instantly consume the information content produced by others and create further from digital commons. The sharing economy encourages people to share specific physical items, which retains the ownership of original idle resources and allows for full social utilization. At the same time, the platform companies as regulators retain overall control, preventing their combinations and flows from going beyond the market scope shaped by the platform. It seems that the two types of production represented by the subcontracting system have developed very different concepts of property rights and institutional logics. Platform subcontracting enables better circulation and recycling of various types of property.

7.3.3 Competition policy

Only Article 12 of the *Anti-Unfair Competition Law* attempts to address the new issues of competition in the Internet market raised by the war between Tencent and Qihoo in 2011, but it is completely unable to cover the various types of unfair competition behaviors that continue to emerge subsequently. Under the two orders of production, issues regarding competitive relationships and market scope have begun to diverge. Under the administrative subcontracting system, the local courts and regulatory authorities tend to determine the competitive relationship and market boundary according to the scope of their own jurisdictions; while under the platform subcontracting system, the doctrine of competitive relationship has gradually been broken through, and the two-sided market model as a theoretical doctrine has begun to be widely recognized. In a large number of cases of unfair competition surrounding the ownership of data, ad blocking, and service interferences, this issue has also gained a broad consensus in judicial practice. The local courts' recognition of a broadly defined competitive relationship is in effect an endorsement of the legitimacy of production through the Internet, making any market conduct conducted through the platform economy model potentially competitive. Paradoxically, however, in a number of Internet antitrust cases, courts have been reluctant to recognize the existence of a bilateral market, arguing instead for finding a suitable unilateral market. The fact is that a single specific market has long been unable to explain the network effect and control of platform companies, and if this is the standard, it will obscure the true source of market control—multi-sided markets and network scale effects, and thus indirectly provide shelter for giant platforms. At the same time, local courts have taken full advantage of the ambiguity of the Principle Clause in Article 2 of the *Anti-Unfair Competition Law* to provide increasingly strong protection for the spatial benefits of the architecture needed by platform companies, an unintended consequence of judicial policy under the platform subcontracting system.

7.3.4 Labor policy

For the first time, the eight departments of the Ministry of Human Resources and Social Security and other departments put forward institutional design and requirements for flexible labor in the *Guiding Opinions on Safeguarding the Rights and Interests of Workers in New Employment Patterns of Labor Security* in 2021. Such policy documents focus on the increasing prominence of new types of labor employment issues brought about by information technology, and mode of production under the platform subcontracting system is quite different from the process of hiring labor in traditional enterprises, which is also known as the shift from the Fordism to the post-Fordism, resulting in an extended labor order. For instance, platform companies continuously design work into modular combinatorial states capable of fragmentation and deep segmentation, coordinate work progress through low-cost information and algorithms, and can measure changes in labor value in real time. On this basis, a plurality of productive agents can enter the loose productive process at scale without being bound to the digital platform by an employment relationship, and the platform's maintenance of a certain degree of organizational integration can respond to possible negative externalities of mobility, both by issuing directives directly and through community collaboration.

Until there is a systematic legislative response, it is often the local courts that help to study and break through new issues at the margins, such as labor relationship determinations for workplace injuries or torts committed by flexible workers in the course of their work, so as to hold the platforms liable for workers' compensation or employer responsibility, or to incentivize preventive inputs into certain *ex ante* compensation insurance. But overall, the platform subcontracting system provides a relaxed development environment and institutional safeguards for new forms of employment.

7.3.5 Infrastructure

Traditional physical infrastructure is often manifested in the form of public infrastructural services in the fields of energy, transportation, water conservancy, environmental protection, municipal engineering, and so on, which are linked to the form of public utilities and are operated and regulated through franchising or public–private partnership. Even the popular "new infrastructure" (such as 5G base station, new energy vehicle, charging piles, data centers, and so on) is mainly managed by local government investment. They tend to emphasize their public service orientation and public nature, belonging to the natural monopoly industry, providing stable and low-cost universal services in accordance with the needs of the general public, with divided management in physical space. However, digital infrastructure under the platform subcontracting system is closer to some kind of digital market infrastructure, owned and operated by private enterprises, and regulated according to the legal status of a general commercial subject. Its capabilities derive more from the network effects of information technology itself, which bring about decreasing marginal costs, and its services are essentially value-added information services based on contracts, and functionally encompass a whole set of abstract systems, especially informational ones, that maintain the functioning of traditional markets and societies. The platform subcontracting system can undoubtedly help to create a national infrastructure that transcends administrative boundaries and facilitates the efficient functioning of a unified market.

7.4 Relationship between platform and administrative subcontracting

The essence of mode of production is a mature value generation and circulation cycle process, the formation of which does not happen overnight and requires a strong internal and external impetus to promote its realization over a considerable territory in China. From the viewpoint of internal dynamics, as contractors, platform companies have earlier discovered the essence of the digital economy's pursuit of scale effects, and have continuously adjusted their internal organizational structure to adapt to the digital expansion process. Unlike the traditional administrative subcontracting system, (1) the platform economy relies more on economic means to get its incentive from the state (rather than administrative personnel policies), and the potential commanding effect of market access is obvious; (2) the platforms cover a wider scope than local governments and manage a huge amount of market players, while lacking nominal enforcement power and legitimacy, and sometimes local governments are required to assist in the enforcement of laws when it comes to the management of local productive resources; (3) the government imposes consequence-oriented assessments on platforms, and also keeps increasing procedures and specific content requirements, while platforms themselves have developed more detailed private rules and user agreements, although they are rarely reviewed for effectiveness by local courts.

The digital platform itself is a combination of three different levels of organization—market, horizontal management, and vertical management—creating a productive virtual space. The horizontal way in which its rules are enforced dictates the need for unified decision-making and enforcement at the level of the enterprise group, unlike the bureaucratic structure of local government, where the platform's headquarters has the power to directly assign enforcement or make rules very quickly. While it may be possible to continue to outsource governance tasks to branches in different regions at times, or to second-tier organizations and agents on the platform (such as popular juries, MCN agencies, rider station managers, advertising franchise agents), with agreed-upon agency through contracts, the effect is generally limited. Platforms are still more likely to reinforce enforcement by shaping market infrastructure, developing network regulations and technical means.

The fundamental reason for these characteristics is that platform companies are still profit-oriented enterprises, aiming to profit from resource mobility that breaks down geographical segregation, and therefore pursuing mainly the idea that mode of production cannot be fundamentally affected by policy and legal changes. Under this conception, the corporate governance structure of platform companies is not horizontally decentralized oriented; there are not too many branch organizations at the local level. Although the public affairs department or the risk control department will interface and partition with the central/local government, important issues will be discussed and decided in the headquarter, which transcends the traditional structure of the head-branch office model, and pursues a uniform execution standard across the country at a fast speed. As a result, the execution structure of platform has not changed particularly due to the influence of the administrative subcontracting section system, and in general it is still a horizontal structure, without the emergence of a vertical structure that is homologous to the government. The immediate institutional advantage of this is centralization of decision-making power, while being organized to respond effectively to local regulation.

In terms of external dynamics, at the outset, Internet governance was the act of regulating media services embedded in traditional regulatory relations, implying that administrative subcontracting did not necessarily produce platform subcontracting. It was only with the expansion of the mobile Internet, which brought huge benefits to all parties in society, that each party was motivated to promote and maintain a basic platform subcontracting structure. First, for local governments, the early Internet issue was managed territorially, which could bring a degree of governance performance and increase infrastructure investment, employment, and tax revenues. In the later years, despite direct subcontracting out to large digital platforms by different central departments, local governments can still enjoy some of the dividends. There are not too many digital economy services managed by specialized local authorities, and local digital economy legislation remains very limited. Second, for the central government, the main reason why it chooses to directly require huge national digital platforms to undertake governance tasks is that, given the national market structure and characteristics of the digital economy itself, if it continues to be regulated by local governments on a hierarchical basis, it will increase the burden on platform companies, and thus is a process of constantly breaking through and bypassing local regulation and traditional industry regulation. Especially when it comes to areas such as public opinion and information security, there is a need to avoid the disadvantages of fragmentation of traditional administrative subcontracting. While localized traditional industry regulation can be left largely to local implementation, the nature of large digital platforms dictates the need for centralized rules to reduce policy communication and implementation costs. Third, for platform companies, allowing them to follow their own explored management style is equivalent to gradually endorsing a new type of mode of production; instead of requiring platforms to convert to a vertical system or mandating outsourcing to lower agency again, the central government has acquiesced to their governance style, and they can trade off their outsourcing tasks for more emerging market entrance as long as they complete the outsourcing tasks.

As a result, the platform subcontracting system has gradually shaped a different governance order from the established mode of production, which is distancing itself from the traditional governance system, more through the interface between the central regulators and the large platform companies, allowing them to carry out the governance process of investment, experimentation, and so on, and thus going beyond the established discussion of the subjective responsibility. However, in terms of practical observation, the governance order implies increasing power of the central regulators, with the upward transfer of license control and approval power, but still needs to rely on the local department for the management of local resources in the physical space, such as digital labor issues. How to rebalance the relationship between the two subcontracting orders is a central issue in the design and operation of the future platform subcontracting system, and a new problem in Chinese constitution as well.

7.5 Concluding remarks

This chapter analyzes the platform subcontracting system as a historical process. The platform subcontracting system is the inevitable result of the development of the platform economy, as well as the confirmation and protection of new mode of production and productive organizations, which gradually dissolves the existing illegitimate emergence problem and retains the state of illegitimate emergence within the platform economic system through subcontracting authorization, thus shifting the legitimacy problem to how to promote the effective flow and utilization of resources into the system. The problem of innovation within the system. It should be noted that this chapter does not believe that there is any social governance system that can solve all or most of the problems once and for all. The platform subcontracting system is nothing more than the emergence of social demand to adapt to the mode of production of digital economy. With emancipation of productive forces being further evolved and replaced, at present we see that such system is beginning to stabilize the state and the economy. The chapter concludes with a brief discussion of the possible consequences of this new governance order.

First, the platform subcontracting system and the administrative subcontracting system may become two grips for the state to govern socioeconomic complexity and advance the national unified market-building, which represent two types of existing modes of production, respectively. The two systems can then compete, constrain, and cooperate with each other in different policy areas. Platform companies are already carrying out autonomous governance activities in response to resource mobility and infrastructure development, and have proposed new governance programs in data resource rights, social credit governance, and infrastructure, which are worth continuing to observe.

Second, the platform subcontracting system could drive the emergence of a hierarchical classification system for platform companies, a process that is beginning to be reflected in the existing hierarchical classification of field regulation on digital economy system. However, issues that need to be resolved include further clarification of the tasks and responsibilities of subcontracting out, with clearer government–enterprise interface, hierarchy, and responsibilities, so that governments at all levels and platform companies have reasonable expectations. The legitimacy of platforms assuming public governance responsibilities can also be further resolved.

Third, the original intention of the platform subcontracting system is to hope that platform companies manage the behaviors and risks occurring in their own platform space, which may also promote the architectural space of the platform to become more closed, and even make the economic and legal status of huge platform companies stable, so that the formulation of rules and standards of the new mode of production will reflect more of the interests of huge enterprises. Therefore, this system also has a double-edged sword effect. On the one hand, it identifies and protects the new mode of production; on the other hand, it may also solidify the rules of the game, and ultimately go to the opposite side of the core spirit of digital economy.

Finally, based on experience in China, the demands and restrictions on platform companies are in the cycle of political and economic transformations. It is easy to let go of the negative externalities brought by platform companies in an environment of loose economic policies, distorting incentives, and therefore it might be difficult to get rid of the cyclical characteristics of the past, causing the phenomenon of "chaos once released, death once regulated". The above problems still need to be gradually recognized and solved in the dynamic adjustment and balance in the long run.

8 Openness and closedness of digital commons

8.1 Introduction

"Openness" has been an ideology ever since the inception of the Internet, and has been embedded, especially since the 1990s, in the neoliberal trend toward globalization of the information economy.[1] To this day, many people still intuitively believe that the Internet needs to be open, even though when this term is used, different people imagine very different things in their minds. For instance, at the political level, the ideology of openness tends to refer to platform companies originating from the United States demanding access to other countries and dominating their local information services in accordance with trade agreements like WTO, whereas if any country asserts cyber sovereignty and autonomy over the governance of digital services on its own territory, this would be perceived as closedness or fragmentation of the cross-border Internet.[2] At the economic or technological level, the ideology of openness means that anyone has the right to unimpeded and equal access to the Internet through telecom cables and end devices, and to innovate and compete at different layers, while if any telecom carrier or platform company imposes traffic control or vertically integrates upstream and downstream resources in a marketplace, it is considered to be heading toward closedness.[3] As a matter of fact, as the Internet is gradually embedded into all aspects of sociopolitical and economic life, and continuously facilitates the connection among various social subjects, forming an increasingly complex network, it is difficult to simply give a one-size-fits-all answer to this question: Whether the Internet is more open or closed? Meanwhile, theorists often intentionally or unintentionally ignore the interests behind the open/closed discourse. For instance, in order to argue for an ideal state of open Internet, the logical starting point is to assume the existence of a

1 The Internet was commercialized at the end of 1980s and promoted globally under the US Information Superhighway Program. It was against this background that China set up an international export channel to connect with the US backbone network, opening up its Internet era till today.

2 Milton Mueller, *Will the Internet Fragment? Sovereignty, Globalization and Cyberspace*, Polity, 2017; Monica Horten, *The Closing of the Net*, Polity, 2016.

3 See Jonathan Zittrain, *The Future of the Internet—and How to Stop It*, Yale University Press, 2008; Tim Wu, "Network Neutrality. Broadband Discrimination", *Journal of Telecommunications and High Technology Law* 2 (2003), 141.

DOI: 10.4324/9781003566243-9

"cyberspace" (now called "metaverse") constructed through information technology. Both anarchists and giant platforms have argued that this virtual space should be left less to the state and allowed to expand in a process of self-governance, which however resulted in the evolution of commercial platforms, wishing to be free from external political constraints on their power. It is such process that the open/closed discourse builds on, whereby the "architecture" making up cyberspace form itself into a kind of expanding autonomous force that continuously absorbs productive resources and therefore needs to become more "open". However, meanwhile, as the competition for productive resources intensifies among digital platforms, in order to prevent other competitors from entering the space dominated by itself, the cyberspace would enter a process of gradually moving toward "closedness" and clearly demarcating the boundaries with others. Therefore, it is not difficult to see that the open/closed discourse is centered around some kind of abstract architectural interests that are constantly changing with competition. Such discourse also changed the ecosystem of digital commons accordingly.

Rather than remaining entangled in the traditional discourse, this chapter aims to trace the changes that have taken place in the shape of the Internet in reality based on Chinese experience. It attempts to figure out the dynamics that determine whether the cyberspace is moving toward an open or closed end as it evolves into an abstract and complex economic and social system, what the possible consequences are, and to what extent the law contributes to, or is responsive to, such a trend. Taking up some of the previous research, this chapter will reshape the open/closed discourse, arguing that such discourse actually directs to the architecture of digital commons. It is necessary to see how the architecture has transformed itself from a simple technological design and connectivity into a complex political–economic interest. Section II briefly reviews the concepts, ideologies, and problems of the original open architecture of the Internet from Western history, which leads to a number of societal resources pushing the architecture's move toward closedness, during which process the transformation in mode of production played a key role. Section III analyzes digital architecture's closedness has expected the law to protect its distinctive rights and interests, therefore causing new legal disputes thereafter. Section IV goes beyond the platform-centered open/closed discourse and return to the substantial issue: How the Internet facilitates resource mobility and builds robust infrastructure, requiring further institutional exploration of how to promote efficient digital commons in which resources flow in a safe and orderly manner on a larger scale.

8.2 Generativity and transformation of Internet architecture

8.2.1 Original Internet architecture and its problems

The original Internet architecture technically adopted an "end-to-end" philosophy, whereby communications were transmitted unimpeded from one endpoint to another through the domain name system and packet switching system. Even if some transmission routes were blocked, other routes would still be available to help complete the transmission. This decentralized philosophy can easily be interpreted as a call to facilitate the free flow of information, especially from neutral transmission conduits such as telecom carriers.[4] The design of an end-to-end hourglass network architecture can also drive a great deal of innovation at the edge of the network, allowing participants to better conduct their activities at different layers of the Internet without interfering with each other.[5] At the heart of the success of this open architecture is the generativity of the network and the powerful operating system at the edge, which facilitate much of the information service innovation we witness today.[6] Another great idea emerging from this process is that anyone can access to communication networks and use software to participate in mass social and cultural production, which is regarded as a new paradigm that goes beyond traditional economic production and creates a new kind of common pool of resources that is conducive to creativity.[7] In particular, these ideas, combined with some traditional anarchist concepts, have led to the creation of mimetic notion such as "cyberspace", which imagines a new type of space free from government authority in physical place, with open technological architectures that give birth to a realm governed entirely by engineers, hackers, anarchists, and so on. The idea is that cyberspace is open to all freedom-fond people, but not to real-world governments.[8] Along with this idea came software designs and practices that has extend to present day, such as open source, anonymity, P2P transmission, and cryptocurrency.

Smart observers are quick to realize that changes in the supporting institutional and technological conditions that underpin many of the rationales for cyberopenness can call these ideas in a vacuum into question. First, cyberspace is not absolutely free; its design architecture inherently implies power relations that can influence and constrain human behavior, and it remains political in nature, no different from the offline world.[9] Second, as Internet services expand and more and more people begin to join this space, the distributed Internet is found to be inherently unstable; there is a steady increase in all kinds of dysfunctional and anonymous behaviors online, which are not subject to the social norms of the original small group of users. Both the creative tools (individuals) and the network (the group) propose uncertain security concerns, which portend the risk of

4 J. H. Saltzer, D. P. Reed, and D. D. Clark, "End-to-end Arguments in System Design", *ACM Transactions on Computer Systems* 2 (1984), 277; Mark A. Lemley and Lawrence Lessig, "The End of End-to-End: Preserving the Architecture of the Internet in the Broadband Era", UC Berkeley Law & Econ Research Paper No. 2000-19 (October 2000).

5 Lawrence B. Solum and Minn Chung, "The Layers Principle: Internet Architecture and the Law", University of San Diego Public Law Research Paper No. 55 (2003).

6 Barbara van Schewick, *Internet Architecture and Innovation*, MIT Press, 2012.

7 Yochai Benkler, "Sharing Nicely: On Shareable Goods and the Emergence of Sharing as a Modality of Economic Production", *Yale Law Journal* 114 (2004), 273; Lawrence Lessig, *The Future of Ideas*, Random House, 2001.

8 John P. Barlow, "A Declaration of Independence of Cyberspace", available at https://www.eff.org/cyberspace-independence.

9 Alexander R. Galloway, *Protocol: How Control Exists after Decentralization*, MIT Press, 2006; Lawrence Lessig, *Code and Other Laws of Cyberspace*, Basic Books, 1999.

interconnectivity/interoperability.[10] Third, the neutrality of the transmission pipeline cannot ensure accuracy of the information and the degree of trustworthiness of the relevant user behavior, and concrete trust in different scenarios cannot replace abstract trust across scenarios, resulting in the need for effective mechanisms that can continuously produce trust among large numbers of strangers. Fourth, while it is true that the value of the Internet is generated by a large amount of edge innovations, it is not the whole story. Robust market infrastructure is still needed to guide the realization of scale and network effects, especially for accurate matching and distribution. Finally, while open access does not lead to the depletion of the online information commons, it could generate a large amount of spam. External intervention is needed to continually expand the scope and stabilize the supply of the commons in high quality.

In the early stages of China's introduction of the Internet, although there was no ideology of cyberspace openness like United States, as the network continued to be commercialized, similar issues concerning security and disorder arose. Because the political ideology against closedness and control is so strong, the openness of network architectures has always been favored and imagined, and has obscured the exploration of possible paths to effectively address their negative externalities. The fact that major digital platforms are gradually addressing the issues surrounding the open/closed nature of the network through their evolving mode of production underscores a fundamental point: Recognizing the political and controlling aspects of network architectural design is not enough. It is equally important to understand that this architecture itself is transforming into new and productive ways of self-organization, thereby resolving many of the challenges posed by the originally open Internet model. Consequently, the open/closed dichotomy of the Internet is inextricably linked to the open/closed nature of its underlying architecture, the economic and commercial dynamics of which will be explored in the following sections.

8.2.2 Architecture as a mode of production

As mentioned earlier, the openness of the network, wishing to enable any two subjects online to be connected, has been gradually enhanced by decreased technological cost, but the application scenarios are very limited and may also be less secure. For instance, in the early days of the Internet, QQ (an instant communication software of Tencent) facilitated connections among strangers, leading to a great deal of fraud and criminal activity. Similarly, essentially one-time transactions on Taobao allowed opportunism to flourish with faking items increasing. All these mean that software that acts as a connecting intermediary may bring about its own loss of potential users and affect the value of the Internet as a whole if it fails to effectively maintain virtual order. How such problems can be effectively addressed is actually at the heart of the concerns of commercially oriented platform companies.

10 Jonathan Zittrain, "The Generative Internet", *Harvard Law Review* 119 (2006), 1974.

The roots of this problem go back to the logic of the emergence of the commercial Internet. The ideology of the open network (for instance, "information wants to be free") actually covers the early practices of "illegal rise" of the Internet, which was needed to obtain productive resources at a low cost and to promote a new mode of production. The transformation of productive resources from traditional physical medium (for instance, recording tapes, paper books, movies) into digitized virtual objects, and the conversion of productive and distributive channels, is a perfect example of the transformation of information flow. In this process, free (pirated) information content attracts users' attention and helps explore a new model of basic plus value-added information services. Consumers, as the end of the traditional production process, were difficult to be turned into accurate statistical objects. While in the digital age, once the consumers become sticky, their behaviors can be continuously tracked and analyzed through the virtual account. Consumers can also be transformed into efficient producers, operating in the same structure through the sharing economy platform, becoming a stable productive group that generates cross-network externalities, thus cognitively contributing to the analytical framework of the "multi-sided market". In this sense, the Internet needs to be open because the new mode of production triggered by the digital economy itself requires a large amount of flexibly dispersed and mobile laborers to contribute from the edges of the network and create network effects. The true meaning of openness in the early days of the Internet was that platform companies, through the creation of architectural space, were constantly absorbing productive resources from outside the architecture (especially those attached to traditional productive organizations) and increasing their mobility.

The socioeconomic significance of mobility is that the fragmentation of the activities of various resources capable of generating value in space and time allows for ever-increasing opportunities for transactions, ideally with every single subject or object connected to the Internet being able to connect with each other continuously and create new possibilities. The early stages of the illegal rise of the Internet in fact broadened the audience for traditional goods or services. Attracting users at zero cost was a necessary price to pay for the widespread establishment of the digital economic model, even though it contradicted with traditional industries. However, even when connected through the Internet, online transactions and cooperation still involve transaction costs and uncertainty. The function of platform companies cannot simply be to provide matching information, but need to help effectively reduce further information asymmetry and other costs, and ensure security throughout the entire process of the transaction, in order to truly utilize the value of the Internet.[11] Platform companies are not only creating a market that facilitates the free flow of resource, but also need to make this market orderly and efficient. Seeing from the perspective of mode of production, the Internet is just an organizational tool to facilitate the cycle of production and consumption. Whether

11 This reasoning is similar to an amplified version of Ronald Coase's research on the nature of the firm, that is, platform companies profit from lower market costs and organize production efficiently.

it is open or closed, as long as it can steadily generate value and reduce mobility risk, it is worth investing and expanding. Openness provides the Internet with low-cost productive resources and an expanding consumer base, and is beginning to show powerful scale effects. How to stabilize the source of productive resources and attract more consumers on a sustainable basis will be an important impetus for the Internet to move toward closedness.

8.2.3 Control and closedness of digital architecture

According to the original ideology of openness, it seems to imply that the Internet is going closed if people cannot be successfully connected through the network. However, this notion clearly ignores the cost of action in the real world. It has been observed that as platform companies have become more sophisticated, especially in the mobile Internet phase, a significant number of APPs have tried to keep productive resources in the architectural space of their own, reluctant to allow them to flow across platforms and other competitors to take possible means to enter their own architecture. This trend allows us to imagine in an abstract sense that a number of closed architectures have begun to form in cyberspace, each of which is internally a marketplace that conforms to the logic of market value exchange. If resources in the architecture are moved to other markets once seduced by a third party, they would be regulated by the platform company. The result is a hybrid state that the architecture continues to open up and expand to more resources, but meanwhile maintains closed borders. Such process is very much close to "feudalization". This again shows that digital markets do not exist in a vacuum, but are constantly being shaped by external forces such as the state and platform companies. When platform companies need the market to function as a resource allocation mechanism, they work to enhance information disclosure and price transparency to facilitate transactions, while when they do not want large-scale resource flow away, they resort to coercive measures in law or technology to ensure that their space is not infringed upon.

The dynamics that have shaped this state of affairs are multifaceted and have intensified along with the growing maturity of the platform economy. First, in order to reduce transaction costs and enable the orderly flow of resources, large platform companies have the ability to develop infrastructural services (for instance, payment, logistics, scoring, authentication, dispute resolution, and so on) embedded in their own markets, which in traditional markets are often invested in by the state. These infrastructures can be more effective in realizing safe and convenient transactions in digital markets, and thus hope to capture the long-term and stable value of resources. Second, platform companies continue to absorb new types of services through expanding practices like corporate mergers and third-party account login, enabling multi-sided market with the aim of creating multiple possibilities within the architectural space, so as to constantly push producers and consumers to change their behaviors and preferences so that the production process can be sustained. Meanwhile, such strategy can also be seen as a defensive substitutable service against competitors. If platform companies are unable to reduce transaction costs in a short period of time, they will need to rely on secondary or tertiary agents in the marketplace (for instance, broker agencies) to help aggregate resources and form a new type of industrial chain. Third, platform companies' inputs, including infrastructure establishment, actually help increase the value of resources because of their credibility and transaction stability, thus creating a competitive advantage over small- and medium-sized platforms. As traditional locally formed economic transaction networks are small and fragile, the denser and more robust networks formed by large platforms will gradually absorb the former. Even as production becomes smarter and human production begins to be replaced by machinery mass production, this logic will remain unchanged. Large and closed platforms may still have a competitive advantage in the future.

Nowadays, it is not difficult to see that the basic model of the digital economy is to promote the mobility of all kinds of resources through productive organizations such as platform, and to take effective measures to reduce the risk of mobility. In less risky scenarios, power of control by platform has not been revealed, and therefore more able to show its openness, while in more risky scenarios, the platform needs to invest more in the construction of digital infrastructure to increase the constraints and control of the resources with both hard and soft measures. Morphologically, it looks much closer to the organizational and managing process of employees by a traditional company.[12] The more obvious manifestation of the open/closed process of network architecture is the contemporary adoption of self-preferencing and blocking of services by third-party competitors, which are not necessarily related to monopoly status. Upon careful consideration of the logic behind these anti-mobility behaviors, it is easy to identify that they all aim to inhibit the flow of resources across platforms, preventing producers on other competing platforms from unauthorized connecting with consumers within their own platforms.

Under the influence of digital economy business model, even the original open distributed technologies may be applied to the closed practices of the platform. Under the original open architecture, distributed technologies were thought to be associated with autonomous mass participation and claimed to enhance abstract social trust (for instance, blockchain technology is pure trust in mathematics). However, the platform model is perfectly capable of absorbing such distributed technologies. For instance, the platform could use blockchain as the underlying technology for the production process, enabling producers to make their production process more granular and quantifiable, while they can still take established business measures to encourage production and enhance resource matching. In this sense, the technical mechanism of distributed ledger will not affect the practice of closing architecture. The question of centralization or not is more about the relationship among resources within the market, a different way of allocating resources, and has no necessary relationship with the closedness of the architecture's boundaries.

12 A great deal of labor law research has focused on how the theory of subordination can be applied to the process of controlling workers on Internet platforms.

Closed architectures have reshaped transactional networks as well. The connection of productive resources is no longer a "link" to a web page as in the traditional desktop computer era, but a translation to a visual interface in an APP. Users are aware of the boundaries of ongoing activity through logging in and staying in that status. Once an operation function transcends the architecture of a given APP by jumping through to another, it often implies collaboration between the two platforms (for instance, open APIs with each other to share users' data). In contrast to the web-mediated connections of the desktop computer era, where the process of jumping from one web page to another could not be controlled or blocked by a specific website, nowadays it can be uniformly controlled by the platform companies through interfaces, thus highlighting the significance of link jumping. In addition, the ideal type of interconnection identified by the traditional concept of openness is to access web links through a browser, but the browser itself cannot mobilize the connection between web content and other software, which is still limited in terms of the breadth of services, while the current built-in app service actually provides more possibilities and facilitates more mobility, and it can be seen that the platform company itself is an integrative power engine that controls different sides of the market. The platform company itself can be seen as a holistic power engine controlling different sides of the market. Transactional and collaborative networks can thus be expanded through the continuous expansion of business and services by large platform companies, with the end result of bringing more and more users into cyberspace, but with a quality and depth of connectivity that far exceeds that of the early open Internet.

In summary, while openness remains a popular ideology, the closedness of architectural boundaries inevitably occurs as the production of digital platforms continues to involve all kinds of complex production and social relations in the architecture. This closedness not only continues to accompany the expansion of the architecture (and thus remains open), but also occurs simultaneously at different levels of visibility—the limited mobility of market resources, the internalization of network connections, the continuous tracking through the consolidation of accounts, the constant extension of infrastructure, and so on. Of course, this process is not a smooth one, and in addition to political economy resources, it also needs to be supported by external law, which involves how the law responds to the open/closed process of the architecture.

8.3 How law responds to the open/closedness of architecture

8.3.1 Architecture as a new type of political–economic interest

Once the digital architecture is formed, it starts to develop a certain sense of autonomy and value, attempting to control the entire space in which the concrete architecture is formed and the holistic benefits brought about by the resources within the space. Although platform companies have the ability to adopt various means to protect such holistic interest, there is a greater need for legal recognition and protection, which can be divided into two dimensions: (1) legitimacy of mode of production and (2) protection of architectural interests. The former is even more crucial to the foundation of the digital economy as a whole. Historically, legislative and judicial activities have played a subordinate role, intentionally or unintentionally, in the rapid expansion of new mode of production, basically in line with the needs of the development of the digital economy.

In terms of the legitimacy of mode of production, the need for platform power and capital to be extended into various traditional industries and services requires the law to constantly recognize legal status (and the historical progressiveness of illicit emergence) in different areas. If licenses are required for entry into traditional areas, licenses are also required for emerging areas (for instance, Internet finance, online car rental), but in general, the state has gradually realized that digital platforms can unleash greater productivity, and that economies of scale and monopolistic effects of the rich getting richer can in fact help to make the cake bigger and accelerate the economic cycle. Under the influence of policies such as "Internet Plus" policy, the legitimacy of the digital economy has gradually been established and consolidated, and has not been hindered by social skepticism (or "digital Luddism"). At the same time, the ideology of innovation and openness has been sustained by the fact that the State as a whole has adopted an experimental approach to observing the operation of different specific types of business, and has called a halt to or clamped down on specific areas in a timely manner.

In terms of the protection of architectural interests, platform companies need to construct a set of abstract emergent interests that need to be continuously protected by the law in various sectors. Such interests are further manifested in two kinds of relationships, one between the architecture and the productive resources active within the architecture, and the other between the architectures. The former manifests itself primarily in the need for architectures to maintain a state of flexible mobility within themselves in order to maximize the value and possibilities of their resources and enable more connectivity, and therefore maintain only a loose relationship of cooperation or software use in their legal relationships; the latter manifests itself primarily in the relationship of unfair competition against architectures attempting to enter into each other's access to resource resources. Due to the nature of the digital economy, illegal practices increasingly continue to occur with small- and medium-sized platform entrepreneurs, which has pushed established and stable platform companies to take measures to protect their own architectures from infringement, as well as to gradually clarify their boundaries legally and technically, which inevitably leads to a further closedness of the architectural space.

8.3.2 Examples of legal responses

Indeed, legislation and justice have responded to the special interests and closedness of architecture in a number of areas, namely, establishing the legitimacy of architectural interests and resolving conflicts of interest between architectural firms and other firms or industries. Specifically on the topic of openness/closedness, which manifests itself in these three dimensions, namely, (1) mobility and efficiency, (2) competitive order, and (3) security, the following are brief illustrative samples of how the law has confronted and resolved these issues in China.

First, as far as mobility and efficiency are concerned, it needs to be legally recognized that users, who ostensibly have a position of autonomy of choice in cyberspace (such as the right to consumer autonomy, the right to be informed, the right to fair deal), do not in reality possess any stable productive resources, and the whole architecture is only of use to the user. This not only ensures that a large amount of flexible virtual work will continue to generate value, but also reduces the platform's liability. Creating such access treats the architecture as a large database service, where users are granted different permissions under different conditions, but are not able to make changes to the software or interface as they see fit. Users are included in the platform's continuous tracking and become one side of a multilateral marketplace, where personal information continues to be utilized even after de-identification or anonymization, and algorithmic recommendations continue to be fed into individual account interfaces. The consumer and labor groups are bound to the same production chain, and the game of interests between them becomes clearer. Especially when the consumer welfare ideology prevails, the laborers can only accept a non-labor-relationship work status. The key question is how to rationalize the distribution of value between the two groups when the consumers themselves may also become producers or reproducers in a circular economy.

Second, as far as the competing order is concerned, architectural rights of platforms have received a great deal of legal recognition as a conceptual core interest, as reflected in many unfair competition cases and formal rules that the architectural space and the market resources within it may not be infringed upon arbitrarily without authorization. The law simply needs to dynamically recognize external architectural property rights encompassing all resources, without granting rights separately to the resources within the architecture, because rights are only one way (and not necessarily the best) of realizing the value of the market resources, and the autonomy of the platform companies allows them to use a combination of means to uncover data from the resources, reserving sufficient space for testing and trying. The biggest contribution of competition law in China to the legitimacy of architectural rights is the recognition of the ubiquitous nature of competitive relationships, which makes any subject's attempt to use resources within the architecture of a particular platform (for instance, the act of obtaining more information about consumers is considered traffic hijacking, and the act of obtaining more free and public content is considered inappropriate creeping) likely to be considered as unfair competition. This makes Article 2 of the *Anti-Unfair Competition Law* the most easily abused Principle Clause. In addition, given the expansive character of the platform economy, antitrust law and its doctrines themselves have been of lesser importance over the past decade or so, until the state began to oppose the uncontrolled expansion of capital in the late 2020s and strengthened antitrust regulation of the platform economy. However, this is also mainly reflected in the negative externalities of operator concentration brought about by the entry of capital into finance, media, technology, and so on, which may impact on the formal power of the state, and the platform economy model is not completely denied at the moment, so the expansion and closedness of the architectural space can be expected to continue.

Third, as far as the security order is concerned, the autonomy of platform companies is also prone to be amplified and strengthened, mainly because the state needs platform companies to constantly assume the subjective responsibility for helping to manage the various types of abnormal behaviors within the market, as well as the responsibility for cybersecurity. The platform companies also have the incentive to build the infrastructure to effectively organize and manage their production in accordance with the security issue.[13] Whether agreed upon through user agreements or enforced through platform rules, the market and social power of platforms is rarely subject to direct administrative and judicial constraints, and this is essentially reflected in the large amount of anti-mobility behaviors of blocking and self-preferential treatment of competitors, which the law has not yet delved into centralized review of such issues. Some rights that are intended to enhance user autonomy such as the transfer of personal information also tend not to be prioritized as a topic in the name of security, unless they lead to a mobility dividend.

All of the above examples illustrate how law, as a superstructure, concretely reflects changes in the mode of economic production, and thus objectively contributes to the continuing open/closed process of the Internet architecture in a unique way. However, this is not to say that the Internet can only evolve along its current sole path toward a completely feudalized territory, and that we can explore possible future breakthroughs from the logic of the networked economy itself, in terms of mobility and infrastructural considerations. This is also not to say that the rules as a superstructure have not attempted to constrain the power of the platforms and balance the different values and choices of consumers, producers, and various other interest groups in society, but rather to point out empirically how the interests of this architectural space have gradually accumulated and formed, and ultimately become unshakeable for the moment.

8.4 Interconnection and interoperation among architectures

As mentioned earlier, the move toward a closed digital architecture did not happen overnight and has largely satisfied consumer demand, increased labor supply, and done everything possible to drive prevalence within the architecture. This process increases the value of the network as a whole, meanwhile subject to relevant state regulatory requirements. As network effects intensify and large platform capital continues to move into more areas, the current deadlock lies in how to make sure

13 For instance, the State Administration for Market Supervision issued the *Guidelines for the Implementation of Main Responsibilities of Internet Platforms* (Draft for Opinion), which puts forward meticulous requirements for mega platforms from nine perspectives, including demonstration of fair competition, equal governance, open ecology, data management, internal governance, risk assessment, risk prevention, security audit, and promotion of innovation. The *Guidelines on Classification and Rating of Internet Platforms* (Draft) released at the same time, on the other hand, grades the platforms, categorizing them into super platforms, large platforms, and small- and medium-sized platforms on the basis of four indicators, namely, the scale of users, the types of business, the economic volume, and the ability to restrict.

at a macro-level that the expanding giant platform architecture will not discourage more emerging platform companies from innovating and competing, as well as how to allow for the mutual sharing of data traffic and services between different ecosystems. In other words, if the architecture of giant platforms has become a potential impediment to innovation and competition, how to maintain their dynamic competitiveness while also being able to promote more cross-platform flows of resources in general.

In the second half of 2021, the State Administration for Market Supervision issued the *Provisions on Prohibition of Unfair Competitive Behavior on the Internet (Draft for Public Comments)*, which intends to prohibit platform companies from "blocking, intercepting, modifying, shutting down, uninstalling, hindering the download, installation, operation, upgrading, forwarding and dissemination of online products or services lawfully provided by other operators and so on, without justifiable reasons". In the subsequent special action of the Ministry of Industry and Information Technology, some of the giant platform companies have also been asked to mutually lift the blocking links as soon as possible, allowing the service content of competing platforms to be opened through the built-in relevant links within the architecture. These measures are widely interpreted as promoting the interconnection of digital platforms, but for the time being, the focus is still mainly on the mandatory data traffic sharing between certain giant platform companies (like Taobao and Byte Dance), for other small- and medium-sized platforms to be able to access traffic on an equal footing remains to be seen. In this sense, the current interconnection policy cannot be limited to exchanging data traffic only, because any traffic has a price and needs to be negotiated among platform companies for better cooperation. Administrative mandatory requirement is not able to last long. If we still wish to play the fundamental role of the market in resource allocation, we need to recognize that the possible ideas lie in the interconnection market itself.

In terms of the path of the Internet's evolution in China, architectural and platform power shaped the digital market, allowing market forces to play a role in cyberspace. Once competition becomes more intense and illegal rise persists, keeping it open in a closed manner becomes the optimal strategy for architectural expansion, and the established market infrastructure plays an important function in privately facilitating the expansion of the market, as Chapter 3 describes. The difficulty of defining the relevant markets precisely in law and economics prevents us from further analyzing infrastructure's externalities. If we want to promote market connectivity, the concept of market should be adopted in the sense of competition law rather than the narrow relevant market in the sense of antitrust law, that is, to view the market as a whole space full of unlimited competition. The architecture itself is the marketplace. Within this overall space, there may be one single market, as well as two-sided or multi-sided markets, and if efforts to assess cross-network externalities are costly, the specifics can be set aside in the first instance, and instead the market can be viewed as a whole that is controlled by the platform companies, and all that needs to be done is to open up the closed architectural space and facilitate the cross-platform flow of market resources from the perspective of regulating the market infrastructure.

Promoting the flow of resources can be done in a number of ways—for instance, through the transfer of personal data in accordance with the provisions of the *Personal Information Protection Law*, through the trading of flows of enterprise data, through the opening of mutual access through API interfaces, through the promotion of trading of data service analysis, and so on. The problem is that, in order for these market resources to be effectively transferred, many supporting infrastructure functions must be utilized to help effectively enhance the value of the resources, otherwise platforms with sound private infrastructure will still have sufficient leverage to control the traffic, thus fundamentally involving the issue of infrastructure interconnectivity, which is key to architecture interconnectivity.

As mentioned earlier, the paradox of digital market infrastructures is that they help to increase the value of resources and the speed of matching flows in the early stages of their establishment, but as the amount of market resources increases, the improvement of the infrastructure instead becomes a sort of anti-mobility mechanism, which can potentially limit the flow of resources and the access to better trading opportunities on other platforms. The important question is therefore how to raise the standard of the market as a whole through infrastructure interconnectivity, thus enabling other smaller markets to access more quality resources while remaining independent. The extension of infrastructure can be done in two ways: One is to turn headline companies into essential facilities that are subject to unified regulation, so that more users can have access to them; the other is to try to break down the space of different architectures, and have external legal and regulatory forces gradually unify the infrastructures that are dispersed within different architectures. China has now accumulated some experience in the second type of path, and specifically, general digital market infrastructure used to be categorized into four main types of models as follows.

The first type of model requires digital platform databases to be gradually docked and opened to the national unified database without discrimination, which mainly involves authentication and dispute resolution functions. For instance, in accordance with the requirements of the *E-Commerce Law*, all platforms have equal access to ID card or e-license databases; or local courts are required to improve the relevant e-litigation platforms, so that evidence on the platform companies can be retained through blockchain and other technological measures to facilitate the cheap flow of evidence. Local governments are also inclined to promote public services through private infrastructure, so that public services and private platforms are more closely integrated. For instance, some public services are provided directly through enterprise platform channels (for instance, Health QR code in public health events, bill payment services, and so on).

The second type of model is licensing, on the basis of which the central regulator takes the lead in mandating interconnection of digital infrastructure operators with specific licenses, which mainly involves payment and credit collection functions in financial issues. For instance, the "Credit Union" requires the establishment of a joint venture company to share personal credit information, unify credit standards and scores, and facilitate mobility among several huge platforms; the "Network Union" also requires the strengthening of supervision of third-party payment clearing activities in the name of a joint venture company, and dynamically grasps the payment and financial services of large payment companies. Although the operation of the "Credit Union" is not working perfectly at present, in the long run, it could be a path that retains the autonomous status of large-scale platform companies while strengthening infrastructure construction through centralized authority.

The third type of model is to require the neutrality of the infrastructure of large platforms through specific regulatory measures, which mainly relate to logistics services and automated recommendation services. Such services are required, for instance, to treat all merchants and consumers on the platform equally and not to discriminate on the basis of the distinction between self-operated and third party-operated.

The fourth type of model is the more traditional mandatory sharing of physical infrastructure and unified national planning to prevent blind and repetitive construction. For instance, in 2014, the three major telecommunication carriers jointly established the China Tower company, realizing the sharing of resources within the industry, and they are not allowed to establish mobile terminal base stations on their own.

Following the above approaches, attempts can be made to gradually promote the connectivity of some existing digital infrastructure services. For instance, the first is trusted account connectivity, whereby the state strengthens the authentication of real identities of various types of accounts, allowing users to log into different platforms with a unified identity to carry out activities, in which the exchange and value-added of account behavior data can occur. The second is payment method connectivity, namely, the state promotes various payment methods, including UnionPay, to enter different ecosystems, allowing consumers to independently choose different payment channels and financial services. Finally, it is the connection of reputational and evaluative information, namely, the assessment of the value of productive resources that needs to be standardized in many scenarios. Just as the traditional price of goods reflects their value, the assessment of labor in the digital market also needs to be standardized, thus helping the resources to maintain a certain degree of market value and competitiveness during the transmission among platforms, which will lead to more platforms to benefit from such mobility.

8.5 Conclusion

This chapter is essentially an examination of the evolution of a new mode of production and its externalities, as well as a brief explanation of how a simple information system can be transformed into a larger complex system. Law, as a superstructure, undoubtedly contributes to this process by helping to achieve order and security in the digital marketplace and making the platform continually function as an effective connector to promote the effective utilization of productive resources. In this sense, the open/closed Internet discourse itself is only a superficial ideology that needs to be transformed into one more substantial issue, namely, the dynamics of the aggregation and dispersion of productive resources that accompany new mode of production, and the kind of power that can play a role within such process.

We want a safe and reliable Internet. We might also want digital commons that is full of innovation and competition and offers a wide range of possibilities. The value of taking into account and balancing the tensions between the two lies in the mobility of the resources that the Internet encountered in the very beginning. We need to think about how to gradually drive all kinds of resources through the extension of the infrastructure to enhance the value of the entire cyberspace. If the policy measures are appropriate, productive resources will be a process of continuous recombination of flow, and ultimately break the invisible boundaries of various existing architectures to form a unified cyberspace. The claim of interconnectivity has helped advance our understanding of the open/closed problem of the Internet. If we are not simply entangled in ideas and semantics, we need to recognize that true connectivity should always revolve around the mobility of productive resources and the extension of infrastructure. The network is no longer a mere pipeline, but a linkage of value. The digital commons, if it needs to further enhance its value, will require the continuous advancement of infrastructure to help absorb more market resources to generate new connections and transactions.

9 Is China's digital commons unique?

9.1 Introduction

So far, this book has broadly established a theoretical framework for observing the formation and governance of digital commons based on China's Internet development experience. Starting from the illegal rise of the digital commons, the framework discusses how the establishment of these legal and technological mechanisms facilitates the flow and integration of productive resources and generates significant scale value, based on the dimensions of changing mode of production, platform organization, networked connectivity, the public nature of resources, and digital infrastructure. In particular, the digital commons have been able to expand rapidly in conjunction with market mechanisms, which is a new phenomenon compared to traditional commons. Another indispensable part of the framework is the external environment in which large platforms survive, that is, how to deal with the relationship with different levels of government, which is crucial for the formation of a stable mode of production. Digital modes of production and business models, driven by private forces, are conducive to the formation and expansion of the digital commons. The paradoxical problem involved is that economic and competitive dynamics can limit interconnectivity while expanding the productive space, leading to the feudalization and closeness of cyberspace, whereby a number of large-scale Internet platforms form a technology and productive system built around themselves. Platform competition then becomes competition between ecosystems. From an economic point of view, this oligarchic network economy seems to be efficient: for central government, the outsourcing system can reduce regulatory costs and enable regulators to focus limited regulatory resources on issues in specific areas, while giving a certain degree of autonomy to giant platforms and allowing them to self-regulate during the process of expansion, which in turn facilitates the formation of networked mode of production, balancing security and development, order and innovation, and production and distribution.

In this sense, the analytical framework established in this book is both descriptive and normative. The effectiveness of this framework is demonstrated by the fact that China has been able to establish a system that fully integrates and utilizes digital resources in a short period of time. The internal logic lies first in the democratization of production allowed first through decentralized end-use technology, which drives productive capacity and scale effects; and then in the integration of

DOI: 10.4324/9781003566243-10

decentralized productive capacity through information, which drives value creation. In this process, until the digital mode of production has stabilized over almost 20 years, the law has played a supporting and complementary role.

This theoretical framework can be used not only to observe China's Internet development, but also, to some extent, to understand Internet governance and digital commons issues in jurisdictions with strong infrastructures, such as the European Union and the United States, and in particular to understand the proper role the law has actually played in the emergence of the Internet. On the surface, it appears that China, like the EU, is a statutory law country. Given China's long history of learning civil law doctrines (first in civil law discipline, later expanding into legal departments such as criminal law and constitutional law) from regions including Germany and Japan, fidelity to a systematic rules-based mindset would seem to lead us to conclude that China is more inclined to regulate the Internet with a belief in statute laws, as the EU has set the example. Curiously, however, the Chinese governance model is in many cases closer to that of the United States, namely, allowing nationally unified digital platforms that transcend territorial jurisdiction to operate with market mechanisms that promote factor mobility. In one sense, the Chinese digital commons model is more like a synthesis of the European and American models; as stated in platform subcontract theory, the state regulates digital market behavior through statutory law in some areas and deregulates in others.

In Anu Bradford's recent book *Digital Empires: The Global Battle to Regulate Technology*,[1] the author presents the United States, China, and the European Union as the digital age's new empires, each with its unique ideological governance model and the drive to extend it globally. These empires have distinct approaches to digital governance: (1) US Market-Driven Model: Rooted in a belief that government regulation can hinder innovation and economic growth, this model prioritizes freedom of speech, Internet freedom, and fostering innovation. (2) Chinese State-Driven Model: This model emphasizes "command and control", aiming to promote economic growth while prioritizing social control over individual rights. (3) EU Rights-Based Model: Based on digital citizenship and human rights, this model seeks to maximize the protection of EU citizens' fundamental rights, balancing government's role in promoting the economy with safeguarding individual liberties. Bradford also analyzes the vertical decentralization between states and platform firms, exploring how digital empires regulate these firms and engage in imperial competition through them. This chapter agrees with the author to a certain extent while seeking to retell the story under the theoretical framework of this book, seeing the broad explanatory power of this framework.

1 Anu Bradford, *Digital Empires: The Global Battle to Regulate Technology*, Oxford University Press, 2023.

9.2 Appropriate place for legal intervention in common

Large jurisdictions always encounter common issues to build flourishing digital commons, like data, personal information, property, antitrust, and market order. In the face of a technological system, the first thing the law needs to determine is whether it is an independent technological tool and object or a set of modes of production. If it represents a mode of production, we have seen that society gradually embeds refined norms of behavior in the productive process based on the acceptance of this mode of production and the legitimacy hereafter, which implies recognition by the legislator. The consequence of this process is that while state sovereignty covers the cyberspace, the law tends to see it as a space dominated by platform companies rather than as a market and social process in which multiple interests are involved. On the one hand, it gradually increases the responsibility of the platform companies as a whole to be the main actors; on the other hand, it strengthens the protection of property rights in the architectural space shaped by platform companies that provide support to the digital infrastructures. At least until the year 2020, a continuous extension of the territory of large digital platforms can be observed, with a considerable number of public policies favoring this trend, culminating in the basic order of digital production seen so far (expansion and self-regulation of large platforms), as well as in disorder at the margins (persistent unfair competition due to the illegal rise).

Within this productive order, new legal norms are emerging in the form of general and special laws in the areas of property, copyright, privacy, labor, competition, monopoly, crime, trade, and so on. Either reflecting the emergence of new types of behavior of social subjects or responding to the need to protect the interests of platform companies in relation to architectural space, these norms isolate a static view of the rights and obligations of social subjects and less directly look at the dynamics of mode of production. Thus, these norms appear to be a semantic continuation of a semantic interpretation of legal doctrines. For instance, in the discussion of gig labor, the issue of concern for legal studies is often how to rationally set the standards of labor relations, as if it is enough to perfectly classify them in legislation. Such way of thinking fails to see changes in reality are forever breaking through established norms. It also focuses solely on how to increase compensation for workers from the perspective of the enterprise, say, by requiring more rest time, upgrading management, and so on.

The problem, however, is that digital platforms are not only entrepreneurially oriented, but also constitute a marketplace. Research has found early on that digital platforms combine the duality of enterprise and market, and different perspectives have led to different legal policies. For instance, the long-standing regulatory thinking on digital platforms has been to treat them as mere enterprises to be regulated, with territorial administrative obligations. According to this line of thinking, platforms occur in response to the mobility of productive resources and to a certain extent facilitate the orderly production of resources, a process that is realized through the exercise of management rights as well as the process of productive organization by the platforms. Platforms are therefore more closed to enterprises controlling the entire process of production. Digital platforms build their own infrastructures if the law lags behind in a relative way. This has led especially large platforms to view self-regulation as superior to direct government regulation, which has given rise to a sort of abstract architectural entitlement that views the ecosystem created by the platform as a space controlled only by the platform company, ultimately ending up in protecting platform as a whole. However, once one recognizes the productive nature of technological systems and looks at the problem from a more systematic perspective, one would realize that the law needs to constrain not only enterprises, but also markets; not only the closed markets formed by specific platforms, but also the need to pay attention to the wider unified markets constituted by different platforms. Platforms represent only a two-sided market model, not a particular enterprise *per se*. Therefore, they can cover a number of relationships formed by various productive resources. The counter-flow mechanisms created by large platforms are not conducive to the realization of a unified market and full resource competition. There is a need to move beyond the idea of mere firms and try to discuss technological systems in terms of market mechanisms.

Once one thinks in terms of the market, one realizes that contemporary laws and policies are in fact advancing slowly along these lines. First, unfair competition in the digital market is constantly changing and increasing due to the intrinsic requirements of start-ups for productive resources, and relying on some principle-based rules. The limited judicial capacity cannot form a uniform and effective deterrent, and can only be relied on to carry out special remediation by administrative power.

Second, it was not until the second half of 2020 that the Chinese state began to pay systematic attention to the uncontrolled expansion of capital in the digital economy in particular, but the state paid more attention to the financial power issues involved and media power issues rather than the general abuse of market dominance. Third, judicial practice, both in competition and antitrust law, also tends to view the digital economy at a holistic level, whereby platforms compete with other platforms on a single service and together belong to the same market. However, the popular ideological discursive strategy remains that platforms are technology-neutral software tools when they need to mitigate their own liability; when they need the state to provide protection or minimize intervention, they argue for a matter of architectural rights and autonomy of enterprises; but when they need to attract market resources, they become public infrastructures. The shift in discourse does not contribute to a complete understanding of digital platforms.

The idea of regulating the unified digital market can go beyond the traditional regulation centered on platform companies, not only avoiding the problem of public power interfering with the autonomous right of enterprises to operate, but also better smoothing the relationship between productive resources and platforms. According to this line of thinking, to solve the new form of employment and labor issues can not only be entangled in the legal nature of the form of labor, but also need to think about how to make use of the market mechanism more fully from the logic of the operation of the entire market, So we need to focus more on the free flow of resources and production-oriented process, so as to ensure resources are under the condition of safe and orderly flow following with the expansion of market scope. We also need to increase more opportunities for cooperation in the transaction, which is the original impetus for the emergence of the Internet, and continue to make the pie bigger. Digital platforms that are gradually moving toward closure have departed from this vision.

There are several legal and policy approaches for market-centered thinking among China, EU, and the United States. The first is to focus on empowerment at the individual level of resources, for instance, either granting individuals property rights or portability rights to personal information, or allowing individual users to authorize third-party subjects as agents to carry for them, or having platform companies take on an overall proposed fiduciary obligation to the data. However, it can also have some problems: (1) The scope of valuable personal information is in fact not broad. Neither the property right nor the right of portability can cover the de-identified or anonymized information produced by users through their accounts, and thus the effect is limited; (2) whether users use such a right to bargain with the platform or allow third parties to capture their information will easily disrupt the existing productive order and create a tragedy of the anti-commons; (3) even if the transferable data resources are of a certain scale, the market structure may not be favorable to small and medium-sized platform companies because they lack the infrastructure services to control the resources, thus resulting in further concentration of data; (4) the subject of the data trust is too broad and the rules of prohibition of conflict of interest in the duty of fidelity cannot be applied to free charge digital market, thus failing to solve the Internet platform's conflict of interest problem.

The second is to promote public supply of productive resources through state power to attract social resources. For instance, providing public data through state-owned enterprises and local governments to guide data transactions with private platforms; or levying taxes on specific data resources to improve development or circulation. But the question is whether such mechanisms can actually sustainably leverage social data resources, and the data price formation mechanism remains to be seen.

The third approach is to restrain the unfair competitive behavior of enterprises from the market perspective, such as banning "choosing one from two", exclusive copyright agreements, self-preferencing, and reducing the degree of dependence of workers on platforms and the cost of cross-platform mobility.

The last approach is to strengthen digital infrastructure and promote interconnectivity and publicity, especially extending infrastructure services between different platform markets, including sharing and standardization of identity authentication, third-party payment, credit data, and labor evaluation data, so as to facilitate the flow of resources instead of fragmentation. In the era of digital economy, a considerable number of social subjects may be constantly faced with the problem of cross-platform mobility and work. Therefore, from the perspective of labor protection, there is a need for the recording and sharing of a minimum amount of labor data between platforms so as to strengthen the authentication and protection of workers.

9.3 The EU and rights-based governance

The European Union, as a political and economic union of global significance, has always paid great attention to and actively participated in Internet governance. The EU is well aware of the importance of Internet governance, which is related to the protection of citizens' rights and interests, fair competition in the market, as well as social stability and security. Therefore, the EU is committed to formulating and implementing a series of laws and regulations to regulate Internet behavior, safeguard the rights and interests of users, and promote the sustainable development of the Internet. The logic of the EU's Internet governance is multilevel and multidimensional, which reflects the EU's comprehensive consideration and long-term planning in dealing with the challenges of the Internet, mainly including the following dimensions.

Maintaining freedom and order. In the age of Internet, free flow of information is crucial. The EU is well aware of this and therefore has always made the preservation of the free flow of information one of its core principles when governing the Internet. However, this does not mean laissez-faire. The EU also emphasizes the need to safeguard freedom while maintaining order and security on the Internet. This implies the need to properly regulate Internet content, combat cybercrime, and protect citizens from cyberthreats.

Promoting fairness and transparency. The rapid development of the Internet has brought about fierce competition in the market, but it may also lead to unfairness and lack of transparency in the market. In governing the Internet, the EU focuses on protecting fair competition in the market and preventing monopolization and unfair competition. By enacting relevant regulations, the EU has ensured the transparency and fairness of the Internet market and provided users with a more just and credible online environment.

Protecting the rights and interests of users. Users are the cornerstone of Internet development. In governing the Internet, the EU has always given top priority to safeguarding the rights and interests of users. This includes the protection of users' right to privacy, data security, and freedom of expression. By formulating strict laws and regulations, the EU requires Internet enterprises to comply with relevant regulations to ensure that the security and privacy of user data are not violated. At the same time, the EU is also committed to providing users with more convenient and efficient network services and enhancing the user experience.

Strengthening international cooperation. The global nature of the Internet makes it difficult for individual countries to govern it. The European Union is well aware of this, and therefore actively advocates and promotes international cooperation to jointly address the global challenges posed by the Internet. Through cooperation with other countries and regions, the EU is working together to combat transnational cybercrime, share cybersecurity information and technology, and jointly promote the healthy development of the Internet.

Compared to China's short period of Internet rule of law construction, the EU's Internet legislation is more continuous, so it is easier to absorb disruptive "illegal rise" into the existing legal system and ensure that Internet platforms accept the rules of traditional production organizations and relevant interest groups, thus limiting to a certain extent the expansion of digital platforms. Expansion of digital platforms is thus limited to a certain extent. First, from the perspective of market elements, the *General Data Protection Regulation* (GDPR), which was formally implemented in 2018, is an important law in the EU in the field of data protection. The GDPR stipulates the principles and obligations that businesses and organizations must follow when processing personal data, including the principle of data protection, the principle of data minimization, and the principle of transparency. In addition, the GDPR gives individuals more control over their own data, such as the right to access, the right to rectify, and the right to erasure. The implementation of this regulation has greatly strengthened the EU's efforts in data protection, providing users with more comprehensive and effective data protection. Second, from the perspective of digital market development, in order to maintain fair competition in the Internet market, the EU has revised and improved the *Unfair Competition Law*. The Act provides for a series of prohibited behaviors, such as misleading publicity and defamation of competitors. Meanwhile, the EU has also strengthened its supervision of the Internet market and cracked down on illegal behaviors. These measures have effectively curbed the occurrence of unfair competition and provided a strong guarantee for the healthy development of the Internet market. The *Digital Services Act* and the *Digital Market Act*, which the EU has been actively promoting the formulation of recently, are both aimed at further regulating the behavior of Internet platforms and safeguarding the rights and interests of users and fair competition in the market. Third, from the perspective of digital security, in the face of increasingly serious cybersecurity threats, the EU released the EU Cybersecurity Strategy in 2013. The Strategy specifies the EU's goals in cybersecurity, including raising awareness of cybersecurity, strengthening the protection of critical information infrastructure, and combating cybercrime. In order to realize these goals, the EU has formulated a series of specific measures, such as establishing a cybersecurity information-sharing platform and strengthening cybersecurity technology research and development. While protecting its own data security, the EU also supports cross-border data flows to promote the development of the global digital economy. By establishing data protection agreements with its partners, the EU seeks to realize the free flow of data under the premise of safeguarding data security. Finally, from the data sovereignty dimension, the EU is also actively seeking to establish its own data infrastructure to reduce its dependence on external data services, including 5G networks and fiber optic networks, to ensure the stable operation of digital services. In addition, the EU supports the development of new digital infrastructure such as edge computing and cloud computing. The EU enhances its competitiveness in key technology areas by investing in R&D and innovation. For example, the EU has launched the "European Horizon" program, which aims to support research and development of cutting-edge technologies to enhance Europe's digital innovation capacity.

As a result, the overall Internet governance legal mechanism of the EU is characterized by the following: First, the EU emphasizes the maintenance of freedom and order, and ensures the free flow of information on the Internet through the enactment of relevant regulations and policies, while at the same time cracking down on cybercrime and protecting its citizens from cyberthreats. Protection based on human rights values and traditional industries is one of the most distinctive features of the EU's digital legislation, which, to a certain extent, raises the cost of digital platforms and explains why world-class large-scale Internet platforms cannot emerge in EU. The EU still adheres to a more traditional conception of the digital commons and wants to limit the impact of large Internet platforms on civil society. Second, the EU focuses on promoting fairness and transparency by strengthening market regulation through a "gatekeeper" mechanism to ensure fair competition in the Internet market and prevent monopolization and unfair competition. This demonstrates the special relationship between the EU and large Internet platforms originating from the United States. Namely, the EU often strengthens its own authority through antitrust and other regulations, but at the same time it is unable to leave the services provided by these platforms. Third, the EU has always prioritized the protection of users' rights and interests, and through the enactment of strict laws and regulations, Internet companies are required to comply with the relevant regulations to ensure that the security and privacy of users' data are not infringed upon. This means that large platforms are unable to mobilize productive resources at will by shifting their business models, and the issue of data ownership is replaced by strong individual control. Rapidly updating technology also poses a huge challenge to governance in the EU. In addition, Internet technologies and business models are being updated at a very fast pace, which makes it difficult for existing laws and regulations to adapt to the new situation.

9.4 US and market-based governance

The United States, as the birthplace of the Internet and one of the most developed countries in the global Internet industry, has explored and practiced Internet governance with far-reaching significance. The logic of Internet governance in the United States is based on a series of core principles, which reflect the basic thinking and value orientation of the US government in addressing the challenges of the Internet, and are mainly characterized by the following features.

Pluralistic co-governance and market power: The Internet governance system of the United States is characterized by pluralism. The government, enterprises, social organizations, and individuals participate together, forming a pattern of pluralistic co-governance guided by the government, led by enterprises, participated by society, and self-regulated by individuals. This governance pattern not only reflects the authority and guiding role of the government, but also fully stimulates the vitality of market players and social organizations.

Flexibility and innovation: Under the premise of following the basic legal principles, the Internet governance of the United States shows great flexibility and innovation. This governance can quickly adapt to the rapid development of Internet technology and market changes, and ensure that Internet governance is always synchronized with the times.

Individual freedom and privacy protection: US Internet governance attaches great importance to individual freedom and privacy protection. In legislation and practice, the United States has continued to strengthen the protection of personal information to ensure that the legitimate rights and interests of individuals are not infringed upon in the Internet age.

In the process of governing the Internet, the United States has continuously improved relevant laws and regulations to provide strong legal protection for the development of the Internet. First, on the issue of data ownership, the US law adopts the concept of "right to privacy", treating personal data as part of personal privacy for protection. For example, the *California Consumer Privacy Act* (CCPA) gives consumers the right to access, delete, and refuse to sell their personal information. Second, in terms of platform liability, US law adopts the "safe harbor" rule in terms of platform liability, namely, as long as the platform is not involved in or aware of the violation of the law, it should not be held liable for the behavior of its users. This principle is fully reflected in the *Communications Decency Act* (CDA) and the *Digital Millennium Copyright Act* (DMCA), and has been the core of promoting free flow of information on platforms. However, in recent years, as the scale and influence of platforms have increased, the United States has also begun to gradually strengthen the regulation of platform liability. For example, the *Social Media Transparency Act* requires platforms to disclose their content review policies and algorithmic decision-making processes to increase platform transparency and accountability. Third, from the perspective of digital infrastructure, US law has adopted a flexible and pragmatic approach to the management of Internet infrastructure. On the one hand, the government ensures the safe and reliable operation of the infrastructure by formulating relevant policies and regulations; on the other hand, the government encourages the private sector to participate in the construction and operation of the infrastructure in order to improve efficiency and innovation capacity. For example, the US Broadband Plan proposes specific measures to improve broadband infrastructure, including promoting competition and increasing investment. Fourth, net neutrality is one of the core principles in Internet governance, aiming to safeguard the openness and innovative vitality of the Internet. US law has gone through a long period of debate and exploration on this standing issue. In 2015, the US Federal Communications Commission (FCC) passed the *Open Internet Act*, which established the principle of net neutrality and required that Internet service providers not discriminate against or prioritize any type of traffic. However, this act was repealed by the FCC in 2017, sparking widespread controversy and discussion. In practice, issues such as how to effectively implement the net neutrality principle, prevent intervention by interest groups, and circumvent regulation still need to be explored in depth. Finally, in terms of market mechanisms, the US government encourages Internet platform enterprises to practice self-discipline and autonomy, and strengthens the construction of industry self-discipline and norms through industry associations and social organizations. These self-regulatory platforms have played an important role in formulating industry standards, regulating industry behavior and maintaining market order. At the same time, the US government has also been strengthening its supervision of Internet enterprises to ensure their compliance and healthy development.

Therefore, it is easy to see the characteristics of the United States' governance of the digital commons. First of all, the flexibility of the US common law ensured that the Internet was able to utilize all kinds of information resources to realize the "illegal rise" at an early stage, and even if there were marginal lawsuits, the court system as a whole did not have the ability to prevent the emergence of a new mode of production.[2] Second, the US legal system as a whole emphasizes the self-regulation of platform enterprises, encourages innovation in the industry, and applies competition and monopoly laws more loosely, which contributes to the rapid expansion of the digital market based on platform enterprises and the provision of services globally. Third, by providing tax incentives, financial support, and other policies, the US government encourages large technology enterprises to conduct R&D and innovation. At the same time, the government also establishes close cooperative relationships with technology enterprises through procurement and cooperative R&D to jointly promote technological development. In addition, science and technology enterprises tend to pursue free flow and open cooperation in the global market, while the US government may adopt protectionist measures due to national security considerations. Such differences have, to a certain extent, exacerbated conflicts and frictions between the two sides.

9.5 Concluding remarks

This chapter briefly extends the theoretical framework of the digital commons based on Chinese experience. In this framework, market infrastructure is the most critical component that can facilitate the orderly flow of factors and the formation of digital modes of production. In turn, the external legal system needs to ensure that digital platforms are sufficiently capable of driving this market building and that the law has the ability to intervene and regulate when it needs to be based on specific values. The interaction and different combinations of these components and laws then constitute the different models of Internet governance in China, the EU, and the United States (and even other countries). One of the value positions supported in this book is seen in the context of the overall historical development of human civilization, namely, that law and public policy must not be an impediment to digital transformation, and in particular to the formation of new mode of production. It is only by constantly adjusting the expectations of human beings

2 See Anupam Chander, "How Law Made Silicon Valley", *Emory Law Journal* 63 (2014), 677; Julie E. Cohen, *Between Truth and Power: The Legal Constructions of Informational Capitalism*, Yale University Press, 2019; Nanna Bonde Thylstrup, *The Politics of Mass Digitization*, MIT Press, 2019.

themselves in the midst of change and developing in tandem with technology that civilization can be pushed forward. In this process, even if there are marginal problems that are not in line with established values, they need to be resolved gradually once the mode of production has stabilized, which is one of the main criteria used in this book to measure the value of law as a superstructure.

Conclusion

In September 2020, *People Magazine* published a report "Takeaway Riders, Stuck in the System", which triggered widespread social concern about new employment forms of labor groups represented by takeaway riders and ride-hailing drivers. The story also caused publication of an official document, *the Guiding Opinions on Safeguarding the Rights and Interests of New Employment Forms of Workers in Labor Security,* jointly issued by the Ministry of Human Resources and Social Security and eight other ministries about one year later (hereinafter "*Guiding Opinions*"), which called for the effective safeguarding of the labor security rights and interests of workers in new employment forms and the promotion of the standardized, healthy, and sustainable development of the platform economy. It is worth noting that the story particularly emphasizes the importance of algorithms as a technological system and power in controlling the labor process of takeaway riders. This has also led to a discussion on the regulation of algorithms in society.

The relationship between technological systems and labor is somewhat reducible to the general problem of technological systems. Philosophy of technology tends to focus on the abstract ethical dimensions of technology, such as risk, safety, efficiency, responsibility, and fairness, whereas for social science, it may be more crucial to understand the internal mechanisms of system operation and the motivations of stakeholders' behaviors. A mature technological system may manifest itself only as a product at the microlevel, with little impact on the overall behavior and expectations of the members of the society; but it may also change the relationships between social agents, at the macro-level through the networked diffusion of technology. In the latter sense, law and public policy, as superstructure in society, will also gradually intervene to respond and adapt to new problems brought about by technological system, and ultimately guide the direction of its development. General information technology, typified by the Internet, is such a system that transcends the mere application of technology. It revolves around the production, dissemination, and use of information, relying on the model of creativity and open platforms to absorb all kinds of fragmented productive resources into the platform for recombination and matching, thus changing the relationship between productive resources and traditional productive organizations, and therefore directly or indirectly changing the relevant legal relations. The new employment pattern (or gig economy), as the latest form of digital economy, can demonstrate in a more

DOI: 10.4324/9781003566243-11

complete way how the law has been responding to problems that have arisen in the evolution of the technological system.

Although the digital economy has from the outset relied on the reintegration of all types of labor (and its outcomes), it is only after the shift from online content services to offline human labor that the use of flexible labor through software platforms has come to the forefront of society's attention. Different disciplines use the concept in different senses: in the vein of the political economy of communication, "labor" is used in a more generalized way ("digital labor" is not literally clear), and can refer to any act that arises within a given productive relation. Thus, it covers activities such as ad clicks and games. Similarly, economic analysis views human capital and other value-producing resources in a framework that is more rhetorical, such as data as labor. The legal and public policy perspective pays more attention to social common sense and established legal perceptions, namely, recognizing whether an activity is a legally protected form of labor through formal criteria (namely, a labor relationship resulting from the conclusion of a labor contract) and enhancing remedies and compensations *ex post* in single case through substantive criteria at the margin (namely, the "subordination" standard). However, both formal and substantive standards are constantly encountering changes in reality. For example, from a formal point of view, it is logically difficult to distinguish a video creator from a gig driver, although the latter is closer to our perception of labor (because of the existence of related industries), but there is no fundamental difference between the two through the software platform for the fragmented production of value, and both entered into with the platform is a user agreement rather than a labor contract. From a substantive point of view, subordination is not the only core element in determining labor relations. Some occupations that meet the criteria for subordination (for instance, civil servants) do not receive full and equal protection under labor law. The *ex post* determination of a labor relationship is merely a way for the court to help a particular worker obtain more interests in particular case. These tensions and logical conflicts suggest that there may not be a one-size-fits-all solution to an economic and social problem such as labor, but rather it needs to be viewed from different dimensions of the technological system.

This book focuses on productive mechanisms of digital commons in China, but there are many theoretical and practical issues that have not been fully discussed. First, the core issue of traditional cyberlaw has been to confirm the legitimacy of the digital economy's mode of production and to resolve the conflict of interests between the old and the new, focusing more on the process of production. With the increase of the digital economy's share in national general production, the goal of the next stage should be to focus more explicitly on the distribution and to deal with the relationship between digital production and distribution. Second, as digital platforms reshape the market and society, the two are deeply intertwined with each other, new forms of employment and labor can help us understand the different logics of the market and society in solving the same problem. Third, while the law is intervening in the technological system, the latter is also changing the former, and the fundamental change is not in the form of the organization of legal services such as the Internet Court, but rather the law needs to adjust itself according to the kind of imaginations of the technological system. If the law does not adapt in time to address new issues such as flexible labor, more effective governance solutions will be adopted by platforms.

It is also necessary to understand how information technology systems have evolved into full-fledged mode of production. From a discursive point of view, technological systems, in order to justify their superiority over traditional mode of production and hoping for special protection from the law, have continuously developed different ideological discourses in an attempt to lead to changes in legal responsibility and regulation. First, technological systems want the law to see them as merely independent and neutral instrumental objects (hardware or software), and therefore separate themselves from social contexts of production, without employer or managerial responsibilities. Second, even if a legal relationship exists between the technological tool and the user, it is a single relationship of service, which can be bound in advance by a consensual contract. Third, behind this loose legal form, technological systems can profit consistently without more direct productive responsibility by tracking the behavior of productive resources, controlling networks of connections and transactions, creating new demand, and enabling resource activities to achieve the productive goals. Finally, even when called to account for their actions, technological systems wish to particularize the object of their responsibility (for instance, automated algorithms) and thus cut themselves off from the potential role of the mode of production.

While the above rhetoric is often very persuasive and can help to obscure the essence of technological systems as a set of productive methods, the reality of the practice is often quite the opposite. First, the development of "free" business models through the commodification process of incorporating various productive resources into the virtual world lays the groundwork for the free production of the masses for the platforms. Second, the technological system is not a neutral and unified technological facility as imagined, but a competing marketplace composed of a number of self-interested digital platforms, each of which constitutes a market/society with boundaries of power, moving from openness to closure through the spatial construction of interests, (such as "architecture"). Third, technological systems cannot grow and develop without traditional productive organizations and networks: Early technological systems obtained their original productive resources from traditional industries at low cost through "illegal rise". The sharing economy is in fact sustained by taking advantage of social security provided by traditional social networks, and is therefore more akin to "free-riding" than simply efficiently utilizing idle resources. Digital platforms continue to absorb traditional networks into seemingly neutral technological networks, while denying their advantages, believing that they represent advanced productivity and innovation, and refusing to give back to traditional networks to achieve win-win outcomes. In this sense, technological systems are actually trying to reconfigure the market and society based on their own will.

The concluding part of this book examines technological systems in terms of the legal concerns of economic efficiency, productive organization, and risk sharing. The main idea is that if efficient markets are constructed, then mobility labor in digital markets as well as digital commons requires public power to reinforce what kinds of guarantees and institutional provisions are needed. While market logics around publicness (for instance, infrastructure and public resource sharing) can help to increase the income of workers in new employment forms to certain extent, they also need to be complemented by secondary distribution. The above *Guiding Opinions* provides multidimensional requirements in this regard, such as implementing a fair employment system and eliminating employment discrimination; improving the minimum wage and payment guarantee system, and promoting the inclusion of workers in new forms of employment who do not fully comply with the conditions for establishing a labor relationship into the scope of the system's protection; improving the rest system, and promoting the clarification of the labor quota standards for the industry, and scientifically determining the workloads and labor intensity of workers; improving and implementing the responsibility system for labor safety and health, and strictly enforcing the national regulations on labor safety and hygiene protection; improving policies related to basic pension insurance and medical insurance; strengthening occupational injury protection for flexibly employed persons on platforms; and so on.

Matching productive resources purely on the basis of efficiency not only neglects the protection of the rights and interests of the workers themselves, but also falls into the myth that the market seems to operate in a vacuum. Market problems cannot be solved purely in a market-oriented manner, as they are also social problems that need to be thought about in the context of a broader perspective on the relationship between the market and society. For instance, the *Guiding Opinions* also stipulate that individualized job placement, vocational guidance, entrepreneurship training, and other services should be actively provided to workers in all types of new employment patterns; social insurance administration should be optimized, and a social insurance administration service model suitable for new employment patterns should be explored; a vocational skills training model suitable for workers in new employment patterns should be established, and their right to training should be guaranteed equally; and the construction of urban integrated service outlets should be accelerated, and the construction of new employment opportunities in areas where workers in new employment patterns are concentrated should be promoted.

A truly open technological system and the digital commons it creates is an interconnected system of production and distribution that is capable of transforming modes of production, in terms of both managerial power, instruments of production, space, productive relations, productive processes, as well as technical standards, infrastructures, resource mobility, security, and order. Digital labor is a particular productive resource that can fully reflect the efficiency-oriented economic model of the digital market. This is used here as an example to focus on the discourses, ideas, and experiences of how the law intervenes in technological systems described in this book. Viewing the technological system as a mode of production as well as unified marketplace, it is possible to think about how market mechanisms can be robust in terms of reinforcing the infrastructure, and how they need to be shared and supplemented by social mechanisms if they are still deficient in a distributive sense.

References or Works Cited

Ananny, Mike, *Networked Press Freedom: Creating Infrastructures for a Public Right to Hear*, The MIT Press, 2018.

Arthur, W. Brian, *The Nature of Technology: What It Is and How It Evolves*, Free Press, 2009.

Arthur, W. Brian, *Complexity and the Economy*, Oxford University Press, 2014.

Barabasi, Albert Laszlo, *Linked: The New Science of Networks*, Perseus Books, 2002.

Barlow, John P., "A Declaration of Independence of Cyberspace", available at https://www.eff.org/cyberspace-independence.

Beinhocker, Eric D., *Origin of Wealth: Evolution, Complexity, and the Radical Remaking of Economics*, Harvard Business Review Press, 2006.

Benkler, Yochai, *The Wealth of Networks: How Social Production Transforms Markets and Freedom*, Yale University Press, 2006.

Benkler, Yochai, "Sharing Nicely: On Shareable Goods and the Emergence of Sharing as a Modality of Economic Production", *Yale Law Journal* 114 (2004), 273.

Benkler, Yochai, "Commons and Growth: The Essential Role of Open Commons in Market Economies", *University of Chicago Law Review* 80 (2013), 1499–1555.

Ben-Shahar, Omri and Schneider, Carl E., *More Than You Wanted to Know: The Failure of Mandated Disclosure*, Princeton University Press, 2014.

Bernasek, Anna and Mongan, D. T., *All You Can Pay: How Companies Use Our Data to Empty Our Wallets*, Nation Books, 2015.

Boyle, James, *The Public Domain: Enclosing the Commons of the Mind*, Yale University Press, 2008.

Calabresi, G., Melamed, A. D., "Property Rules, Liability Rules, and Inalienability: One View of the Cathedral", *Harvard Law Review* 85, no. 6 (1972), 1089–1128

Castells, Manuel, *The Rise of the Network Society*, 2nd ed., Wiley-Blackwell, 2009.

Chander, A., "How Law Made Silicon Valley", *Emory Law Journal* 63 (2014), 677.

Chen, Long, "Labor Order Under 'Digital Control'–A Study of Labor Control of Takeaway Riders", *Sociological Research* 35, no. 6 (2020), 13–135.

Cheney-Lippold, John, *We Are Data: Algorithms and The Making of Our Digital Selves*, New York University Press, 2017.

Chi, I. D., et al. "A Study of the Impact of Internet Use on the Wage Earnings of Flexibly Employed Persons in the Age of Digital Economy", *Social Science Series* 1, no. 1 (2022), 36–37.

Chu, Huijuan, *Storytellers and Dream Factories: Technology, Law, and Online Literary Production*, Social Science Literature Press, 2019.

Cohen, J. E., *Configuring the Networked Self: Law, Code, and the Play of Everyday Practice*, Yale University Press, 2012.

Cohen, J. E., *Between Truth and Power: The Legal Constructions of Informational Capitalism*, Yale University Press, 2019.

Cui, Guobin, "The Underlying Theory of Limited Exclusion Rights in Big Data", *Legal Studies* 5, no. 5 (2019), 3–24.
Easterbrook, Frank H., "Cyberspace and the Law of the Horse", University of Chicago Legal Forum (1996), 207.
Evans, D. S., Schmalensee, R., *Matchmakers: The New Economics of Multisided Platforms*, Harvard Business School Press, 2006.
Fairfield, Joshua A. T., *Owned: Property, Privacy, and the New Digital Serfdom*, Cambridge University Press, 2017.
Frischmann, B. M., *Infrastructure: The Social Value of Shared Resources*, Oxford University Press, 2012.
Fuchs, C., "The Digital Commons and the Digital Public Sphere: How to Advance Digital Democracy Today", *Westminster Papers in Communication and Culture* 16, no. 1 (2021), 9–26.
Fuchs, Christian, *Social Media: A Critical Introduction*, 2nd ed., SAGE Publications Ltd, 2017.
Granovetter, Mark, *Society and Economy: Framework and Principles*, Belknap Press, 2017.
Hart, H. L. A., *The Concept of Law*, Oxford University Press, 2012.
He, Bo, "The Problematic Dilemma Facing the Definition of Data Ownership and Cracking Ideas", *Big Data* 7 (2021), 3–13.
Horten, Monica, *The Closing of the Net*, Polity, 2016.
Hu, Ling, "Public Sphere or Private Asset? The Nature of Digital Commons in China", *Peking University Law Journal* 11, no. 2 (2024), 185–198.
Hu, Yong, *Crowd Voices: Individual Expression and Public Discussion in the Age of Networks*, Guangxi Normal University Press, 2008.
Huang, Yiping (ed.), *Platform Economy: Innovation, Governance and Prosperity*, CITIC Press, 2022.
Jia, Kai, "Distributive Impacts and Governance Reforms of the Digital Platform Economy", *E-Government* 5, no. 5 (2022), 69–78.
Jiang, Qiping, *An Introduction to the Theory of a New Civilization*, Commercial Press, 2012.
Kreiczer-Levy, S., *Destabilized Property: Property Law in the Sharing Economy*, Cambridge University Press, 2019.
Lemley, Mark A. and Lessig, Lawrence, *The End of End-to-End: Preserving the Architecture of the Internet in the Broadband Era*, UC Berkeley Law & Econ Research Paper No. 2000-19, October 2000.
Lemley, M. A., Weiser, P. J., "Should Property or Liability Rules Govern Information", *Texas Law Review* 85, no. 4 (2007), 783–842.
Lessig, Lawrence, *The Future of Ideas: The Fate of the Commons in a Connected World*, Random House, 2001.
Lessig, Lawrence, "The Architecture of Privacy", *Duke Law Journal* 51 (2002), 1783.
Lazzarato, Maurizio, "Immaterial Labor", in Virno, P., Hardt, M. (eds.), *Radical Thought in Italy: A Potential Politics*, University of Minnesota Press, 1996, pp. 142–157.
Leenes, Ronald, et al. (eds.), *Data Protection and Privacy: (In)visibilities and Infrastructures*, Springer International Publishing, 2017.
Liu, Quan, "On the Main Responsibility of Internet Platforms", *Journal of East China University of Political Science and Law* 5 (2022). https://doi.org/10.14330/jeail.2008.1.2.02.
Liu, Xinhai, *Credit Collection and Big Data: How to Reshape the Credit System in the Era of Mobile Internet*, CITIC Publishing House, 2016.
Liu, Wenjie, *From Haven of Responsibility to Obligation of Safety and Security: A Study on the Intermediary Liability of Network Service Providers*, China Social Science Press, 2016.
Luhmann, Niklas, *Trust and Power*, Polity, 2017.

Marx, Karl and Engels, Friedrich, *Manifesto of the Communist Party,* 2nd revised ed., Progress Press, 1977 [1848].

Mau, Steffen, *The Metric Society: On the Quantification of the Social*, Polity, 2019.

Mueller, Milton, *Will the Internet Fragment? Sovereignty, Globalization and Cyberspace*, Polity, 2017.

Musiani, Francesca, et al. (ed.), *The Turn to Infrastructure in Internet Governance*, Palgrave Macmillan, 2016.

Pasquale, Frank, *The Black Box Society: The Secret Algorithms That Control Money and Information*, Harvard University Press, 2015.

Perzanowski, A. and Schultz, J., *The End of Ownership: Personal Property in the Digital Economy*, MIT Press, 2014.

Pistor, Katharina, *The Code of Capital: How the Law Creates Wealth and Inequality*, Princeton University Press, 2020.

Posner, Eric A. and Weyl, E., Glen, *Radical Markets: Uprooting Capitalism and Democracy for a Just Society*, Princeton University Press, 2018.

Prassl, J., *Humans as a Service: The Promise and Perils of Work in the Gig Economy*, Oxford University Press, 2018.

Reidenberg, Joel, "Lex Informatica: The Formulation of Information Policy Rules Through Technology", *Texas Law Review* 76 (1998), 553.

Rochet, J. C. and Tirole, J., "Platform Competition in Two-Sided Markets", *Journal of the European Economic Association* 1, no. 4 (2003), 990–1029.

Saltzer, J. H., Reed, D. P. and Clark, D. D., "End-to-end Arguments in System Design", *ACM Transactions on Computer Systems* 2 (1984), 277.

Schewick, Barbara van, *Internet Architecture and Innovation*, MIT Press, 2012.

Scholz, T., *Platform Cooperativism: Challenging the Corporate Sharing Economy*, Rosa Luxemburg Stiftung, 2016.

Shapiro, Carl and Varian, Hal R., *Information Rules: A Strategic Guide to the Network Economy*, Harvard Business School Press, 1999.

Shirky, C., *Here Comes Everybody: The Power of Organizing Without Organizations*, Penguin Press, 2008.

Shirky, C., *Cognitive Surplus: Creativity and Generosity in a Connected Age*, Penguin Press, 2010.

Scholz, Trebor (ed.), *Digital Labor: The Internet as Playground and Factory*, Routledge, 2012.

Scholz, Trebor, *Uberworked and Underpaid: How Workers Are Disrupting the Digital Economy*, Polity, 2016.

Solum, Lawrence B. and Chung, Minn, *The Layers Principle: Internet Architecture and the Law*, U San Diego Public Law Research Paper No. 55, 2003.

Srnicek, N., *Platform Capitalism*, Polity Press, 2017.

Sundararajan, Arun, *The Sharing Economy: The End of Employment and the Rise of Crowd-Based Capitalism*, MIT Press, 2017.

Sunstein, Cass, *Republic.com 2.0*, Princeton University Press, 2007.

Sunstein, Cass, *#Republic: Divided Democracy in the Age of Social Media*, Princeton University Press, 2017.

Thierer, A. Koopman, et al., "How the Internet, the Sharing Economy, and Reputational Feedback Mechanisms Solve the 'Lemons Problem'", *University of Miami Law Review* 70, no. 3 (2016), 1–47.

Thylstrup, N. B., *The Politics of Mass Digitization*, MIT Press, 2019.

Vogel, Steven K., *Marketcraft: How Governments Make Markets Work*, Oxford University Press, 2018.

Wang, Tianyu, "The Determination of Labor Relationship Based on the Provision of Labor Services on the Internet Platform", *Jurisprudence* no. 6, 2016, 50–51.

Weinberger, David, *Too Big to Know*, Basic Books, 2014.

Yee, Andy, "Internet Architecture and the Layers Principle: A Conceptual Framework for Regulating Bitcoin", *Internet Policy Review* 3 (2014), 3.
Yoo, C. S., *The Dynamic Internet: How Technology, Users, and Businesses are Transforming the Network*, AEI Press, 2012.
Zeng, Zheng and Wang, Lei, *Data Market Governance: Theories and Policies for Constructing a Foundational System*, Social Science Literature Press, 2021.
Yao, Zhiwei, "Havens in the Shadow of Public Law-focusing on the Censorship Obligations of Online Service Providers", *Global Law Review* 1, no. 1 (2018),68–72.
Zhang, Yicheng, Lv, Linyuan, and Zhou, Tao, *Reinvention: The Structure of the Information Economy*, Sichuan People's Publishing House, 2018.
Zhang, Angela Huyue, *High Wire: How China Regulates Big Tech and Governs Its Economy*, Oxford University Press, 2024.
Zhao, Peng, "Beyond Platform Liability: Rethinking the Regulatory Model of Online Food Transactions", *Journal of East China University of Political Science and Law* 11, no. 1 (2017), 145–146.
Zhou, Hanhua, "On Internet Law", *China Law Journal* 3, no. 3 (2015), 1–5.
Zhou, Hanhua, "Exploring an Incentive-Compatible Approach to Personal Data Governance", *Legal Studies* 2, no. 2 (2018), 3–23.
Zhou, Li'an, "Administrative Subcontracting System", *Society*, no. 6 (2014), 43–55.
Zhou, Li'an, *Local Government in Transition*, Gezhi Publishing House, 2017.
Zhou, Li'an, "One Body, Many Faces: Re-examining State-Society Relations During the Chinese Imperial Period", *Society* 42, no. 5 (2022), 1.
Zittrain, Jonathan, "Internet Points of Control", *Boston College Law Review* 44 (2003), 653.
Zittrain, Jonathan, *The Future of the Internet–And How to Stop It*, Yale University Press, 2008.
Zittrain, Jonathan, "The Generative Internet", Harvard Law Review 119 (2006), 1974.
Zuboff, S., *The Age of Surveillance Capitalism: The Fight for a Human Future at the New Frontier of Power*, PublicAffairs, 2019.

Index

FSC
www.fsc.org
MIX
Papier | Fördert gute Waldnutzung
FSC® C083411

Kolibri 360 GmbH
Ferdinand-Jühlke-Straße 7
99095 Erfurt, Deutschland
produktsicherheit@kolibri360.de